DEMOCRACY IN IMMIGRANT AMERICA

Democracy in Immigrant America

*Changing Demographics and
Political Participation*

S. KARTHICK RAMAKRISHNAN

STANFORD UNIVERSITY PRESS

STANFORD, CALIFORNIA

Stanford University Press
Stanford, California
www.sup.org

Library of Congress Cataloging-in-Publication Data

Ramakrishnan, S. Karthick (Subramanian Karthick), 1975–
    Democracy in immigrant America : changing demographics and political participation / S. Karthick Ramakrishnan.
        p. cm.
    Includes bibliographical references and index.
    ISBN 0-8047-5044-0 (cloth)
    ISBN 0-8047-5592-2 (paper)
        1. Immigrants—United States—Political activity.   I. Title.
JV6477.R35 2005
323'.042'0869120973—dc22   2004009114

Printed in the United States of America on acid-free, archival-quality paper.
Original Printing 2005

Last figure below indicates year of this printing:
14   13   12   11   10   09   08   07   06

Designed and typeset at Stanford University Press in 10 / 12.5 Palatino.

To my immigrant parents

Contents

Tables

Figures

Acknowledgments

There are few places in the United States like California, where immigration has had a sustained and profound effect on society and politics. In the past decade, the state has not only witnessed various ballot propositions relating to immigrants but has also seen the rise of various elected officials who are first-generation immigrants, with Governor Arnold Schwarzenegger among them. The Public Policy Institute of California has been a wonderful place to work on issues of immigration, race, and ethnicity. Working across the street from the Bureau of Citizenship and Immigration Services provides me with a daily reminder of the demographic and political transformations currently under way in the United States. I hope that this book sheds some light on the significant and growing role of immigrants and their descendants in the American electorate.

I thank the many friends, colleagues, and mentors who gave me guidance over the years that it took to research and write this book. My first thanks go to my parents, Tarakad and Rani Ramakrishnan. I owe my education and this book to their loving guidance and their decision to leave India and start a new life halfway across the globe. Next, I thank Larry Bartels, Jennifer Hochschild, Thomas Espenshade, and Eric Oliver—my graduate advisors at Princeton University, who prodded me to improve my arguments and defend my claims. I also thank the various institutions and programs that have made this book possible. Princeton University provided four years of financial support for coursework and research, and Harvard University offered one year of support through its Visiting Fellows program. At Princeton, the Office of Population Research was a great interdisciplinary environment in which to explore issues of immigrant incorporation. The same can be said for the Public Policy Institute of California (PPIC) in San Francisco. This research was also made possible by the generous assistance of the following grants and fellowships: the Woodrow Wilson School Summer Research Grant, the conference and training grants offered by the Office of Population Research, the scholarly travel grants of the Graduate School at Princeton, and the Mellon Foundation summer research grant for dissertation research. I am also grateful to the following people for easing the financial burdens of fieldwork by offering their homes and extending their hospitality: Suresh Venkateswaran, Chitra and Sukumar Ramanan, and the Thottam family.

I thank David Lyon for making academic research a high priority at PPIC. During my time there, I benefited from conversations with fellow researchers from various disciplines such as economics, political science, public policy, and sociology. In particular, I thank Mark Baldassare, Paul Lewis, and Belinda Reyes for their support of this project and my other research on immigrant civic and political participation. I also thank Amanda Moran, Tony Hicks, and Mary Ray Worley at Stanford University Press for guiding this book from its initial proposal to its present form, and Nikesh Patel and Peter Richardson at PPIC for assistance with manuscript preparation.

Finally, I also thank various scholars and colleagues for their feedback and advice on various aspects of this book. Although I cannot name them all, I wish to acknowledge the contributions of Andrew Aoki, R. Douglas Arnold, Irene Bloemraad, Louis DeSipio, Taeku Lee, Pei-te Lien, Tali Mendelberg, Ricardo Ramírez, Reuel Rogers, Kay Schlozman, Marta Tienda, Sidney Verba, and Janelle Wong; colleagues at the Public Policy Institute of California; and colleagues from graduate school such as Michael Fortner, Cybelle Fox, Chris Karpowitz, Deborah Schildkraut, Okiyoshi Takeda, and Vesla Weaver.

I am also grateful for the support of friends outside my discipline, and outside academia altogether—my loving partner, Brinda Sarathy, who helped in preparing this book; my brother, Sunder Ramakrishnan; friends at Princeton University such as Lauren Hale, Jason Brownlee, Anjum Hossain, Kushanava Choudhury, Kunal Sarkar, and Sachin Shah; and others such as Jeremy Eichler, Angela Romans, Aparna Vootkur, and Tracy Thottam. There are many others who helped me in small but significant ways over the years, and I apologize for not acknowledging them in a formal manner. Needless to say, any limitations to the arguments and analyses presented here are entirely my own.

DEMOCRACY IN IMMIGRANT AMERICA

CHAPTER 1

Introduction

Hundreds of thousands of immigrants take the oath of citizenship every year. Each has come not only to take but to give. They come asking for a chance to work hard, support their families, and to rise in the world. And together they make our nation more, not less, American. . . . In the life of an immigrant, citizenship is a defining event. In the life of our nation, new citizens bring renewal.

George W. Bush (Ellis Island, July 10, 2001)

Good people who are living here, working hard, and paying taxes should have a path to equal citizenship in the American community. And families should be reunited more quickly.

John Kerry (Washington, D.C, June 26, 2004)

Who votes, who does not participate, and why?

For nearly five decades, political scientists have devoted considerable attention to these questions regarding democratic participation in the United States. Questions regarding electoral participation take on increased significance during eras in which there are substantial changes in the size and composition of the electorate—for instance, with the entry of women into electoral participation following suffrage in 1920 (Andersen 1996), with the rise in participation among European immigrants after the New Deal (Erie 1988; Gamm 1989), and with the entry of southern black voters into the electorate following the civil rights movement and the Voting Rights Acts of the 1960s (Davidson and Grofman 1994; Rosenstone and Hansen 1993).

Now, in the early twenty-first century, we are once again witnessing a sea change in the composition of the American electorate, this time caused by processes related to immigration and racial diversification. In the past three decades the number of immigrants living in the United States has grown enormously, from about 10 million in 1970 to about 32 million, or more than 11 percent of the U.S. population (U.S. Census Bureau 2001). Although the foreign-born constitute a smaller proportion of voting-age citizens (about 6 percent in 2000), this proportion has increased remarkably in the past few years thanks to an upsurge in naturalizations beginning in 1996. This wave has yet to recede, with immigrants naturalizing at a rate of well over five hundred thousand per year (U.S. Citizenship and Immigration Services 2002). The surge in immigration since 1965 has also altered the shape of the American citizenry through the children of the foreign-born (or second-generation immigrants). Together, these two groups account for about 15 percent of the adult citizen population today and will grow to about one-quarter of the national electorate by 2020 (Passel and Van Hook 2000). Finally, the growth of the "new" second generation, combined with the entry of naturalized citizens into the electorate, is also creating a shift in the racial, ethnic, and national-origin composition of the American electorate—away from the predominance of a "black-white" dynamic to a "black-white-brown-yellow" dynamic.

The significance of first- and second-generation immigrants to the electoral process has not been lost either on the media or on national political leaders (Greenhouse 2000). Recognizing the value of immigrants in the American electorate, both Republican and Democratic presidential candidates in 2000 sought to garner votes among immigrant citizens. The desire to woo immigrant voters was especially strong for the Republican Party, which endeavored to undo the political damage wrought by the party's prior support for legislation that restricted immigrant access to public benefits. For instance, George W. Bush distanced himself from the restrictionist policies advocated by Republican governors such as Pete Wilson of California and spent considerable sums of money on Spanish-language advertisements in immigrant-rich states such as California (Segal 2003). Even after the 2000 election, Bush sought to make Republican inroads into current and future immigrant voters. In 2001, he asked Congress to extend the deadline for a limited amnesty allowing undocumented immigrants with family in the United States to apply for legal status and then declared his support for the idea of a broader amnesty for undocumented immigrants. The September 11 attacks complicated Republican attempts to attract immigrant votes while retaining the support of the party's conservative base. At the same time that the administration deported thousands of South Asian and Arab immigrants who overstayed their visas, it proposed to reclassify undocumented immigrants from Mexico as temporary workers and sought to restore immigrant access to food stamps, the provision of which was initially restricted by the 1996 welfare reform law (Pear 2002).[1]

Despite a few efforts to reach out to immigrant voters, many Republicans and Democrats still harbor a deep uncertainty about the likely participation of these relative newcomers to the electoral process (Edsall and Thompson 2001; Gimpel and Kaufmann 2001). A similar uncertainty is found among many political scientists, who rarely have examined the issue of immigrant political participation in a comprehensive manner. While there are many studies that focus on the political participation of either Latinos or Asian Americans, very few works in political science have studied immigrant political participation across racial groups and national origins. This paucity stands in stark contrast to the burgeoning number of studies in sociology and economics on the experiences and outcomes of first-, second-, and third-generation immigrants in a cross-racial perspective (Portes and Rumbaut 1996; Borjas 1999; Waldinger 2001; Alba and Nee 2003).

As a consequence of this gap in scholarship, there are still several unanswered questions regarding the political participation of immigrants in the United States. For instance, some political theorists have argued that policies of dual nationality are detrimental to civic participation among immigrants in the United States. And yet few studies have examined whether such policies actually do entail lower rates of participation. Similarly, many political observers have remarked that immigrants from communist regimes are highly engaged in the political life of the United States, based largely on impressionistic evidence from the experience of Cuban immigrants in Florida. And yet, the question of communist country origin has not been asked more generally for immigrants of different racial groups and national origins.

This work is an attempt to provide answers to these and other questions relating to the political participation of immigrants and their descendants in the United States. In doing so, I examine whether traditional models of voting participation can account for the political behavior of immigrants. I also analyze whether new factors related to immigrant adaptation add significantly to our theoretical understandings of voter turnout. Finally, I consider the relationships between race, immigration, and participation inequality, shifting the analysis beyond voting to other forms of political participation. (Note that the terms *race* and *ethnicity* are used interchangeably in this book.)

This study of immigrant political participation focuses on four central sets of questions:

1. *How do immigrant numbers relate to the overall population and the voting-age population in particular?*

The number of immigrants in the United States has grown rapidly since the liberalization of immigration policy in 1965. The demographics of immigrant residents have received considerable attention from studies in sociology, economics, and public policy. And yet there has not been a sufficient accounting of immigrants and their share of the national electorate and various state electorates.

2. *Do traditional models of voting participation account for the political behavior of immigrants?*

Some contemporary studies have suggested that traditional models of voting participation, especially those that emphasize the importance of age and socioeconomic status, do not sufficiently explain the participatory behavior of immigrant and minority populations.[2]

3. *Do factors related to immigrant adaptation add significantly to the existing theoretical knowledge of voter turnout?*

A growing literature in Latino and Asian American politics, and the larger literature on immigrant outcomes in the United States, suggests that various factors regarding immigrant adaptation may bear a significant relationship to political participation. These factors include duration of stay in the United States, various country-of-origin characteristics, and contextual factors related to immigrant life in the United States.

4. *How do group disparities in voting compare to inequalities in other forms of political participation?*

Participation in democratic politics extends well beyond the ballot box to include activities such as writing to elected officials, giving money to political causes, and working on political campaigns. As in the case of voting, involvement in these activities is unevenly distributed across racial groups and immigrant generations. Some activities may exacerbate group inequalities in political participation, while others may serve to mitigate such inequalities.

Before examining these questions, I shall first present an overview of prior work in the field of immigrant electoral participation. In Chapter 2, I summarize the findings of scholars who analyze the adaptation of

European immigrants to American social and political life in the early twentieth century. I also review the contributions from contemporary studies of voting participation among Latinos and Asian Americans. I note that even though these studies provide testable hypotheses regarding immigrant political participation, the external validity of many of their findings is limited by the fact that they are confined to particular groups or geographic areas or that they are derived from elections prior to the massive increase in naturalizations of the mid-1990s. This study attempts to provide a more systematic analysis of the dynamics that govern immigrant political participation in the contemporary period, primarily using national data from recent elections. Chapter 2 ends with an introduction to the data sources used in this book—with surveys such as the Current Population Survey Voter Supplement (CPS), the National Election Studies (NES), the Washington Post/ Kaiser Family Foundation/Harvard University (or PKH) Survey of Latinos, and the Pilot National Asian American Political Survey (PNAAPS); field interviews with leaders of ethnic organizations in various cities; and newspaper coverage of immigrant-related issues in three states.

In Chapter 3, I provide a detailed examination of immigrant numbers in the national population and various state populations, as well as their corresponding electorates. I also compare the contemporary levels of first- and second-generation immigrants to those found earlier in the twentieth century. While the analysis confirms a rising tide of first-generation citizens in the past forty years, it also tempers some of the inflated rhetoric referring to immigrants as "sleeping giants" or "awakening giants" in the American electorate.

Chapter 4 examines the question of whether traditional models of participation can account for voter turnout among first- and second-generation immigrants. Many contemporary studies of electoral participation suggest that models that emphasize the importance of age and socioeconomic status cannot account for the political behavior of immigrants. First, I test the validity of what I term the hypothesis of "immigrant exceptionalism." Next, I test the consistency of other factors that have been shown to be significant predictors of participation among native-born populations (factors related to social incorporation, rules governing registration deadlines and absentee ballots, and party mobilization at the statewide level).

The analysis then proceeds to consider a new model of immigrant participation. In Chapter 5, I introduce and examine the effects of immigrant-related factors such as (1) immigrant generation, (2) duration of stay in the United States, (3) country-of-origin characteristics such as policies of dual citizenship and histories of nondemocratic rule, and (4) U.S.-based characteristics such as residential ethnic concentration and access to bilingual ballots. Many of these factors have been hypothesized to have significant effects but have not yet been systematically tested. For instance, some political theorists have voiced the concern that access to dual citizenship lowers immigrant participation in U.S. politics. I find that immigrants from countries that allow for dual citizenship actually have a higher level of participation than do immigrants from other countries. For these and several other factors, this book provides the first comprehensive test of the effects of immigrant adaptation on political participation.

After examining the role of various immigrant-related factors on voting participation as found in national surveys, I consider in more detail the effects of political threat and institutional mobilization on the likelihood of immigrant participation. The mid-1990s were watershed years in the contemporary era of immigration and naturalization, as the United States considered and passed legislation that restricted immigrant access to public benefits. The trend started in 1994 with the passage of Proposition 187 in California and continued in 1996 with national legislation that made even legal immigrants ineligible for most welfare benefits. These measures (hereby termed "anti-immigrant legislation") produced a sense of political threat among many first- and second-generation citizens and have largely been credited for an immigrant backlash at the polls against the Republican Party. In Chapter 6, I provide a structured case study comparison of threat and mobilization across groups in California, Texas, and New York. This comparative analysis relies on newspaper coverage of immigrant-related issues prior to each general election and on interviews with leaders of ethnopolitical organizations. Finally, I combine these contextual and group-specific measures of threat and mobilization with individual-level data on participation from the Current Population Survey, thus providing a cross-regional analysis of the relative importance of each factor in stimulating voter turnout among immigrants.

Chapter 7 addresses the question of immigrant participation in political activities beyond the ballot box. Using recent data from the Public Policy Institute of California, the analysis focuses on whether disparities in participation across racial groups and immigrant generations get better or worse when the scope of relevant activities includes not just voting but also other types of political activities that may have a substantial impact on election and policy outcomes. Finally, Chapter 8 considers the future of immigrant political participation, paying particular attention to policies aimed at reducing participation inequality and the partisan consequences of immigration in the United States. This final chapter also considers the ways that immigrant political participation is prompting reformulations of theories of political participation as well as the more general literature on immigrant adaptation. As will be clear from the analysis, not only are immigrants transforming the demographic and political landscape of the United States; they are also transforming our very understandings of the factors that motivate electoral participation.

While this book treats the question of immigrant political participation from an empirical perspective using survey data and elite interviews, the issue of political participation is not merely of academic interest. For the immigrants themselves, the extent of their political participation is often important to securing their economic, social, and political footholds in the United States. Some may argue otherwise—that the primary goal of immigrants entering the United States is to seek a better life defined in terms of wealth and social mobility and that political participation is not necessary for the foreign-born to attain these goals. In my fieldwork in California, Texas, and New York, a common refrain among leaders of party organizations and middle-class Asian community organizations was that it was difficult to get more Asian immigrants involved in politics because they were already enjoying considerable success in the economic realm. Some may argue that this kind of behavior—giving primacy to economic activity over political participation—is perfectly rational. With economic advancement as the primary yardstick for immigrant success, low levels of political participation should not be a cause for concern. Others may extend these arguments of economic primacy even further, rationalizing away low levels of participation even among those immigrants with limited socioeconomic mobility. Indeed, the focus on economic or professional advancement may be seen as even more pressing among those immigrants who have not yet fulfilled the "American Dream," with political participation seen as an afterthought.

This apologia for low levels of participation among immigrants certainly has an intuitive appeal, especially given the centrality of the "American Dream" in the mythologizing of social relations in the United States—both by individuals and institutions of the host society and by the immigrants themselves. However, the argument of economic primacy is limited in several ways. First, political activism is indeed necessary for the economic advancement of many immigrants who face racial and ethnic discrimination in areas such as housing, lending, and the workplace (see, for instance, activism among undocumented immigrants in California to secure driver's licenses and to obtain compensation for work-related injuries). Far from being an unnecessary diversion, political participation for these immigrants is integral to the mission of securing an economic foothold in the United States. Political participation may also be necessary for the economic advancement of those immigrants who have enjoyed some degree of economic success but who nevertheless continue to face barriers such as glass ceilings in the workplace. Finally, political activism is also important for those immigrants who have succeeded in economic terms but who have not yet secured a legal foothold in the United States and who do not enjoy the same protections as native-born whites (see, for instance, the detention of many Arab and South Asian immigrants during the months following September 11, 2001).

With low levels of political participation, immigrants may find themselves trapped in what Claire Jean Kim (1999, 2000) has called systems of "racial triangulation." They may be valorized in relation to other subordinate groups such as native-born blacks, yet ostracized as foreigners and kept outside the realm of the body politic. During periods of economic decline or crisis in national security, the political vulnerability of immigrants intensifies, with attempts by the state and various social actors to restrict immigrant rights and erect even greater barriers to citizenship. Higher levels of political participation and strategic activism among immigrant communities challenge such policies of political marginalization. Activities such as participating in public protests, writing letters to elected officials, and attending meetings of local government can provide immigrants with the skills necessary to defend their rights during times of political vulnerability. Also, immigrant participation in political and civic activities can lessen the ability of states and social actors to paint immigrants as alien to the American body politic. Thus, political participation need not be marginal to the concerns of immigrants. Indeed, in many ways it is central to the goal of immigrants to secure a better life in the United States for themselves and their children.

CHAPTER 2

Studying the Newcomers

MANY OF OUR UNDERSTANDINGS of immigrant political incorporation are still derived from studies of earlier waves of European immigrants, although there have also been some significant contributions from recent studies of particular racial and ethnic groups. In this chapter, I summarize the key insights from the scholarship on political participation among immigrants in the earlier part of the twentieth century. I also review contemporary studies of political participation among immigrants arriving after World War II. Many of these contemporary studies have shed considerable light on processes related to immigrant political participation. Still, they are often limited by the fact that their analyses are confined to particular racial or ethnic groups (Asian Americans or Latinos) or to particular geographic areas (states such as California or metropolitan areas such as New York and Los Angeles). This book therefore draws upon the findings and insights from early and contemporary studies of immigrant electoral participation. At the same time, it provides a more systematic test for some of the hypotheses offered and also introduces some new factors related to immigrant adaptation that have not previously been considered.

Scholarship on Early European Immigrants

Many of the early works on immigrant adaptation situate the study of political participation within the larger processes of cultural assimilation and changes in socioeconomic status. One of the earliest treatments of the subject of immigrant incorporation in the United States is *The Up-rooted* (1951), a historical study by Oscar Handlin. Handlin portrays the archetypical story of immigrants as peasants uprooted from their traditional structures and forced to create new relationships and institutions in the United States. While immigrants found it relatively easy to form voluntary associations in the New World, Handlin argues that it was more difficult for them to participate in politics because they had no prior experience in democratic government. As Handlin notes, "In the Old World (except perhaps in France), the state had been completely external to the peasant's consciousness. In the business of ruling he did not act, was only acted upon" (202). According to Handlin, even when immigrants overcame their distrust of the state, their inherited political values were ill suited for political participation—they had been brought up in a system that legitimized rank and hierarchy and therefore needed several years to internalize the egalitarian norms of American democracy. Prior to that internalization, immigrants had to rely on an intermediate system in which their participation and preferences were mediated through political machines and their bosses.

Handlin's archetype of the early immigrant experience finds a more formal expression in Milton Gordon's *Assimilation in American Life* (1964). Although political participation is marginal to much of Gordon's analysis, he does consider the issue as part of the larger process of immigrant assimilation. He presents a framework in which assimilation can be differentiated into seven components: (1) *cultural assimilation*, whereby immigrants discard the language and customs of their home countries and acquire those of the host society; (2) *structural assimilation*, in which immigrants assimilate into existing formal and informal institutions; (3) *marital assimilation*, or large-scale intermarriage; (4) *identificational assimilation*, in which immigrants develop a sense of identity based exclusively on the host society; (5) *attitude receptional assimilation*, in which the host society no longer maintains prejudice against the immigrant group; (6) *behavioral receptional assimilation*, or the absence of discrimination by the host society; and (7) *civic assimilation*, or the absence of conflicts over values and power.

According to Gordon, some components of assimilation proceed more quickly than others. He suggests that cultural assimilation is likely to be the first and easiest type of assimilation, one that occurs largely during the first and second generation. On the other hand, structural assimilation occurs much later because it requires that immigrant groups share the same social cliques and membership associations as those of the host society. Finally, according to Gordon, civic assimilation proceeds at a more rapid pace than structural assimilation because of the relative openness of the political system and the disappearance of ethnic bloc voting in the face of socioeconomic differentiation (1964, 35). Thus, for both Gordon and Handlin, the extent and shape of immigrant political participation is largely determined by processes related to assimilation—as immigrants spend more years and more generations in the United States, their political behavior begins to approximate that of the native-born population.[1]

In addition to historians and sociologists, political scientists have also paid attention to the incorporation of European immigrants into the American electorate. The seminal work among early studies in political science is Robert Dahl's *Who Governs? Democracy and Power in an American City* (1961). In his study of political power in New Haven, Connecticut, Dahl argues that while immigrant groups may have initially lacked social prestige and economic power, they were able to gain political power through the mobilization of ethnic votes: "Whatever else the ethnics lacked, they had numbers. Hence politicians took the initiative; they made it easy for immigrants to become citizens, encouraged ethnics to register, put them on the party rolls" (1961, 34). Dahl sees the political rise of immigrants as supportive of his pluralist theoretical framework of political power, in which political systems move from a pattern of cumulated inequality (rule by a cohesive set of social and economic elites) to one of dispersed inequality (rule by different groups of leaders with access to various sets of political resources).

While Dahl's study addresses the question of political power, it remains relatively silent on the issue of voter turnout among immigrants.[2] For instance, he outlines three phases in the development of ethnic politics (mobilization by native-born politicians, the election of ethnic leaders, and the disappearance of ethnicity-based political appeals). However, he does not examine whether the level of participation changes across these different phases of immigrant political incorporation. Furthermore, Dahl makes no mention of any variation in the level of voting participation for members of different national-origin groups in New Haven. However, one can infer from his pluralist analysis that the path to electoral participation for European immigrants was relatively straightforward and free of barriers. Under a pluralist framework, the mere presence of immigrants as potential voters would be sufficient for political challengers to mobilize them and for incumbents to be attentive to their concerns.

Steven Erie challenges these pluralist assumptions in his study of Irish-dominated urban machines, *Rainbow's End* (1988). Erie argues that analyses such as Dahl's overstate the extent to which political machines incorporated new immigrants into the political process. Instead, he suggests that factors such as the lack of party competition and the desire to minimize the size of winning electoral coalitions discouraged many party machines from enfranchising immigrants and mobilizing them to vote. He points out that Irish bosses in machine-dominated cities were interested in mobilizing only Irish voters, not immigrants from Southern and Eastern Europe: "The entrenched Irish big-city bosses had no intention of churning out new citizens and voters. . . . Once they had consolidated power they had little incentive to mobilize the newcomers" (94). With the exit of middle-class "Yankee" voters to the suburbs and the association of Republicans with anti-immigrant policies, Irish Democrat machines in most major cities did not fear competition from local Republican parties. What they did fear were demands from new immigrants to have a share in the distribution of power and patronage at the local level. So even though the incorporation of new voters would have cemented the control of Democrats over city governments, party bosses were reluctant to register and mobilize immigrant voters because new constituencies would undermine the control of Irish Americans over government patronage. Only in a few cities where Irish Americans had not consolidated their hold over city governments were local Democrat organizations eager to aid immigrants in the processes of naturalization and registration. As a consequence, immigrants living in cities with high party competition were more likely to participate than those living in machine-dominated cities. Indeed, Erie argues that it was not until the New Deal era and the weakening autonomy of local party machines that immigrants from Southern Europe and Eastern Europe began to participate in electoral politics in large numbers.

The importance of the New Deal to immigrant mobilization receives a more thorough consideration in Gerald Gamm's *The Making of New Deal Democrats* (1989). Gamm provides a detailed precinct-level analysis of electoral participation among members of different immigrant and ethnic groups in Boston between 1920 and 1940. He shows that the early years of the New Deal prompted Italian immigrants to join the electorate in large numbers, but that the same was not true of Jewish or Irish immigrants. Gamm argues that these differences are due to Italian immigrants having low levels of registration and voting during the 1920s, while Irish and Jewish immigrants already had relatively high levels of participation.[3] While Gamm does not explain why participation was high among Jewish immigrants and low among Italians, others have noted that this difference is due primarily to Italians' high degree of return migration, whereas Jewish immigrants did not anticipate returning to Europe (Erie 1988). Furthermore, Italian immigrants had lower levels of English-language ability, making it more difficult for them to pass literacy tests for naturalization and voting. Whatever the reason for these initial differences among different national-origin groups, the New Deal era led to widespread mobilization among all immigrants that finally put their participation on par with those of the native-born "Yankees."

To sum up the scholarship on political participation for earlier waves of European immigrants, we see that various authors emphasize different sets of factors that influence the extent and timing of immigrants' entry into the political process. For Gordon and Handlin, immigrant participation in American politics increases over time, as newcomers shed their old customs and institutions and adopt those of the host society. For pluralists such as Dahl, what drives immigrant participation is not cultural assimilation (which determines only the forms that ethnic politics take) but instead the processes of contestation and mobilization that are inherent to a democratic political system. Finally, party-oriented scholars such as Erie and Gamm argue that the political incorporation of immigrant groups is not the inevitable result either of cultural assimilation or of processes related to pluralism. Instead, they draw attention to the role of party competition at the local level, the shifting fortunes and strategies of national parties, and the degree of control by party bosses over the provision of government jobs and contracts.

Scholarship on Contemporary Immigrants

The post-1965 surge in immigration has prompted a flurry of research on the issue of immigrant adaptation, most notably in the fields of demography, economics, and sociology. Demographers have studied differences in fertility behavior between the foreign-born and the native-born and have also examined variations in health outcomes across immigrant generations (Guendelman et al. 1990; Hill and Johnson 2002; Kahn 1994). Studies of economic outcomes have focused on questions of educational attainment among immigrants, differences in earnings between the native-born and the foreign-born. They have also vigorously debated the nature of occupational mobility across immigrant generations (Chiswick 1977; Borjas 1987, 1999; Portes and Zhou 1993; Tsuda, Valdez, and Cornelius 2003). Finally, sociologists have trained their attention on issues such as intermarriage, residential segregation and mobility, English language acquisition, and racial and ethnic identification (Massey and Denton 1987; Frey 1996; Portes and Rumbaut 1996, 2001; Alba and Nee 2003).[4] Across these various studies, a common set of questions emerges: How do the foreign-born and the immigrant second generation fare in the United States, how do their outcomes compare to those whose parents were born in the United States, and how do their trajectories of adaptation compare to those in previous immigrant waves?

By contrast, the study of political behavior among immigrants is still in relative infancy. Although the post-1965 surge in immigration has had a substantial influence on the American electorate, few studies have explicitly addressed the issue of immigrant political participation until recently. Granted, there have been several studies in the past twenty years that have examined naturalization rates across national origin groups (Portes and Mozo 1985; Liang 1994; Yang 1994; Johnson et al. 1999). However, questions of what happens after naturalization have been relatively rare (DeSipio 1996b; Uhlaner, Cain, and Kiewiet 1989; Tam Cho 1999). Indeed, most studies in political science approach the issue of immigrant adaptation only indirectly—not as a topic unto itself, but as part of a more general study of political participation among Latinos or Asian Americans. As we shall soon see, even those few studies that have focused on issues of immigrant adaptation are limited by the fact that they are confined to a particular racial or ethnic group or to particular states and metropolitan areas. Thus, while these contemporary studies offer important insights and hypotheses regarding the role of immigrant-related variables on participation, a true test of immigrant electoral participation requires a comparative study across racial and ethnic groups.

There have been several studies of Latino participation in the past decade that have touched upon dynamics that are specific to first-generation immigrants. In *Latino Voices*, Rodolfo de la Garza and his coinvestigators (1992) present tabulated results from the Latino National Political Survey (LNPS), the first comprehensive survey of political attitudes and participation among Latino citizens at the national level. While the survey itself has questions on nativity that allow scholars to disaggregate levels of participation by immigrant generation, the authors' presentation of the tabulated results delineates political participation only according to national-origin group (Mexican, Puerto Rican, and Cuban).[5] Subsequent analyses of the LNPS do, however, provide a deeper examination of questions related to immigrant political participation among Latinos. In an article in the *Hispanic Journal of Behavioral Sciences*, Louis DeSipio (1996b) considers differences in participation between naturalized citizens and the native-born. From his analysis of the LNPS, DeSipio finds that after controlling for various demographic and social factors, naturalized Latinos are less likely to be registered to vote than their native-born counterparts. He notes, however, that the effects of age and education on voting are stronger than those related to nativity, indicating that the "economic betterment of Latino immigrants, as well as their steady aging, can overcome the negative influence of naturalization" (1996b, 208). Kevin Hill and Dario Moreno's (1996) analysis of general political activity among Cuban Americans echoes the findings of DeSipio regarding electoral participation—those born in Cuba are less likely to participate than those born in the United States. More important, they disaggregate the effects of age and length of stay in the United States and find both to be statistically significant. Thus, in addition to showing that the foreign-born are less likely to participate than the native-born, they note that even among first-generation immigrants, participation increases as respondents live longer in the United States. More recently, however, some studies have challenged the notion of first-generation Latinos as politically less active than the native-born population, with evidence that naturalized Latinos in California have an unusually high level of participation (Pantoja, Ramirez, and Segura 2001).

In addition to these studies of Latino political participation, scholars in Asian American politics have also examined the issue of voting participation among immigrants. For instance, Pei-te Lien (1994) analyzes voting participation among Asian Americans based on a 1984 survey of California respondents that contains an oversampling of Asian and Mexican Americans. In her analysis, Lien controls for factors such as age, national origin, partisanship, ethnic ties, and acculturation. She finds that first-generation Asian immigrants are just as likely to vote as those in later immigrant generations.[6] Even in a subsequent study of a 1993 survey from southern California, Lien (1997) shows that there is no difference in the likelihood of participation between foreign-born and native-born citizens. Finally, a recent multicity study of Asian American participation reveals modest differences in voter registration between the foreign-born and native-born, but no significant differences in voter turnout (Lien, Conway, and Wong 2004). These results stand in contrast to the findings among Latinos that naturalized citizens are generally less likely to vote than native-born citizens. One should, however, be cautious about reading too much into these differences because the Asian American findings are based on surveys in a limited set of cities or regions.[7]

There have been a few studies in recent years that have compared participation outcomes between Latinos and Asian immigrants. In a 1989 study, Carole Uhlaner, Bruce Cain, and Roderick Kiewiet present the initial findings of their 1984 California-wide survey that includes 317 whites, 335 blacks, 574 Latinos, and 308 Asian Americans. The authors measure immigrant adaptation through the use of two variables: (1) the percentage of one's life spent in the United States, and (2) the use of English as a primary language. In their analysis, both immigrant-related factors have a significant effect on participation, although duration of stay in the United States has a stronger effect on Asian immigrants while English-language speaking ability has a stronger impact on participation among Latinos.[8] These results therefore lend support to theories of immigrant adaptation that link political participation to broader processes of cultural and socioeconomic assimilation. While these results provide important insights regarding the effect of immigrant-related variables on participation, their external validity is limited. First, the findings about duration of stay in the United States are inconsistent with Lien's analysis of the same survey, which indicates that first-generation Asian immigrants are not less likely to vote than their native-born counterparts. This indicates that some of the findings are sensitive to model specification, producing seemingly inconsistent results even from the same survey.

Finally, other studies comparing the political behavior of Latino and Asian immigrants have examined the relevance of traditional models of voting participation in explaining turnout among the foreign-born. For instance, Wendy Tam Cho's (1999) analysis of Latino and Asian immigrants relies on the same 1984 survey of California residents. In addition to noting that voting among immigrants is influenced by the duration of their stay in the United States and their ability to speak English, Tam Cho argues that the traditional variables of age and education do not have the same effect among Asian and Latino immigrants as they do among the native-born population. Finally, Jane Junn (1999) presents an analysis of system-directed political activity (voting, contacting government officials, working on political campaigns, and contributing money) using data from the 1990 Citizen Participation Study. Her analysis of the composite measure of system-directed activity indicates that immigrants of all racial groups are less likely to participate than their native-born counterparts. Unlike Tam Cho's analysis, however, Junn's study does not consider whether factors such as age and education have the same effect on immigrants as they do on the native-born population, although she does note weaker effects among Asian Americans.[9] While these comparative studies of Asian and Latino immigrants offer up important questions regarding participation among the foreign-born, they are still limited by their reliance on data from 1984 and 1990, years in which immigrant numbers were considerably smaller and the political climate surrounding immigration considerably different from those found in recent years.[10]

Studies of political participation among contemporary black immigrants have been relatively rare. Even the few studies of Afro-Caribbean immigrants in New York do not address the issue of voting participation per se. For instance, Philip Kasinitz (1992) highlights changes in the leadership of the Caribbean community and evaluates the likelihood of their building political coalitions with native-born blacks. Similarly, Reuel Rogers (2000) analyzes differences in political ideology, mobilization, and party identification between Afro-Caribbeans and African Americans. Finally, Mary Waters (2001) addresses the issue of socioeconomic mobility and racial identification among first- and second-generation Afro-Caribbeans. Missing from most of these studies, however, is any analysis of how the participation levels of first-generation Afro-Caribbeans compare with those in other immigrant generations, or whether the same factors that motivate turnout among African Americans also motivate turnout among Afro-Caribbean immigrants.

Finally, there have been virtually no studies of voting participation among contemporary white immigrants.[11] Scholarship on political participation among white immigrants is still primarily focused on the earlier eras of party machines and the New Deal (Erie 1988; Gamm 1989). This reflects the fact that first-generation immigrants constituted a much larger proportion of the white electorate in the early 1900s than they do today.[12] Furthermore, there are significantly fewer immigrants from Europe in the post-1965 period than in the earlier part of the twentieth century. As Table 2.1 indicates, however, white immigrants still constitute a sizable portion of first- and second-generation citizens who

TABLE 2.1

First- and Second-Generation Immigrants Among Adult
Citizens, by Race and Ethnicity, 1994–2000

	Percentage of First-Generation (Naturalized) Citizens		Percentage of Second-Generation Citizens
	Less Than 15 Years in the U.S.	15 Years or More in the U.S.	
White	23	42	75
Black	10	5	2
Latino	29	30	18
Asian	37	22	5

SOURCE: Current Population Survey, 1994–2000 (weighted tabulations) .

are eligible to vote. Among first-generation immigrants who have lived
less than fifteen years in the United States, white immigrants constitute
about 23 percent of those eligible to vote in the 1994–2000 period.

Among those who have lived for more than fifteen years in the
United States, the proportion of white immigrants increases to 42 percent, making whites the largest racial group among naturalized citizens
in earlier cohorts. Finally, the voting-age population among second-
generation adults is still heavily influenced by the early-century waves
of European immigration. Since second-generation children of immigrants who arrived in the United States after 1965 are still relatively
young, whites constitute an overwhelming proportion of second-generation adult respondents. Thus, there is no empirical justification to exclude the political behavior of whites when studying contemporary
trends in immigrant electoral participation. Of course, there may be important national-origin differences among white immigrants, something to consider in the chapters that follow. This study therefore breaks
new ground in the scholarly understanding of immigrant political participation by including whites as part of a cross-racial and cross-gener-
ational analysis.

The literature on political participation among contemporary immi-

grants in the United States has thus been steadily getting more volumi-
nous, with political scientists assessing the extent to which traditional
understandings of electoral participation are sufficient to understand
voter turnout among first- and second-generation immigrants. As this
review has indicated, however, we still do not have a systematic and
comparative understanding of immigrant electoral participation across
racial groups. This study seeks to provide such a systematic understanding—by relying primarily on various data sources at the national
level or cross-regional level and by comparing the effects of various factors using the same explanatory models. These data sources provide
important information about the rising presence of immigrants in the
national electorate and various state electorates. Furthermore, they enable us to address the central questions that motivate this study—
whether standard models of electoral participation account for the voting behavior of immigrants, whether participation rises or falls after the
first immigrant generation, whether new factors related to immigrant
adaptation add significantly to the existing theoretical knowledge on
voter turnout, and finally, whether group differences for campaign contributions and other forms of political engagement mirror those found
at the ballot box.

Data on Contemporary Immigrants

Prior to conducting these analyses, however, it is worth considering the
data sources used in this book. First, data on immigrant demographics
are derived from historical U.S. Census data, figures from the most recent Census, as well as data from recent Current Population Surveys.
The primary sources of information about voting among contemporary
immigrants are the Current Population Survey Voter Supplements
(CPS), beginning in November 1994, when the CPS began to ask questions regarding the nativity of respondents and their parents. The CPS
datasets are enhanced by adding various contextual-level variables relating to racial concentration, poverty levels, electoral dynamics, and
institutional rules regarding registration and turnout.[13]

The CPS offers several advantages in the study of voting participation across racial groups and immigrant generations. First, it is the only
national survey since 1994 that has consistently asked questions on the
nativity of respondents and their parents. The nativity of respondents is
important to ascertain the generational status of respondents, since

those who are born outside the United States are first-generation, those born in the United States with foreign-born parents are second-generation, and those born in the United States to native-born parents are in the third generation or later. Questions on the nativity of respondents and their parents cannot be found in the National Black Election Study or in the National Election Studies (NES) since 1994. National surveys of Latino participation do have questions that differentiate respondents of different immigrant generations, but they have been conducted far less frequently and regularly than the CPS; the Latino National Political Survey was conducted in 1990, followed by the Washington Post / Kaiser / Harvard University Survey of Latinos (PKH) in 1999. Surveys of Asian American political participation are even more rare, and no study has yet been conducted at the national level. Thus, the Current Population Survey holds several advantages as the only national source of information on voting in recent elections that has consistently asked questions on the generational status of respondents.

Another advantage to the CPS is that it is the only national survey of political participation that includes sizable samples of whites, blacks, Latinos, and Asian Americans of different immigrant generations. Table A.1 in the Appendix indicates the number of respondents from pooled data in the CPS for members of different racial groups and different immigrant generations. Among first-generation immigrants, there are at least seven hundred respondents in each major racial category, and among second-generation immigrants there are at least five hundred respondents. Even when the population is divided into national origin groups, the samples for first- and second-generation respondents are large enough to produce reliable estimates of voting participation and analyses of the relationship of voting to factors such as age and socio-economic status.

The CPS also has advantages in the richness of data regarding immigrant characteristics. For instance, the survey contains questions on both country of origin and year of entry into the United States. These measures are important because they enable researchers to ask whether factors such as coming from repressive regimes or from nations that allow dual citizenship influence the likelihood of immigrant participation in American politics. As I shall indicate in Chapter 5, there are some scholars who suggest that those who come from communist regimes are more likely to participate in American politics than those who come from democratic regimes. Knowing the immigrant's country of origin and year of immigration enables us to test this hypothesis in a systematic manner, a hypothesis which until now has been asserted only in regard to the Cuban American population. Since surveys such as the National Election Studies do not contain such measures, we cannot test the effects of factors such as duration of stay, communist country origin, or dual citizenship policies on political participation. Finally, another advantage of the Current Population Survey is that it has greater variation than datasets such as the Post / Kaiser / Harvard survey on factors such as state concentration of Latinos and access to Spanish-language ballots. This is because the CPS is a truly national survey, getting responses from all fifty states, whereas the PKH survey is limited to five states and the District of Columbia. Thus the advantages of the CPS (size, national scope, racial diversity of respondents, richness of data regarding immigrants, and consistency of questions regarding nativity in recent elections) make it a valuable dataset to study immigrant electoral participation.

There are, however, some limitations to using the Current Population Survey. First, it is not possible to discern the national origins of those in the third generation and later because there are no questions on ethnic identity or country of origin separate from questions of nativity. The only exception is for Latinos, for whom all respondents are asked about their ethnic identity. Also, the CPS does not include any individual-level information on political attitudes or party contact that have been known to lead to greater participation. It has been well documented that individual contact with party organizations, strong party identification and feelings of political efficacy increase the likelihood that a person will vote (Rosenstone and Hansen 1993; Miller and Shanks 1996; Verba, Schlozman, and Brady 1995). I address the absence of individual-level mobilization measures by incorporating contextual measures such as the competitiveness of statewide elections and the history of voting participation in the state. However, I cannot find a similar contextual variable that captures the effects of other attitudinal factors such as political efficacy and party identification. Thus, through the use of contextual measures from external data sources, I am able to solve some but not all of the problems associated with political attitudes that are missing in the CPS.

Some scholars argue that the CPS is also limited because it does not include validated measures of voting that confirm whether an individual's reported vote matches public records of registration and voting. However, vote misreporting in the CPS is considerably lower than misreporting in other surveys such as the National Election Studies

(Presser, Traugott, and Traugott 1990). Also, the problem of misreporting U.S. citizenship in the CPS can largely be solved by excluding those foreign-born respondents who claim U.S. citizenship yet have spent less than six years in the United States (Passel and Clark 1998). Still, group biases in vote misreporting among U.S. citizens may remain a concern. For instance, some studies have shown that levels of misreporting among blacks and Latinos are higher than those among whites (Abramson and Claggett 1992; Shaw, de la Garza, and Lee 2000). However, there is considerable disagreement over whether the higher level of mismatch between reported and validated votes among minorities is due to their higher propensity to misreport (Abramson and Claggett 1992) or to the fact that racial minorities are more likely to live in areas with poor record-keeping of voter registration or unreliable voting systems (Presser, Traugott, and Traugott 1990; Brady 2003). Even if systems of vote validation are accurate, examination of results from surveys with validated vote measures indicate that the findings regarding immigrant generation are not weakened. Thus, for instance, an examination of validated data in a three-state survey of Latinos in 1996 (Tomás Rivera Policy Institute Survey 1996) shows no significant differences in vote misreporting across immigrant generations. I also used the NES to examine vote misreporting only for white respondents (the size of the black, Asian American, and Latino subsamples were too small for a similar analysis). Second-generation whites in the NES are less likely to misreport their votes than those in other immigrant generations. However, this only serves to strengthen the effects of generational status and does not nullify the other findings presented in this book.

In addition to the Current Population Survey, I also rely on the National Election Studies to provide a measure of external validity to the findings in the CPS. One significant advantage of the NES over the Current Population Survey is that the former contains several questions relating to political attitudes and mobilization. On the other hand, the NES does have its limitations, the most significant of which is that there are not large enough sample sizes of blacks, Latinos, and Asian Americans from different immigrant generations to provide reliable measures of participation. Thus I use the NES to examine participation among white immigrants in more detail. The National Election Studies are based on in-person interviews of a random sample of American citizens of voting age. Between 1964 and 1994, the NES consistently asked questions on whether respondents and their parents were born in the United States. Thus, it is possible to combine the fifteen election years between 1964 and 1994 to construct a pooled dataset of responses related to public opinion and participation. In such a pooled dataset, there is a sufficiently large number of responses among first- and second-generation citizens to make reliable estimates of participation and its determinants. As can be seen from Table A.2 in the Appendix, there are over one thousand responses from first-generation white immigrants and more than three thousand responses from second-generation immigrants.

The National Election Studies also make it possible to examine immigrant participation for members of different national origins, but only 48 percent of respondents in this pooled dataset provided an answer to a question on the respondent's ethnicity or nationality. As a consequence, the number of cases of first-generation Polish and Irish immigrants is too small for multivariate analyses of electoral participation. However, there are sufficient numbers of respondents in other immigrant generations to make comparisons between second-generation immigrants and those in the third generation and later.

Just as the National Election Study is a good source of data on political attitudes and participation for white immigrants, the Post / Kaiser / Harvard (PKH) survey is a good data source for Latinos. The PKH survey is based on telephone interviews in July and August of 1999 conducted in five states (California, Florida, Illinois, New York, and Texas) and the District of Columbia. Together, these six areas account for about 70 percent of Latino citizens in the United States. In its multistate sample of Latino and non-Latino adults, the PKH survey contains 1,443 Latino citizens and 974 noncitizens. As indicated by Table A.2 in the Appendix, there are sizable samples of first- and second-generation citizens among all major national-origin groups. However, among those respondents in the third and later generations, there are only ten respondents who are of Cuban or Central / South American origin. Thus, the CPS retains its advantage in sample size for Latino populations, even though it is not a survey that attempts to oversample Latinos. Furthermore, there are several contextual factors in the CPS related to immigrant incorporation that are absent from the PKH survey. Still, the PKH survey retains the advantage of including basic measures of party identification and other political attitudes relevant to participation. Thus it should be possible to discern whether some of the patterns uncovered in the national CPS data are reflected in other surveys that include measures of political attitudes and voting participation.

This study also makes occasional use of the Pilot National Asian

American Political Survey (PNAAPS), a multicity survey from the 2000 election (Lien 2004). The PNAAPS was conducted in various Asian languages and utilized a dual sampling frame of random-digit dialing in Asian-heavy zip codes and listed-surname frames. As noted in Table A.2 in the Appendix, the sample size of the survey is smaller than the Asian subsample of the Current Population Survey and is more heavily weighted toward first-generation immigrants. Also, unlike the CPS, the PNAAPS is not national in scope but is focused instead on a set of immigrant-heavy zip codes. The particular sampling method of the Asian American survey may also skew the respondents toward those with limited English proficiency. Still, the PNAAPS retains certain advantages with respect to the CPS. It includes measures of party identification and political attitudes that allow us to test for the consistency of the CPS findings when controlling for these measures. Also, its support of various Asian languages captures the responses of Asian immigrants who have limited English proficiency or who prefer to be interviewed in their native language.

In addition to the NES and ethnic-specific surveys, this study also uses data from the Public Policy Institute of California (PPIC) Statewide Surveys to see whether generational patterns in voting also apply to other forms of political engagement. Questions on campaign contributions and other forms of political participation are absent from other recent surveys such as the 1999 PKH survey. The PPIC surveys, conducted between August and October 2002, have the advantage of containing various measures of participation for members of different racial groups and immigrant generations in California. The random-digit dial survey contains approximately two thousand respondents in each month. Here, I pool across three surveys in consecutive months, yielding a sample size of 6,004 respondents, including 746 Latinos, 195 Asian Americans, and 258 whites who are first-generation immigrants.

Finally, this study goes beyond survey data to include interviews with leaders of various ethnopolitical organizations that have immigrants as their primary members. Interviews of Latino and Asian organization leaders are based on my fieldwork during the summer of 2000 in the following metropolitan areas: Orange County, Los Angeles, and San Francisco in California; San Antonio, Houston, and Austin in Texas; and New York City. Names of organizations were obtained using community directories as well as the snowball method. The community directory used for Latino organizations is the *Anuario Hispano-Hispanic Yearbook* (2000), those for Asian American organizations is the *OCA Na-*

tional Directory of Asian Pacific American Organizations (1999). State and local organizations were chosen for interview if they engaged in any of the following activities: voter registration, voter education, and get-out-the-vote efforts. Overall, leaders or staff members from forty-one organizations were interviewed, which included twenty-two Latino organizations and nineteen Asian American organizations.[14] This study therefore takes advantage of several data sources, including qualitative data, to examine various issues related to immigrant adaptation and political participation in the United States.

CHAPTER 3

A Matter of Numbers

Immigrant Demographics and the Electoral Process

The sleeping giant now awakened. Many Hispanics who have not registered to vote are now doing so—and going to the polls. This includes many immigrants, who waited five years for residency and then became naturalized citizens. Between 80–90% of these new citizens have become registered voters, and most of them will show up at their polling place on Election Day.

Horton Scioneaux

The first step to understanding the political participation of immigrants is to consider their growing numbers at the state and national levels. This chapter addresses some fundamental questions regarding the demographic strengths of first- and second-generation immigrants in the United States. How many immigrants currently live in the United States, and how has their share of the total population changed in the past century? In which states do most immigrants now reside, and what proportion of the population do they represent in those states? Finally, how much do immigrants account for the voting-eligible population at the state and national level?

As the following analysis demonstrates, the rise in immigrant numbers has indeed led to a significant growth in the share of first- and second-generation immigrants in the national electorate and various state electorates since 1970. In many instances, however, the magnitude of these increases has been exaggerated, with overly optimistic rhetoric referring to immigrants as "sleeping giants" or "awakening giants" in the American electorate. First, the proportion of first- and second-generation immigrants in the total population is considerably smaller today than it was during the early 1900s. Furthermore, the foreign-born constitute a smaller share of the overall electorate (adult citizens) than of the resident population. So, while immigrants may in some cases resemble "awakening giants" in the American electorate, they do not loom as large as their numbers would suggest. At the same time, one should not discount the significant transformations wrought by immigration since 1965, such as the changes in the racial composition of the American electorate and in the politics of various states.

National Trends

The importance of immigrants to the electoral process has grown considerably in the past two decades, with substantial increases in the size of the foreign-born population and demographic shifts among the immigrant second generation. Since the liberalization of immigration policy in 1965, the number of first-generation immigrants living in the United States has more than tripled, from 9.6 million in 1970 to 31.2 million today. Just as their numbers have grown, so too has their share of the total population. Table 3.1 presents historical census data on first- and second-generation immigrants from 1850 to 2000. As the data indicate, first-generation immigrants now account for more than one in every ten residents in the United States. Thus, with a tripling of their numbers in the last twenty years and a doubling of their share of the resident population during the same time period, immigrants constitute an increasingly important demographic group in the United States.

While first-generation immigrants enjoy a substantial presence in the United States today, they account for a smaller proportion of the total population now than they did in the early part of the twentieth century. During the peak of the last great wave of migration to the United States, the foreign-born accounted for one out of every seven persons living in the country. With the onset of the Great Depression and World War II, however, the number of people entering the United States diminished sharply. By the middle of the century, the foreign-born population had dwindled to less than 6 percent of the total population. Since the mid-1960s, however, the proportion of immigrants in the population has swung higher once again, with the foreign-born now accounting for

TABLE 3.1

First- and Second-Generation Immigrants as a Proportion of the U.S.
Resident Population, 1850–2000

	Total Population (millions)	First Generation		Second Generation	
		Millions	% of Total	Millions	% of Total
2000	281.4	31.2	11.1	29.0	10.3
1990	248.7	19.6	7.9	—	—
1980	226.5	14.0	6.2	—	—
1970	203.2	9.6	4.7	24.0	11.8
1960	179.3	9.7	5.4	24.4	13.6
1950	150.2	10.4	6.9	—	—
1940	131.7	11.6	8.8	—	—
1930	122.8	14.2	11.6	26.0	21.2
1920	105.7	14.0	13.2	22.8	21.6
1910	92.0	13.5	14.7	18.9	20.6
1900	76.0	10.3	13.6	15.7	20.7
1890	62.6	9.3	14.8	11.5	18.4
1880	50.2	6.7	13.3	—	—
1870	38.6	5.6	14.4	—	—
1860	31.4	4.2	13.2	—	—
1850	23.2	2.2	9.7	—	—

SOURCE: Campbell J. Gibson and Emily Lennon, "Historical Census Statistics on the Foreign-Born Population of the United States: 1850–1990," *Population Division Working Paper No. 29* (Washington, DC: U.S. Census Bureau, 1999); and Current Population Survey (November 2000).

about 11 percent of the U.S. resident population. Furthermore, evidence from population projections indicates that the number of first-generation immigrants will continue to rise in the next two decades, reaching over 12 percent (or 41 million) by 2020 (Passel and Van Hook 2000).

The demographic effects of immigration are also evident in the growth of the immigrant second generation—native-born children whose parents were born outside the United States. Second-generation immigrants today number over 29 million residents, or about 10 percent of the total population. In the early part of the twentieth century, second-generation immigrants accounted for a still greater proportion of the population than they do today. Historical census estimates of the immigrant second generation are far more spotty than census figures on the foreign-born because questions on the nativity of respondents' parents were not included in many recent censuses (Table 3.1).[1] Still, the evidence indicates that from the 1900s to the 1930s the share of second-generation immigrants in the resident population was more than twice as large as it is today, with proportions reaching more than 20 percent of the total population. Also unlike in the past, the second generation today is not considerably larger than the foreign-born population. Indeed, in 2000, first-generation immigrants actually accounted for a slightly larger share of the resident population (11 percent) than did second-generation immigrants (10 percent).

This recent parity of the two populations is a result of several factors. First, there has been no drastic reduction in the flow of the foreign-born since the 1960s, whereas there were substantial drops in immigration during the Great Depression and World War II. Thus, while the growth of second-generation immigrants outpaced the inflow of the foreign-born in the early 1900s, the same is not true today. Another reason for the recent parity of the two populations is that the children of many first-generation immigrants have yet to be born. Nearly a third of foreign-born women in the United States are under the age of thirty, so there will be a substantial lag between the rise of the first generation and the growth of the immigrant second generation. Finally, the foreign-born population in the early 1920s had much higher levels of fertility than immigrants do today, leading to a greater equalization in the relative size of the first- and second-generation populations. Because of all these factors, the growth of the second generation from the post-1965 wave of immigration will be relatively modest, with the share of the total population rising to 13 percent by 2020. Still, with the addition of the foreign-born population, first- and second-generation immigrants will account for more than a quarter of the U.S. population within the next two decades.

So far, we have seen that first- and second-generation immigrants constitute a sizable and growing presence in the United States, although their share of the total population is lower now than during the period of massive immigration in the early 1900s. It should be noted, however, that the net effect of immigration on American society and politics does not depend on numbers alone; it also depends on the relationship between immigration and the changing racial composition of the U.S. population (McClain and Stewart 1999). During the early 1900s, immigrants to the United States came primarily from countries in Eastern and Southern Europe. While these national-origin groups differed from previous waves of German and Irish immigrants, they soon became amalgamated into a common white, European-origin identity (Jacobson 1999).

The majority of immigrants in the United States today trace their origins to countries outside of Europe. Data from the U.S. Census Bureau indicate that in 1900 about 86 percent of the foreign-born population came from Europe. Today that proportion is a meager 15 percent. By contrast, immigrants from Asia and Latin America now constitute 26 percent and 51 percent, respectively, of the first-generation population. Mirroring these differences in national origins, the racial composition of first-generation immigrants today is markedly different than in the past. In 2000, for instance, non-Hispanic whites constituted about 26 percent of foreign-born residents, while they accounted for over 95 percent of immigrants a century earlier. Also, about two-thirds of the foreign-born today identify as either Asian or Hispanic. Such proportions were unimaginable in the early 1900s when the United States implemented various policies of racial exclusion. Although earlier racial classification schemes differ from those used today, we can infer that less than 3 percent of immigrants in 1900 would have identified as Asian or Hispanic.[2] As other scholars have noted, these changes in the racial composition of the United States resulting from immigration have presented new challenges to politics and intergroup relations in various parts of the country (McClain and Stewart 1999; Yamamoto 1999; Kim 2000; Lien 2001).

The effects of immigration on the racial composition of the United States are also evident in the transformations of the immigrant second generation. The second generation today continues to bear the imprint of the earlier waves of European immigration, with whites now accounting for 50 percent of those who are the children of immigrants. However, among younger members of the second immigrant generation, whites account for a considerably smaller proportion of the population. Data from recent Current Population Surveys indicate that only 23 percent of second-generation respondents under the age of eighteen identify as white, while 53 percent identify as Latino, 16 percent as Asian, and 8 percent as black. Thus, even though the second generation may not grow to represent as large a share of the total population as in the early 1900s, it will still play a significant role in transforming the

TABLE 3.2

States in Which First- and Second-Generation Immigrants
Are 25 Percent or More of the Total Population, 2000

	First Generation (%)	Second Generation (%)	Total (%)
California	26	20	46
New York	20	16	36
Hawaii	16	18	34
Florida	20	13	33
Nevada	16	15	31
New Jersey	16	15	31
Arizona	14	14	28
Connecticut	13	15	28
Massachusetts	12	15	27
Texas	13	13	26
Rhode Island	8	17	25

SOURCE: Current Population Survey (November 2000).

racial composition of the United States, as the old second generation of
European ancestry gradually passes away and the "new second generation" enters young adulthood.

State-Level Trends

In addition to constituting an important and growing share of the national population, immigrants have also fundamentally reshaped the
demographic contours of several states. As Table 3.2 indicates, in 2000
first- and second-generation immigrants already accounted for over
one-quarter of the population in eleven states. California, the state with
the largest number of immigrants, is also the state with the greatest
proportion, with first- and second-generation immigrants accounting
for nearly one-half of the state's population. Other high-immigrant
states include New York, Hawaii, and Florida, where first- and second-
generation immigrants account for at least one-third of their respective
state populations. Rounding out the rest are Nevada, New Jersey, Arizona, Connecticut, Massachusetts, Texas, and Rhode Island, all states in

which first- and second-generation immigrations constitute over 25 percent of the resident population.

The demographic strengths of immigrants in these various states have had significant implications for policies in areas such as education, affirmative action, and immigration. In some instances, the effects of immigrants on state policies have been based primarily on their roles as taxpayers and consumers of public goods, while in other cases, the effects have been the result of their political participation. We shall address the issue of immigrant political participation later in this chapter and in the chapters that follow. For now, however, we can note that immigrants are already having a significant impact on the politics and societies of several states and will continue to do so for the foreseeable future.

In examining the geographic concentration of immigrants today, it is also instructive to compare these state-level patterns to those found in the United States a century ago. Scholarship on immigrants in the early twentieth century has largely focused on cities and states in the Northeast and Midwest. Indeed, a significant proportion of immigrants in pre–World War I America lived in cities such as New York and Chicago and in states such as Massachusetts and Rhode Island. Yet, as Table 3.3 indicates, the states with the largest proportion of immigrants during the turn of the twentieth century were rural states in the Midwest, such as North Dakota, Minnesota, and Wisconsin. Immigrants and their children living in these rural states came primarily from Germany and Scandinavia and vastly outnumbered the native-stock population in these areas. However, during the great wave of immigration in the early twentieth century, most immigrants settled in the cities of the Northeast, making Rhode Island, Massachusetts, Connecticut, and New York the states with the highest proportion of first- and second-generation immigrants by 1930. Indeed, in most of these states, the foreign-born and their children accounted for over one-half of the total state population, with proportions in a few states reaching nearly two-thirds.

The sizable presence of immigrants in the Northeast during the 1920s and 1930s also had significant implications for their political incorporation, since many of these cities and states were dominated by party machines. As Steven Erie (1988) and Gerald Gamm (1989) have shown, the presence of party machines did not necessarily mean the easy incorporation of immigrants into processes of state and local governance. Indeed, as Erie notes, the myth of the party boss drawing im-

TABLE 3.3

Top Ten States by Proportion of First- and Second-Generation Immigrants, 1900 and 1930

	First Generation (%)	Second Generation (%)	Total (%)
1900 Census			
North Dakota	35	42	77
Minnesota	29	46	75
Wisconsin	25	46	71
Rhode Island	31	33	64
Massachusetts	30	32	62
South Dakota	22	39	61
Utah	19	42	61
New York	26	33	59
Connecticut	26	31	57
Michigan	22	34	57
1930 Census			
Rhode Island	25	43	68
Massachusetts	25	40	65
Connecticut	24	41	65
New York	25	36	61
North Dakota	15	45	61
New Jersey	21	35	56
Minnesota	15	40	56
Wisconsin	13	37	50
New Hampshire	18	31	48
Michigan	17	30	47

SOURCE: U.S. Citizenship and Immigration Services, 2002, p. 162.

migrants into the political process was often belied by the attempts of various Irish-dominated machines to limit the size of their patronage circles and to prevent the entry of immigrants from Italy, Russia, and elsewhere. It was not until the Great Depression and the arrival of the New Deal that many immigrants were able to overcome the barriers to entry set up by party machines. Even then, however, most immigrants from Asia and Latin America were excluded from participation in politics through measures such as citizenship exclusion, loss of property rights, and racial gerrymandering (Espiritu 1992; Hero 1992; Smith 1997).

Party machines are less relevant to the political incorporation of immigrants today for two reasons. First, with the creation of a nationally controlled merit-based bureaucracy during the New Deal, party bosses had considerably fewer opportunities to reward political support with patronage jobs. Furthermore, settlement patterns of immigrants in the last few decades have meant that immigrants are a significant proportion of the total population in states such as California, Florida, Arizona, and Texas—states that have never had a tradition of party machines similar to those found in the Northeast. Thus, even if there are remnants of party machines in New York, Rhode Island, and Massachusetts, immigrants constitute a smaller presence in those states when compared to others such as California and Florida. We shall examine the role of state residential contexts on immigrant participation in Chapters 5 and 6. For now, however, we see that the states with the highest proportion of immigrants today are less likely to be those with party machines, or even the present-day remnants of older machines.

Translating Numbers to Power

So far, we have seen that even though first- and second-generation immigrants account for a sizable proportion of the national population and various state populations, their shares are still smaller than those found in the early decades of the twentieth century. Thus, whatever declarations we may find of "awakening giants" in states such as California, such giants are still modest when compared to those found in 1900 or 1930. The impact of immigration on the contemporary electorate is also limited in two other respects—by the citizenship status of the first generation and the age structure of the second generation.

Citizenship is the most significant factor that accounts for the gap between the share of first-generation immigrants in the resident population and their proportion of the American electorate. Although the officially required minimum time to acquire citizenship is five years for permanent residents of the United States, figures from the U.S. Citizenship and Immigration Services (or USCIS, formerly the Immigration

TABLE 3.4

Years in the United States Prior to Naturalization for Select Years, by
Region of Origin, 1970–2002

	2002	2000	1995	1990	1980	1970
Overall	8	10	9	8	8	8
Africa	7	8	6	7	7	6
Asia	8	8	7	7	7	6
Europe	7	8	9	10	10	9
North America	11	11	14	11	11	7
South America	8	10	10	9	9	7

SOURCE: U.S. Citizenship and Immigration Services, 2002, p. 162.

and Naturalization Service, or INS) indicate that the average length of
stay before acquiring citizenship has recently hovered around nine to
ten years (Table 3.4). There are also important country-of-origin differences in the speed with which immigrants become U.S. citizens. As
Table 3.4 indicates, immigrants from Africa and Asia acquire citizenship
the fastest, followed by those from Europe, South America, and finally,
from North America. More generally, those coming from far away regions and from repressive regimes acquire citizenship relatively quickly
because they have no plans to return home. Also, dual citizenship policies among democratic regimes lead to higher U.S. citizenship because
they allow immigrants to naturalize without giving up their privileges
in their countries of origin (Yang 1994; Jones-Correa 2002). Still, for
many immigrants, factors such as limited English proficiency, low educational attainment, and lack of familiarity with mainstream institutions tend to prolong the gap between qualification for citizenship and
naturalization (Yang 1994; Johnson et al. 1999). Finally, the gap between
residency and citizenship is nearly insurmountable for the over 8 million undocumented immigrants currently living in the United States
(Cohn 2001).

So, for various reasons, we can expect to see significant gaps between immigrants' share of the resident population and their share of
the voting-eligible population. Data from the Current Population Survey confirm that this is indeed the case. While the foreign-born now

Naturalizations
(millions)

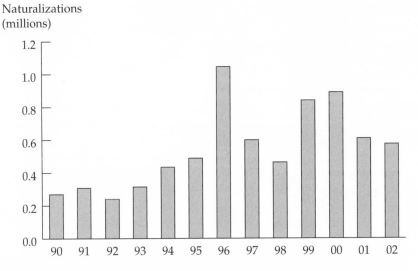

Figure 3.1. Number of Naturalizations, 1990–2002
SOURCE: U.S. Citizenship and Immigration Services, 2002, p. 163.

constitute about 10 percent of the overall population, they make up only 6 percent of the voting-eligible citizenry. This discrepancy is due primarily to the fact that nearly 40 percent of the foreign-born had entered the United States during the 1990s, leaving many of them either ineligible for naturalization by the end of the decade or still in the process of applying for citizenship. In recent years, however, the proportion of the foreign-born in the electorate has grown substantially, thanks to sharp increases in the number of naturalizations (Figure 3.1).[3]

With immigrants now acquiring citizenship at a rate of over five hundred thousand per year, the share of the foreign-born citizens in the electorate will continue to rise in the years to come. Indeed, if present rates of naturalization are sustained, the share of first-generation immigrants among the American citizenry will reach 10 percent within the next twenty years. Still, there will continue to be a gap between immigrant residents and naturalized citizens because undocumented immigrants account for over one-quarter of the foreign-born population today. So, barring any large-scale return of undocumented immigrants to their countries of origin, and without any provisions for amnesty along the lines of the Immigration Reform and Control Act of 1986, the gap between residency and citizenship will persist for first-generation immigrants. Thus, even though the foreign-born will grow as a proportion of the electorate in the next twenty years, their ability to translate numbers to political power will be limited by the size of the undocumented immigrant population.

In addition to the foreign-born, the second generation will also grow as a proportion of the American electorate in the next twenty years. At present, the second generation accounts for a smaller proportion of the adult citizen population (8 percent) than of the resident population (10 percent). This is because many in the immigrant second generation are the children of those who arrived in the United States after 1980. Citizenship is not a barrier to participation among these second-generation immigrants, but age is certainly a consideration, as those with foreign-born parents account for a greater share of the under-eighteen population than those with native-born parents. As this new population reaches young adulthood, the proportion of second-generation citizens in the American electorate will begin to grow and is expected to account for about 13 percent of those eligible to participate in elections. Taken together, first- and second-generation citizens will therefore account for nearly a quarter of the American electorate within the next two decades. So, even though the age structure of the new second generation may hinder its political participation, it will be less of a liability in the next two decades. Similarly, citizenship status may limit the participation of first-generation immigrants, but sustained levels of high naturalization will mean that immigrants will soon grow to be an important part of the voting-eligible population.

In the meantime, the impact of immigration and naturalization on the voting-eligible population is already evident in states like California, New York, and Florida. As Table 3.5 indicates, there are now nine states where first- and second-generation immigrants account for at least one out of every five adult citizens. More pointedly, in five of the states—Hawaii, California, New York, Florida, and New Jersey—naturalized citizens account for more than 10 percent of the voting-eligible population. The growing presence of immigrants in state electorates also points to their potential to affect national politics. For instance, the nine states with a large proportion of first- and second-generation immigrants in the electorate account for 34 percent of the seats in the House of Representatives (147 out of 435 seats) and 31% of those in the Electoral College (165 out of 538 seats). Similarly, the five states with a significant proportion of naturalized citizens account for 28 percent of

TABLE 3.5

First- and Second-Generation Citizens as a Proportion of
the Adult Citizen Population, by State of Residence, 2004
(weighted tabulations)

	First Generation (%)	Second Generation (%)	Total (%)
Overall	6.5	8.5	15
Hawaii	15.6	22.1	38
California	17.2	16.5	34
New York	15.1	15.8	31
New Jersey	11.4	13.8	25
Rhode Island	6.8	15.8	23
Massachusetts	7.9	14.5	22
Florida	11.1	10.7	22
Connecticut	7.4	13.7	21
Arizona	7.3	12.4	20

SOURCE: Current Population Survey, April 2004.

the House of Representatives and a quarter of the Electoral College.
With the proportion of first- and second-generation immigrants growing in Sunbelt states that already have high overall populations, the impact of immigration on politics at the national level will continue to
grow at a modest but significant pace in the years to come.

CHAPTER 4

Are the Newcomers Exceptional?

The Applicability of Traditional Models to Immigrant Political Participation

> Citizens of higher social and economic status participate more in politics. This generalization has been confirmed many times in many nations. And it generally holds true whether one uses level of education, income, or occupation as the measure of social status.
>
> Sidney Verba and Norman Nie

> Socioeconomic theories have long been the cornerstone of political participation studies. However, these studies are incomplete and particularly unsuited to explaining behavior found within immigrant minority communities.
>
> Wendy Tam Cho

Voting is the least costly and most widespread form of political participation in the United States. Yet voting participation is by no means a universal act. In recent elections, participation rates in presidential elections have hovered between 50 and 60 percent, while voting in midterm elections has dipped below the 40 percent mark. Given that about one-half of the voting-eligible population does not participate in elections, the question naturally arises as to why this is so. Scholars of American politics have devoted considerable attention to the question of who votes and who does not participate in electoral politics. Studies of electoral participation in the past two decades have tended to emphasize one or more of the following sets of factors: (1) demographic characteristics and individual resources related to socioeconomic status, (2) the incorporation of individuals into social networks, (3) institutional barriers to registering and voting, (4) contexts of political mobilization and political culture, and (5) attitudinal factors such as party identification and political efficacy.[1]

In recent years, some scholars have questioned the relevance of these traditional models to explain the voting behavior of nonwhite immigrants.[2] For instance, recent studies of voting among immigrant minorities challenge the standard finding that the likelihood of voting increases with age, education, and income. Some have shown that education has a weak or inconsistent effect on voting (Lien 1994; Junn 1999) and that age does not always lead to higher participation (Hritzuk and Park 2000). Indeed, one study indicates that age actually has a negative relationship to voting for Asian and Latino immigrants (Tam Cho 1999). These findings therefore suggest an "immigrant exceptionalism" when it comes to the effects of socioeconomic status on voting.

While these findings may challenge the relevance of traditional models in explaining political participation among immigrant and minority populations, they do have significant limitations. First, many of these studies have not applied the same explanatory framework to members of different racial groups and immigrant generations using the same data source. Thus, it is quite possible that inconsistencies in the relationship of traditional variables to voting are due more to differences in the collection of survey data and in the construction of explanatory models than to any systematic differences between whites and nonwhites or between people of different immigrant generations. Another limitation to these studies is that they use single point-in-time estimates of electoral participation, leaving the findings vulnerable to the vagaries of particular election years. Finally, the findings of immigrant exceptionalism are based on survey data that are more than a decade old—indeed, two of the studies are based on a 1984 survey in California (Tam Cho 1999; Lien 1994). The timing of survey data is especially important in the study of immigrant political participation because the naturalized population is considerably larger today than it was in the mid-1980s, with a substantial portion of immigrants having lived in the United States for fifteen years or more.[3] Indeed, more recent analyses based on the 2000 multicity Asian American survey show education to be a strong predictor of voting (Lien, Conway, and Wong 2004). Thus, it is important to use data from recent elections to provide a definitive assessment of whether traditional models of voting apply to first- and second-generation immigrants across racial and ethnic groups.

In considering the traditional set of factors that explain voter participation, we have the advantage of utilizing the Current Population Survey (CPS), a data source with sufficient numbers of respondents across racial groups and immigrant generations to provide reliable estimates of group differences. As noted in Chapter 2, however, the CPS is limited in that it does not contain measures of individual-level political attitudes and orientations. Thus, in considering the effects of factors such as party identification on voting, it will be necessary to use other datasets such as the National Election Studies (NES), the Post / Kaiser / Harvard (PKH) survey of Latinos, and the Pilot National Asian American Political Survey (PNAAPS).

SES Models of Participation

The likelihood of voting increases among those who are older, wealthier, and more educated. These findings have constituted the bedrock of studies of voting participation since the 1960s. The significant effects of socioeconomic status and age (hereafter SES variables) have withstood not only the test of time; they have also been shown to be consistent across surveys as disparate as the Current Population Survey, the National Election Study, and the Citizen Participation Study. As Sidney Verba and Norman Nie note in their 1972 study *Participation in America*, "Citizens of higher social and economic status participate more in politics. This generalization has been confirmed many times in many nations" (125). Over the years, scholars have refined the findings regarding SES variables by more clearly specifying the mechanisms through which such variables operate, whether it be through the acquisition of relevant skills (Verba, Schlozman, and Brady 1995) or through the likelihood of being mobilized (Rosenstone and Hansen 1993). The applicability of SES models to racial and ethnic minority groups has also been refined, with scholars noting that there are significant residual effects of race and political context that remain even after controlling for factors such as age, education, and income (Bobo and Gilliam 1990; Leighley 2001; Arvizu and Garcia 1996).

However, some recent studies of voting among immigrant minorities go beyond the assertion that controlling for SES still leaves significant residual effects of race and political context (Lien 1994; Junn 1999; Tam Cho 1999). These studies stake a more ambitious claim—that factors such as age and education have inconsistent or null effects on voting among contemporary immigrants. This section tests the validity of such claims of immigrant exceptionalism by conducting a deep and systematic examination of the effects of factors such as age, education, and income across racial groups, national origins, and immigrant generations.

Age

Several studies have shown that age has a significant and positive relationship to the likelihood of voting. In their early, seminal work on political participation, Verba and Nie (1972) note that age has a significant relationship to voting even after controlling for education, income, and length of residence. Raymond Wolfinger and Steven Rosenstone (1980) find similar results in their study of CPS data from the 1970s, noting that life experience can serve as a sort of substitute for education, providing people with skills and information relevant to voting participation. One difference between the two studies is that the former shows a slight decline in participation among the elderly, lending support to the "life cycle hypothesis," which predicts a decline in psychological engagement and participation among the elderly. On the other hand, Wolfinger and Rosenstone note that there is a positive relationship between age and voting even among the very old. Subsequent analyses of pooled data from the National Election Studies show that participation increases in a monotonic fashion throughout the age scale, casting doubt on the life cycle hypothesis (Rosenstone and Hansen 1993). Finally, even newer models of participation that control for factors such as "civic skills" and "political engagement" find that age is significantly and positively related to voting participation throughout the age range (Verba, Schlozman, and Brady 1995).

Studies of racial and ethnic groups have shown mixed results with respect to the significance of age and voting participation. In her analysis of participation as reported in the National Black Election Study, Katherine Tate (1991) finds that age is a significant predictor of voting in only two of four elections. On the other hand, the results of Lawrence Bobo and Franklin Gilliam Jr. (1990) indicate that age is a significant predictor of overall political participation. Studies of participation among Latinos have shown age to be significantly and positively related to voting, a finding that is consistent across national-origin groups (Calvo and Rosenstone 1989; Arvizu and Garcia 1996; DeSipio 1996a).

Challenges to the presumed relationship between age and voting get stronger, however, when the analysis is restricted to naturalized citizens. In her study of voting among Asian Americans and Latinos in California, Wendy Tam Cho (1999) shows that age has a negative relationship to voting among immigrants. She attributes this negative effect to dynamics that are particular to the immigration process, arguing that younger immigrants are more likely to be socialized into American political institutions and norms than older immigrants. The issue of immigrant exceptionalism with respect to the effects of age on voting resonates with traditional theories of straight-line immigrant assimilation, and it has yet to be examined at the national level or in recent elections.

Education

In addition to age, education has also been shown to be a powerful predictor of participation among the general citizenry. Wolfinger and Rosenstone (1980) find education to have the strongest effects on voting, especially among those with low incomes. Rosenstone and Hansen (1993) affirm the importance of education, finding it to be an indicator both of political skills and of the likelihood of being mobilized. A similar argument is found in *Education and Democratic Citizenship in America* (Nie, Junn, and Stehlik-Barry 1996), in which the authors argue that education increases the likelihood of participation through two causal pathways: verbal cognitive proficiency and social network centrality. Once again, however, the picture is mixed with regard to ethnic and immigrant populations. In her analysis of voting participation in the National Black Election Study, Tate shows education to be significant in only one of the four elections under consideration. Similarly, studies based on the Latino National Political Survey show that education is significantly related to participation for Mexican Americans and Puerto Ricans, but not for Cuban Americans (Arvizu and Garcia 1996). Another study of Latinos in the 1990 Citizen Participation Survey finds that education has no effects on the likelihood of voting after controlling for factors such as group size and contexts of mobilization (Leighley 2001). Finally, some analyses of Asian American participation have pointed to an insignificant relationship for education (Lien 1994; Junn 1999), and one study actually finds a negative relationship between education and voting (Tam Cho 1999).

Although there are no studies that restrict their analysis to the effects of education among immigrant respondents, Tam Cho suggests that the lack of significant effect among Asian Americans may be due to the fact that they are more likely to be educated abroad and that "in other countries, especially non-democratic ones, very different ideals of government and society are inculcated" (1999, 1154). As noted earlier, however, some of these null findings may be due instead to factors unique to particular states such as California, or to periods in which naturalized citizens were less numerous and less well established than they are today. Some of the inconsistencies in the effects of education may be also due to variation in the collection of survey data and in the construction of explanatory models, barriers that can be overcome with the use of the Current Population Survey.

Income

Studies of voting among the general citizenry have also shown income to be a significant predictor of participation, although the effects are often weaker than those of age or education. Wolfinger and Rosenstone (1980) note that the impact of income is modest compared to that of education, raising probabilities of turnout by only 14 percent over the entire income range. In their analysis of the National Election Studies, Rosenstone and Hansen (1993) show mixed results for income in their analysis of pooled NES data from 1956 to 1988. During midterm elections, the effect of income on turnout is weak, but during presidential elections, the effect of income is comparable to that of education. Finally, Sidney Verba, Kay Lehman Schlozman, and Henry Brady (1995) also show income to be a weak but significant predictor of voting participation. Studies of political participation among blacks show that income is not statistically significant—Tate's analysis (1991) shows income to be significant only during presidential primaries, while Bobo and Gilliam (1990) do not find any significant relationship between income and overall participation. Similarly, studies of Asian American and Latino participation reveal insignificant relationships between income and voting (Lien 1994), a finding that is sustained when the analysis is restricted to naturalized immigrants (Tam Cho 1999).

Thus studies of voting participation among the overall population, as well as among ethnic groups, reveal a mixed picture regarding the effects of income. Income is significant in certain types of elections but not in others, or it is significant for certain groups but not others. As noted earlier, differences among the several findings may be due to variation in the collection of survey data or in the construction of explanatory models. In the case of income, however, they may also be due to inconsistencies in the reporting and coding of income variables. For example, the CPS allows for eleven income categories, whereas the NES has only four. By using the same explanatory model and by using the same measure of income across ethnic groups, we can thus hope to ascertain whether these differences in the impact of income on voting participation are systematic.

SES Models and Immigrant Voting

I examine the effects of SES on voting by conducting logit regressions for twelve subsamples (four racial groups and three immigrant generations) that control for various factors related to demographic characteristics, social incorporation, institutional barriers to participation, and contexts of mobilization. The coefficients from the logit regressions can be found in the Appendix. For the sake of ease of interpretation, I present the results here as a set of predicted probabilities for each subsample. These predicted probabilities are generated by holding all the other independent variables at their means for each subsample and assigning different values to the variable in question.

Age

Figure 4.1 presents a series of results for the effect of age on participation among whites, blacks, Latinos, and Asian Americans of different immigrant generations. For all racial groups and all immigrant generations, age has a significant and positive relationship to voting. Among first-generation Latino immigrants, the predicted probability of participation increases by nearly over 100 percent over the age range. Similarly for Asian immigrants, the probability of participation increases by 92 percent, while for first-generation blacks and whites the increase in participation is 51 percent and 55 percent respectively. It is also important to note that for virtually every group the relationship between age and voting is curvilinear, declining among the elderly.[4] This consistent decline in participation among the very old is in line with Verba and Nie's findings from 1972 and the predictions of the "life cycle hypothesis," which posits a decline in psychological engagement and participation among the elderly. Thus the results enable us to reject hypotheses that predict a negative or null relationship between age and voting among immigrants and racial minorities; what emerges from the findings is a consistently positive relationship with declines in participation among the very old. It should also be noted that the consistent relationship between age and voting among different immigrant generations is not limited to the CPS dataset.

Separate analyses of voting participation among white immigrants in the National Election Studies and among Latino immigrants in the Washington Post / Kaiser / Harvard survey also reveal that age is significantly and positively related to voting (see Table A.11 in the Appendix). The same is also true for first- and second-generation immigrants in the 2000 multicity survey of Asian Americans. These findings among whites, Latinos, and Asian Americans are significant even when controlling for attitudinal factors such as party identification and political efficacy. Furthermore, in most cases the likelihood of voting declines among the very old—a finding that is similar to the findings based on analyses from the Current Population Survey.

While age has a significant effect on voting for all groups, the magnitude of the relationship does vary (Figure 4.1). First, age has the strongest effect on participation among Latinos regardless of immigrant generation, followed by Asian Americans, whites, and blacks. It is important to note, however, that a stronger relationship does not necessarily mean higher participation. For instance, Asian Americans have the second-largest increases in the likelihood of voting because of age. Still, elderly Asian Americans of all immigrant generations lag in participation behind their Latino, white, and black counterparts.

Another significant pattern to note in Figure 4.1 is that the effect of age is weaker among first-generation immigrants than among later immigrant generations. This finding holds true across the different racial and ethnic groups. These results lend some support to the hypothesis that higher age does not lead to the same sets of skills relevant to participation among first-generation immigrants as it does for later-generation immigrants. It is important to note, however, that the immigrant exception is not so strong that it renders null the relationship between age and voting. Instead of *differences in kind* between first-generation immigrants and later immigrant generations, we see *differences in degree* (hereafter "immigrant distinction"). Thus, the effect of age on voting is statistically significant for the first generation but still weaker than for those in the second and later generations.

What is the relationship between age and voting for members of different national-origin groups? Conducting the analysis across different national-origin samples indicates that age has a consistently significant relationship to voting. In results not reported here, age is positively re-

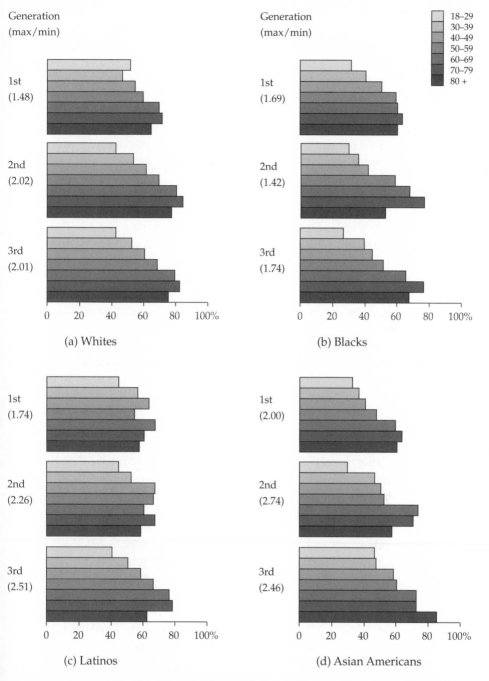

Figure 4.1. Age and Predicted Probabilities of Voting by Race and Immigrant Generation. Controlling for all other factors and holding other variables at their group-specific means.
SOURCE: See Tables A.3–A.5 in the Appendix.

lated to the likelihood of voting for members of all but two national-origin groups.[5] Even the more precise finding of "immigrant distinction" holds true for many of the national-origin groups considered: white immigrants of German, British, and Polish origin; Asian immigrants of Chinese, Filipino, and South Asian origin; and Latino immigrants other than those of Cuban origin.[6] Thus, regardless of whether we analyze voting among immigrants of particular racial groups or national origins, the effects of age on voting are consistently positive.

Education

Turning next to the effects of education (Figure 4.2), we also see a consistently significant and positive relationship to voting across racial groups and immigrant generations. Depending on the racial group, first-generation immigrants with a college degree are 45 percent to 98 percent more likely to vote than those without a high school diploma. The results from recent CPS data therefore challenge the findings of other studies (Lien 1994; Junn 1999; Tam Cho 1999) that find education to have an insignificant relationship to voting among Asian Americans.[7] Here, the results show education to have a strong and positive effect on voting for Asians of all immigrant generations. Finally, just as in the case of age and voting, the effects of education on participation grow stronger from the first generation to later immigrant generations. Thus we find no support for the strong version of immigrant exceptionalism, which predicts a null relationship between education and voting for first-generation immigrants. Instead, we find support for a weaker version of immigrant distinction, in which the effects of education on voting are statistically significant but weaker for the first generation than for later generations.

These consistently significant effects of education on voting are also found in other surveys—such as among whites in the National Election Studies, Latinos in the Post/Kaiser/Harvard survey, and Asian Americans in the 2000 multicity survey. As reported in Table A.11 in the Appendix, the effects of education on voting among whites in the NES is stronger among third-generation immigrants than among those in the first generation. The same is also true for Latinos and Asian Americans in their ethnic-specific surveys (Table A.11). Thus, regardless of the data source and the racial or ethnic group considered, we can state that the effect of education on voting is significant for members of different immigrant generations and that there is support for the hypothesis of "immigrant distinction."

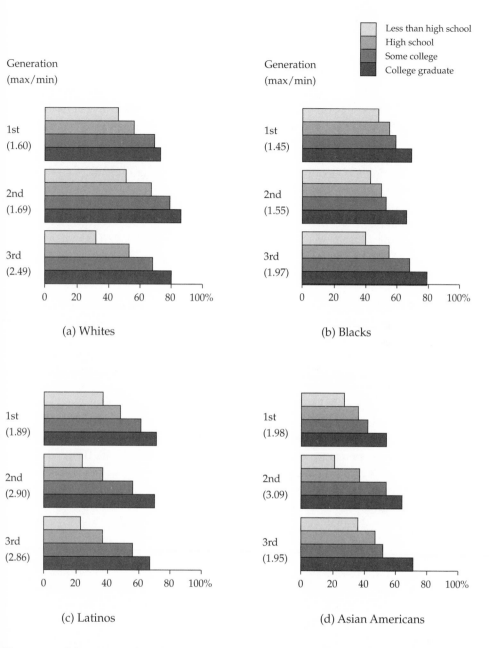

Figure 4.2. Education and Predicted Probabilities of Voting by Race and Immigrant Generation. Controlling for all other factors and holding other variables at their group-specific means.

SOURCE: See Tables A.3–A.5 in the Appendix.

Does education have a consistently positive effect on voting among immigrants of different national origins? Conducting the analysis across national-origin groups reveals that education has a positive effect on voting among members of most groups. The only exceptions are for Korean immigrants, who display a null relationship between education and voting, and Japanese and Italian immigrants, who display an increase in participation up to the college level but not beyond. Finally, among the groups that display a positive relationship between education and voting, the effects are weaker for first-generation respondents than for second-generation respondents. Thus, just as in the case of age and voting, I find consistent support for the hypothesis of immigrant distinction.

Income

I turn finally to the effects of income on voting across racial groups and immigrant generations. As indicated earlier, studies of voting among the general citizenry have shown income to be a statistically significant predictor of participation, although its effects are often weaker than those of age or education. In this analysis, I find that income has a similar effect on participation across racial groups and immigrant generations (Figure 4.3). With the exception of first-generation Latino immigrants, the effects of income on voting are statistically significant for all groups. Among first-generation whites, the probability of voting increases by 23 percent from the lowest income group to the highest, with similar increases for those in later immigrant generations. The same is also true for Asian Americans, although the effects are slightly weaker for second-generation respondents than for those in other immigrant generations. Higher income also increases the probability of voting for black immigrants, although the effects are less consistent than in the case of white and Asian immigrants and fail tests of statistical significance. Finally, for Latinos, income has a progressively stronger effect on participation—among first-generation respondents it does not have any effect on participation, whereas for those in the third and later generations the probability of voting increases by over 60 percent from the lowest income category to the highest. This analysis of voting participation across racial groups and immigrant generations therefore reveals patterns for income that are similar to those found in previous studies of the overall population—higher income is associated with

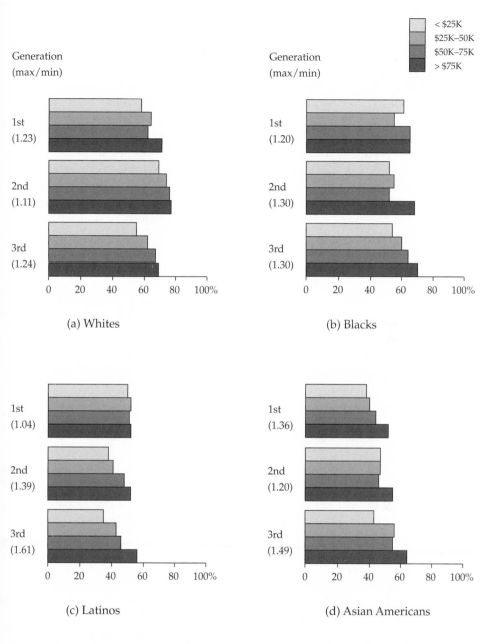

Figure 4.3. Income and Predicted Probabilities of Voting by Race and Immigrant Generation. Controlling for all other factors and holding other variables at their group-specific means.

SOURCE: See Tables A.3–A.5 in the Appendix.

higher levels of participation, although the effects are weaker than is the case for age and education.

The relationship between income and voting among white respondents in the NES is similar to findings from the CPS—the effects are significant for all immigrant generations, although there is no difference in the magnitude of those effects. For Latinos in the Post/Kaiser/Harvard survey, the relationship between income and voting is less consistent across immigrant generations. The same is also true for respondents in the 2000 Pilot National Asian American Political Survey. It is possible that the lack of significant effect is due to misreporting or nonreporting of income among respondents in the Latino and Asian American surveys. In the Latino survey, about 7 percent of respondents in each immigrant generation did not report their income. Of these, about 50 percent had some college education or a four-year college degree. About 25 percent of the respondents in the PNAAPS survey did not report their income, and nearly two-thirds of these respondents had been educated beyond the high school level. It is also possible that the difference may be due to factors that are particular to elections involved or the differences in sampling methods for the ethnic-specific surveys. Whatever the reason, income does not have a significant relationship to voting among Latinos and Asian Americans in the ethnic-specific surveys, findings that differ from those in the Current Population Survey.

Finally, confining the analysis to members of particular national-origin groups in the CPS reveals a less consistent picture between income and voting. Among first-generation immigrants, the relationship between income and voting is significant and positive for about half of the groups considered (Chinese, Filipino, Southeast Asian, German, British, and Jamaican) and null or inconsistent for the rest. Similar results hold for second-generation respondents, as higher income is associated with higher voting levels for more than half of the national-origin groups (Mexican, Cuban, Filipino, Japanese, British, Polish, Italian, and Jamaican). Even for these groups, the effects of income on voting are weaker than those for age and education, in line with findings from analyses of participation among the overall population.

To sum up the findings so far, we find that the returns to voting from SES factors are weaker for first-generation immigrants than for those in later immigrant generations, but these effects are still positive and significant. These findings are also generally borne out in subsequent analyses of data from the National Election Studies, the PKH survey of Latinos, and the Pilot National Asian American Political Survey. There have been several reasons offered as to why factors related to immigrant socialization may dampen the levels of skills or political efficacy associated with age and education. Some have noted that many naturalized citizens still retain political ties to their countries of origin (Jones-Correa 1998), while others also point to the lack of English-language ability among first-generation immigrants (Junn 1999) and their political socialization under nondemocratic regimes (Tam Cho 1999). The analysis here controls for such immigrant-related factors as dual citizenship, language use, and repressive regime origin. And still, the relationships between age, socioeconomic status, and voting remain positive and statistically significant across racial groups and immigrant generations. There is one other possible explanation for these weaker SES effects, one rooted in the selection mechanisms for naturalization. The pool of naturalized immigrants is biased toward the foreign-born who are of higher socioeconomic status. This, in turn, may cause the effects of SES on voting to be weaker among naturalized citizens than they would be if we included those immigrant residents who are eligible for U.S. citizenship (hereafter the "eligibles"). Indeed, adding the eligibles to the naturalized population does strengthen the effects of age and education on voting. Still, we find the same pattern of "immigrant distinction," in which the effects of SES on voting are positive and significant for first-generation respondents, but at the same time weaker than for later-generation immigrants.

Beyond SES and Individual-Level Influences

While socioeconomic factors are important to explain voting participation, such individual-level resources are not, in and of themselves, sufficient to account for differences in participation among the citizenry. It is certainly true that voting in the United States is ultimately an individual act, thanks to rules relating to ballot secrecy in national and state elections. And yet individual resources cannot fully account for variations in political participation, or for why Americans even go to the ballot box in the first place.

As the game theory literature on voting and other forms of collective action has shown, an individual's share of a collective outcome is not sufficient to explain participation to achieve that collective outcome (Downs 1957; Olson 1965). In the case of voting, even if an individual has a preference for the Republican candidate over the Democratic candidate, it is likely that she will receive the same benefit (or loss) regardless of her participation. This is because the individual's vote has virtually no impact on the likelihood that the preferred candidate will win or lose. And yet the voter expends costs related to the acquisition of political information and participation. Age and socioeconomic status may reduce the costs related to voting by providing citizens with higher levels of skills that are relevant to participation, but they do not eliminate such costs. Thus focusing exclusively on the individual-level cost and the share of a collective benefit cannot account for why it is rational for citizens to vote.

Some scholars have pointed a way out of the paradox of rational voting by drawing attention to factors such as social incorporation and political mobilization (Uhlaner 1989; Rosenstone and Hansen 1993). According to these scholars, it is important to treat voters as having individual relationships not only to political candidates, but also to other persons and groups with whom they have contact. As Carole Uhlaner (1989) notes, groups have an incentive to participate because they have a bigger stake in collective outcomes than do individual citizens. At the same time, group leaders can induce individual participation by offering selective benefits to participants and even sanctioning those who do not. Rosenstone and Hansen (1993) offer a similar argument, tying the mechanisms of mobilization to micro-level processes of social pressure: "Indirect mobilization promotes participation, then, by allowing political leaders to exploit citizens' ongoing obligations to friends, neighbors and social groups. . . . Contact through social networks adds the power of social expectations to the message of mobilization" (29).

While people's predisposition to participate may be influenced by their individual skills and their incorporation into social networks, the actual extent of their participation also varies by the political milieu in which they reside. As many scholars have argued, levels of voting change markedly across different political contexts, characterized as they are by variations either in institutional barriers to participation or in the level of mobilization by parties, candidates, and other political organizations. Also, as we shall see in this chapter, some scholars in recent years have drawn attention to the role of state-level political cultures in shaping civic and political participation. In states with traditions of high participation, the argument goes, residents face greater expectations from their social environments to participate in politics. In

states with histories of low political interest and participation, in
uals face fewer stimuli to participate from others.

In this section, I shall evaluate the extent to which all of thes
textual factors (social incorporation, institutional barriers to participation, political mobilization, and political culture) can account for the
voting participation of members of different racial groups and immigrant generations. From assimilationist theories of immigrant adaptation, we might expect domestic social and political contexts to have a
weaker influence on first-generation immigrants than among those in
the third generation and later. However, if immigrants participate in
separate sets of social networks which in turn encourage political participation, then the standard measures of social incorporation and political mobilization may account for immigrant voting just as much as
they do the participation of those in the third and later generations.

Social Incorporation

In the past two decades, scholars of political participation have given
considerable weight to factors related to the incorporation of individuals into communities and other social contexts that encourage or discourage political participation. Social ties and networks alter the logic
of participation in several ways. First, they reduce the costs of obtaining
information that is relevant to voting. Since citizens can obtain political
information from their friends, family members, and colleagues at
work, it is not necessary for all members of a social network to possess
the same initial levels of information on a particular issue or election.
Thus, as Steven Rosenstone and Mark Hansen (1993) note, "each person bears the cost of collecting only a fraction of the political information she receives" (24). Social networks also change the logic of participation by providing selective benefits for participation (or sanctions for
nonparticipation). Being on the winning side of a preferred candidate
or issue outcome is usually considered a collective benefit, because individuals can enjoy such a benefit regardless of whether they participate. However, when one's spouse or friends express social disapproval
for failing to participate in elections or for not being sufficiently aware
of a certain issue, the benefit of participation is a selective one because
individuals cannot enjoy social approval without voting or obtaining
relevant political information. Thus factors related to social incorporation play an important role in structuring the decision of individuals to
participate in elections. While peer influences can indeed operate in the

opposite direction (toward political apathy and abstention from voting), past evidence from both the CPS and the NES indicates that those who are more embedded in social networks are indeed more likely to vote (Wolfinger and Rosenstone 1980; Rosenstone and Hansen 1993).

There are different ways of measuring social incorporation, and the Current Population Survey provides three variables to do so: employment status, residential stability, and marital status.[8] The unemployed are less likely to participate in politics, not just because they tend to have lower incomes, but also because they do not participate in social networks in the workplace that reward political participation (Wolfinger and Rosenstone 1980; Rosenstone and Hansen 1993). The workplace stimulates participation, not only by reducing the costs of acquiring political information among colleagues, but also by creating expectations to participate in various forms of participation related to elections—company Political Action Committee (PAC) giving, union get-out-the-vote (GOTV) efforts, and so on. In addition to employment status, residential stability is another indicator of social incorporation that has been shown to affect the likelihood of political participation. Citizens who live longer in a particular neighborhood are more likely to participate in elections because they are more likely to be vested in their community and are more likely to have stable networks of friends and neighbors. Finally, past research has shown that married citizens are more likely to vote than those who are not married. As Wolfinger and Rosenstone (1980) note, marriage has the strongest effect on voting among those who need a slight push to go to the polls—that is, those with low to moderate levels of education and political interest. Thus, "if someone has a weak inclination to vote, the presence of another family member who has some tendency in the same direction will raise the probability that both will vote" (45).

How consistently do models of social incorporation account for voting participation across immigrant generations? Table 4.1 presents the results of multivariate models that control for various factors related to individual resources and social incorporation. The results for employment status indicate that it is a significant predictor of participation only among respondents in the third and later immigrant generations. The difference between being employed and not being employed also has a significant effect on voting among Asian American respondents of all immigrant generations, but the results are not statistically significant at the 0.10 level. Thus, the results seem to indicate that the workplace does

TABLE 4.1

Social Incorporation and Voting, by Race and Immigrant
Generation (ratio of predicted probabilities when holding other
variables at their means)

	First Generation	Second Generation	Third and Later Generations
Employment Status[a]			
White	0.99	1.04*	1.04***
Black	1.14	0.98	1.08***
Latino	0.99	1.01	1.10**
Asian	1.13*	1.15	1.18
Length of Residence[b]			
White	1.28***	1.30***	1.28***
Black	1.38***	1.27***	1.24***
Latino	1.23***	1.28***	1.31***
Asian	1.13**	1.06	1.31***
Marital Status[c]			
White	1.13***	1.20***	1.14***
Black	1.27**	1.08	1.06***
Latino	1.16***	1.15***	1.15***
Asian	0.96	1.20**	1.30***

SOURCE: See Appendix, Tables A.3–A.5.
    [a]Ratio is p(voting) if employed divided by p(voting) if not employed.
    [b]Ratio is p(voting) if long-term resident divided by p(voting) if not long-term resident.
    [c]Ratio is p(voting) if married divided by p(voting) if not married.
    *** $p < .01$; ** $p < .05$; * $p < .10$

not serve as a spur to participation among first- and second-generation immigrants as it does for those in the third and later generations.

These results should, however, be interpreted with caution. Part of the reason why employment may not be significant among first- and second-generation respondents is that the retired account for a greater proportion of those who are not employed than they do for respondents in the third and later generations. Separating out the retired from the "not employed" category does provide more consistent results for the effect of employment on the likelihood of voting for whites and Asian Americans of all immigrant generations. Still, for blacks and Latinos, employment status is not a significant predictor of participation for first- and second-generation immigrants even after separating out the retired from others who are not employed. It is possible that the insignificance of employment on participation among blacks and Latinos is because the workplace does not serve as a spur to participation for those who work in low-skill service jobs. However, separating out those with postsecondary degrees from those with a high school diploma or less reveals no differences in the effect of employment on participation for black and Latino immigrants. So it remains unclear why employment has a bigger effect on participation among first-generation white and Asian immigrants than among blacks and Latinos—the effects may relate to other aspects of the work environment that are not adequately captured in this analysis.

Turning next to the effects of residential stability, we see that those who live for five years or more in a particular address are indeed more likely to vote than short- and medium-term residents (Table 4.1). For most groups, longer residential duration increases the likelihood of participation by 25 to 30 percent. Among Asian Americans, however, comparable increases in participation can be found only among respondents in the third and later generations. Among first-generation Asian citizens, the likelihood of participation increases by 13 percent, while for second-generation respondents, the increase is even smaller—6 percent. This may be because Asian immigrants are more likely to maintain ties to ethnic enclaves long after moving out to the suburbs (Zhou 2001).[9] Thus we can expect them to have a smaller stake in local politics than immigrants from other racial groups. The weak relationship to residential stability among Asian immigrants may also be because local party organizations are less likely to make efforts to reach out to them (Wong 2001). Whatever the reason, the results here indicate that residential stability at a given address leads to a significant increase in participation across racial groups and immigrant generations, with the notable exception of first- and second-generation Asian immigrants.

Finally, those who are married are more likely to vote than those who are not married. This finding is consistent across immigrant generations for white and Latino respondents. However, marital status is not significant for first-generation Asian Americans and for black respondents after the first generation. The reason for this latter finding may be because native-born blacks have the lowest rates of marriage—32 percent for the second generation and 37 percent for those in the third and later generations. If being unmarried is a relatively widespread phenomenon for certain groups, then it is possible that unmarried adults in such groups find bases of social support that can compensate for the absence of a spouse.[10] In such circumstances, being married may not serve as the necessary spur to participation as originally noted by Wolfinger and Rosenstone (1980). However, the authors' assertion that marital status has its strongest effects among those with low levels of education does indeed hold true. In results not reported here, the effect of marital status on the likelihood of voting is stronger among those who do not have a college degree than among those with postsecondary education. This is true for virtually every racial group and immigrant generation.[11]

To sum up the findings regarding models of social incorporation, we see that the effects are generally weaker than those found for age and education. Still, there are important differences across racial groups and immigrant generations. Employment status holds a weak relationship to the likelihood of voting, especially among immigrant blacks and Latinos. Also, Asian immigrants are exceptional in that longer residential duration does not lead to a higher likelihood of voting, and marital status does not bear a significant relationship to participation. There may be several explanations for this Asian immigrant exception regarding the effects of marital status and residential duration on voting. Given the limitations of the CPS data, however, these explanations remain plausible hypotheses in need of further exploration and testing through ethnographic research and specialized surveys.

Institutional Barriers

While an individual's resources and degree of social incorporation can have a significant influence on the likelihood of voting, macropolitical contexts may also matter. Institutional barriers to voting can have a substantial impact on voting participation, as witnessed by low levels of black turnout during the Jim Crow era of poll taxes and literacy tests. Most of these formal institutional barriers to voting were lifted in 1965, with the passage of the Voting Rights Act. Today the most significant barriers are those relating to registration deadlines and absentee voting.[12] Since each state determines its own laws regarding registration procedures and deadlines, there is considerable variation in the ease with which citizens can remain eligible to vote in any given election. In states such as Mississippi, the deadline to register is a full month prior to the general election, whereas states such as New Hampshire, Wyoming, and Wisconsin allow citizens to register on Election Day.[13] The process of registration is further complicated by the fact that states often require residents to reregister when they change their address. Furthermore, many states require citizens to establish residence for a year before they are eligible to register. Since registration is a required step in electoral participation, we can expect variation in state registration deadlines to also produce differences in the likelihood of voting. Finally, as Wolfinger and Rosenstone (1980) argue, variations in the difficulty of registering will have a greater impact on citizens who are "least able to cope with bureaucratic problems—those with the least education" (62).

The likelihood of voting can also depend on the extent to which states allow citizens to vote by absentee ballot. Most states allow absentee balloting when residents are physically unable to get to a polling place. However, a handful of states such as Maine, Michigan, and New Mexico allow absentee ballots for all elderly voters, while eleven states allow all registered voters to vote absentee (Oliver 1996). We can expect citizens living in states with liberal absentee eligibility requirements to have a higher likelihood of voting than those who do not live in such states, although research by Eric Oliver (1996) indicates that the effects are weak in the absence of party efforts to mail out absentee ballots to eligible citizens.

How well do institutional rules regarding registration and absentee ballots affect the likelihood of voting across racial groups and immigrant generations? As is evident from Table 4.2, state-level factors on rules relating to absentee ballot eligibility and registration deadlines do not have a consistent or significant impact on the likelihood of participation. The findings on liberal absentee eligibility are generally in line with those found by Eric Oliver (1996); expanding eligibility for absentee ballots does not, in and of itself, lead to higher levels of voter turnout.[14] However, even these findings are extremely sensitive to the race and immigrant generation of respondents. Among first-generation immigrants, for instance, Asian Americans living in states with liberal absentee eligibility have a 26 percent higher probability of voting than those living in other states. However, the same advantage does not hold for second-generation Asian immigrants. Similarly, first-generation

TABLE 4.2

Institutional Barriers and Voting, by Race and Immigrant
Generation (ratio of predicted probabilities when holding other
variables at their means)

	First Generation	Second Generation	Third and Later Generations
Liberal Absentee Eligibility[a]			
White	1.05	1.05***	1.04***
Black	0.54**	1.00	1.02
Latino	0.87**	1.01*	1.05
Asian	1.26***	1.01	1.20
Early Registration Deadline[b]			
White	0.95	1.00	0.97***
Black	0.78	1.17	1.03
Latino	0.94	1.20	0.99
Asian	0.92	0.95	1.42

SOURCE: See Appendix, Tables A.3–A.5.
[a]Ratio is p(voting) if resides in state with liberal absentee eligibility divided by
p(voting) if resides in state without.
[b]Ratio is p(voting) if resides in state with early registration divided by p(voting) if resides in state without.
*** $p < .01$; ** $p < .05$; * $p < .10$

blacks and Latinos seem to actually have lower probabilities of voting
when they live in states with liberal absentee ballot eligibility. However,
the same disadvantage is not found among respondents in later immigrant generations.

The reason for this inconsistency in relationships across immigrant
generations is likely that most of the states that have liberal absentee eligibility also have very small populations of nonwhite immigrants. For
example, of the sixteen states that have liberal eligibility for absentee
ballots, only four have populations that are greater than 10 percent
black. Moreover, in these four states (Alabama, Ohio, Arizona, and
Texas) less than 1 percent of all black respondents are first-generation
immigrants, and 1.3 percent are in the second generation. Similarly,

only three states out of the sixteen with liberal absentee eligibility have populations that are greater than 5 percent Asian American (California, Hawaii, and Washington). On the flip side, there are very few states with strict absentee ballot rules that also have sizable proportions of first- and second-generation Latino immigrants. Thus, given the high degree of correlation between liberal absentee eligibility and the proportion of black, Asian, and Latino immigrants, it is not surprising that the analysis produces unreliable estimates with inconsistent signs across race and immigrant generation.

Inconsistent results can also be found in the relationship between early registration deadlines and the likelihood of voting. Having to register at least twenty-one days before the general election reduces the likelihood of voting in only seven of the twelve subsamples considered (Table 4.2). Furthermore, even in these cases the relationship between early registration deadlines and voting participation is statistically significant in only one instance—white respondents in the third and later generations. It is possible, as Wolfinger and Rosenstone (1980) note, that the impact of registration rules on participation is apparent more among those who have low levels of education than among those who are college educated. Conducting separate regressions for those with and without postsecondary degrees does reveal significant differences in the effects of registration deadlines on voting among white respondents of different immigrant generations. For all other groups, however, the inconclusive relationship between registration deadlines and voting participation remains true, regardless of education. Thus, in the case of institutional barriers to participation, neither absentee eligibility nor registration deadlines display a strong or systematic relationship to the likelihood of voting for members of different racial groups and immigrant generations.[15]

Political Mobilization

In addition to institutional barriers to participation, we also need to pay attention to contexts of political mobilization. The level of political mobilization in a given state or congressional district can have a significant influence on voter turnout. From the early works of V. O. Key and E. E. Schattschneider, political scientists have noted the importance of political mobilization and party competition in inducing higher levels of voter turnout (Key 1949; Schattschneider 1960).[16] Recent studies of electoral turnout have also emphasized the importance of party competition and mobilization on voter turnout (Rosenstone and Hansen 1993; Schachar and Nalebuff 1999). They show that individuals who live in states where presidential contests are close are more likely to vote than those living in states where there is a clear favorite. This is due largely to differences in state-level mobilization by political actors. As Rosenstone and Hansen (1993) put it, "campaigns, interest groups, and the media . . . contest every inch in campaigns that stand to be decided by tenths of percentage points, and they tacitly concede campaigns that look to be blowouts" (179). Political mobilization also varies by the closeness of statewide races, particularly those for governor and senator. States that have a governor's race or a senate race concurrent with presidential or house elections have a higher level of political mobilization and voter turnout. The effects can be especially strong during midterm elections when there is no presidential contest to generate interest among potential voters (Rosenstone and Hansen 1993).

However, the effects of close elections may not be the same across racial groups and immigrant generations. On the one hand, mobilization associated with close elections may have its strongest impact on those who are otherwise the least likely to participate. Thus, for instance, close electoral contexts may have their greatest impacts on first- and second-generation Asian immigrants, who tend to have the lowest likelihood of voting. On the other hand, it is possible that the higher level of mobilization associated with close elections never reaches groups who have traditionally been excluded from networks of party mobilization. Thus, for groups such as Asian immigrants and black immigrants who have been shown to have less contact with party organizations (Rogers 2000; Wong 2001), the presence or absence of close electoral contests may make less of a difference in the likelihood of participation. Under this latter scenario, then, the closeness of electoral contests should serve as a stronger spur to participation for members of groups that have traditionally been contacted by party organizations.

Analyses of CPS data do not reveal much support for either contention (Table 4.3). To test for the effects of mobilization contexts on participation, I use the index of electoral competitiveness from *Congressional Quarterly* for congressional and gubernatorial races and the Associated Press for presidential contests. Each source ranks races as competitive or noncompetitive based on opinion polls and surveys of candidate and party organizations a few months before Election Day (see Appendix). Table 4.3 indicates that the closeness of presidential elections does not have a substantial impact on voting for most of the groups considered, even including third-generation whites. The closeness of senate and governor elections does have a significant effect on voting for many groups. However, there is no clear picture that emerges across immigrant generations that supports either of the contentions mentioned above. While the magnitudes for blacks, Latinos, and Asian Americans reveal stronger effects for third-generation immigrants than for first-generation immigrants, these differences are not statistically significant. However, there is some support for the contention that close electoral contexts have their greatest effects on low-propensity voters. The largest increases associated with competitive senate and governor elections are found among Asian Americans in the second and third generations and Latinos of all immigrant generations. Indeed, among third-generation Latinos, residing in a state with a competitive statewide contest raises the likelihood of participation by nearly 30 percent. So, even though there is no clear generational picture that emerges from the CPS data, there is some support for the contention that close elections have a disproportionately stronger impact on groups that would otherwise be among the least likely to vote.

Political Culture

The decision of citizens to participate in elections may be shaped not only by short-term factors at the state level such as mobilization over electoral contests, but also by more long-term factors such as the history of voting participation in the state. In the past few decades, political scientists have drawn attention to the role of state and regional political cultures in shaping the likelihood of electoral participation. Scholars during the 1970s and 1980s noted a kind of regional political culture in the South, a vestige of one-party competition and racial disenfranchisement that led to lower turnout among southern blacks and whites. More recently, the work of scholars such as Robert Putnam (2000) suggests that differences in civic and political culture are present even at the state level, with states such as North Dakota and Vermont exhibiting the highest levels of civic engagement and those such as Nevada and Mississippi exhibiting the lowest.

The effect of political and civic culture on voting participation may indeed vary by immigrant generation. For instance, assimilationist perspectives would suggest that state-level variations in political culture would have a weaker effect among first-generation immigrants than

TABLE 4.3

Mobilization Contexts and Voting, by Race and Immigrant
Generation (ratio of predicted probabilities when holding other
variables at their means)

	First Generation	Second Generation	Third and Later Generations
Competitive Presidential Election[a]			
White	1.06	1.06***	1.01***
Black	1.19	0.95	1.03
Latino	0.97	0.99	1.01
Asian	1.23**	1.21	0.91
Competitive Senate/ Governor Election[b]			
White	1.07**	1.07***	1.06***
Black	0.88	1.08	1.05***
Latino	1.15***	1.10*	1.28***
Asian	1.04	1.25**	1.21

SOURCE: See Appendix, Tables A.3–A.5.

The results presented here are for pooled data from 1994 to 2000. Similar
results are found when the analysis is restricted to only presidential elections in
order to gauge the effect of residence in presidential toss-up states. Also, no clear
picture emerges across immigrant generations when the analysis of competitive
senate and governor races is confined to midterm elections during this period.

[a]Ratio is p(voting) if resides in state with presidential tossup divided by p(voting) if resides in state without.

[b]Ratio is p(voting) if resides in state with senate/governor tossup divided by p(voting) if resides in state without.

*** $p < .01$; ** $p < .05$; * $p < .10$

among those in later immigrant generations. According to such a perspective, the foreign-born are less likely to be incorporated into mainstream social and political institutions than the children of immigrants born in the United States. This latter group, in turn, would be less affected by a state's political culture than those who are born in the United States to native-born parents.

In order to test the effects of a state's political and civic culture on voting, I consider measures such as the index of social capital utilized by Robert Putnam in *Bowling Alone* (2000). Putnam's index of social capital includes measures such as turnout in recent presidential elections, as well as other factors related to civic engagement found in sources such as the General Social Survey and the Roper Social and Political Trends archive. While this comprehensive measure of civic engagement includes various forms of voluntarism and political participation, it is limited in that many of the factors do not include valid measures for states such as Alaska, Hawaii, New Mexico, and Nevada.[17]

The only measures of political and civic culture that have universal coverage across states are the level of voting participation in recent presidential elections and the number of nonprofits per capita in each state. I utilize a modified version of the first measure of state political culture: the average level of voting participation in presidential elections between 1972 and 1992. I also utilize Putnam's measure of the density of nonprofits in each state, defined as the number of 501(c)(3) organizations per capita. These two measures of state political and civic culture (voting history and nonprofits per capita) are superior to the earlier characterization of "South" versus "non-South" states. Both have the advantage of looking at contemporary patterns in political and civic behavior, taking into account changes in participation in the South after the civil rights era and the Voting Rights Act of 1965. Furthermore, the two measures allow for state-level variation and do not limit the effect of political or civic culture to one regional bloc—namely the Confederate South.

How do state political cultures influence the likelihood of individual citizens to participate in elections? Furthermore, do these effects vary across immigrant generations? As Table 4.4 indicates, the history of voting participation in a state has a strong effect on the likelihood of voting among respondents in the third and later generations. Indeed, the effects are among the strongest for state-level measures considered so far. At the same time, the effects of state voting history on participation are generally weaker for first-generation immigrants than for those in later immigrant generations. For example, among first-generation Latino immigrants, a subject living in the state with the legacy of greatest voter participation is 28 percent more likely to vote than a subject living in the state with the legacy of least voter participation. However, for Latinos in the third and later generations, a similar shift means a 158 percent increase in the probability of participation. Note that these effects are found *after* controlling for factors such as socioeconomic status, so-

TABLE 4.4

State Political Culture and Voting, by Race and Immigrant
Generation (ratio of predicted probabilities when holding other
variables at their means)

	First Generation	Second Generation	Third and Later Generations
State Voting History[a]			
White	1.08	1.28***	1.36***
Black	1.08	1.20	1.54***
Latino	1.28	1.85***	2.58***
Asian	1.59**	1.45	2.45***
Nonprofits per Capita[b]			
White	1.26**	1.18***	1.28***
Black	1.23	2.30**	1.01
Latino	0.76	1.68**	1.03
Asian	1.37	1.00	2.41***

[a]Ratio is p(voting) if subject resides in state with maximum level of voter participation (Minnesota) divided by p(voting) if subject resides in state with minimum level of voter participation (Delaware).

[b]Ratio is p(voting) if subject resides in state with maximum level of nonprofits per capita (Vermont) divided by p(voting) if subject resides in state with minimum level of nonprofits per capita (Mississippi).

*** $p < .01$; ** $p < .05$; * $p < .10$

cial incorporation, and the competitiveness of presidential and state-wide elections.

Similar differences in the effect of state political culture can be found for whites, blacks, and Asian Americans of different immigrant generations, with the weakest effects generally found among first-generation immigrants and the strongest effects found among those in the third and later generations. These findings therefore support the expectations of assimilationist theories of immigrant adaptation, which suggest that first-generation citizens are less likely to be incorporated into mainstream social and political institutions than those in later immigrant generations. With first-generation immigrants less likely to be incorporated into mainstream institutions, the effects of state political culture are more muted because there are fewer social and organizational ties for such factors to have an influence on individual participation.

Finally, as Table 4.4 indicates, state civic culture as measured by the number of nonprofits per capita in a state also tends to be significantly related to the probability of individual voting participation. At the same time, the effects are less consistent across racial groups and immigrant generations, and there is no clear generational pattern in the significance of this measure. For instance, among white immigrants, the effect of nonprofit density on voting is roughly the same across different immigrant generations, while for blacks and Latinos the variable is significant only for second-generation immigrants. The lack of a clear pattern for nonprofit density and voting participation may be reflective of a larger disconnect between political participation and participation in civic associations. Or it may reflect the fact that mainstream measures of civic culture do little to explain behavior or outcomes among nonwhites (Hero 2003), possibly because they focus on formal civic organizations and ignore the role of informal associations in immigrant communities. Thus it is unclear what to make of Putnam's measure of civic culture and its relationship to voting. Still, what is clear is that political culture as measured by state traditions of voter participation has consistently weaker effects on voting among first-generation immigrants than among those in the third and later generations.

Party Identification

Party identification bears a strong relationship to the likelihood of voting. This finding has been confirmed time and again in studies of voting participation in the United States. In *The American Voter*, one of the earliest studies of mass political participation in the United States, Angus Campbell and his colleagues (1960) find party attachment to be highly stable and strongly predictive of participation in elections. As the authors note, "few factors are of greater importance for our national elections than the lasting attachment of tens of millions of Americans to one of the parties" (121). Subsequent studies have confirmed the importance of party identification to electoral participation, with party independents considerably less likely to vote than those attached to either the Democratic or Republican Party. Indeed, the importance of party identification to voting seems to have remained strong despite the rising number of people who identify themselves as independents during the latter half of the twentieth century (Bartels 2000; Abramson, Aldrich, and Rohde 1998; Wattenberg 1998).

Party identification has received considerable attention from scholars of Latino and Asian American politics (Cain, Kiewiet, and Uhlaner 1991; DeSipio 1996a; Uhlaner, Gray, and García 2000; Wong 2000; Alvarez and García Bedolla 2003; Lien, Conway, and Wong 2003). However, most of these studies have focused on the determinants of partisanship acquisition, with studies from various surveys indicating that the likelihood of being a partisan increases with time spent in the United States and is generally higher among the native-born than among the foreign-born. Some have even suggested that models of partisanship acquisition may be different for immigrant nonwhites than for whites (Uhlaner, Gray, and García 2000; Hajnal and Lee 2003), with factors such as issue positions, involvement in civic organizations, and residence in ethnic enclaves playing important roles in shaping party choice.

The differential impact of party identification on voting has received considerably less attention from scholars of Latino and Asian American politics. And yet there are reasons to believe that the effect of party identification on voting may vary according to one's immigrant generation. For instance, first-generation immigrant voters may have a clearer sense of where they stand on particular issues such as abortion and the role of government in society than on what party they belong to (Hajnal and Lee 2003). Thus issue positions may play a stronger role than party identification in their decision to vote. Differences across immigrant generations may also arise if the generational patterns in voting do not match generational patterns in the strength of party identification. For instance, if the first generation has a lower level of party identification than the native-born but a similar level of participation, then the effects of party identification should be weaker for the first generation than for later immigrant generations.

There is no dataset such as the Current Population Survey that contains sufficient information on party identification as well as sufficient numbers of respondents of different racial groups and immigrant generations. However, we can compare results between whites in the National Election Studies, Latinos in the Post/Kaiser/Harvard survey, and Asian Americans in the PNAAPS survey to provide some preliminary results regarding the effects of party identification on voting across immigrant generations. However, given the differences in sampling methodology between the various surveys, any comparisons here can only be preliminary, awaiting validation by national datasets with sizable samples across racial groups and immigrant generations.

Results from the NES indicate that there is no difference among whites in the effects of partisanship on voting across immigrant generations (Table A.11 in the Appendix). Generational patterns in voting closely track those patterns found for party identification among whites, and so the effects of partisanship on voting do not change from the first generation to later immigrant generations.[18] For Asian Americans, by contrast, the effects of partisanship on voting vary across immigrant generations. They are weakest among third-generation immigrants because even though they have the highest levels of participation, they are less likely than second-generation immigrants to identify with a political party. The effects of partisanship on voting among first-generation Asian immigrants are also weaker than for second-generation immigrants because the difference between the two groups in voter participation is steeper than the difference in party identification. Finally, even for Latinos there is a significant difference in the effects of partisanship on voting across immigrant generations. Identification with a political party is strongly associated with voting among third-generation Latinos but is not significantly related to voting among first-generation immigrants (Table A.11). Note that these findings hold even after adding additional controls for national origin or excluding Cuban Americans from the sample. Also, the weaker effect of party identification on voting is evident even when using alternative measures that differentiate between strong and weak partisans.

The apparently weak relationship between party identification and voting among first-generation Latinos may be due to the overriding importance of other factors such as beliefs regarding the role of government in society (Alvarez and García Bedolla 2003) or to the immigrant backlash at the ballot box in response to various measures deemed to be political threats (see Chapter 6). These results should, however, be interpreted with caution—similar results regarding the weaker effects of party identification on voting are found in some surveys such as the three-state Tomás Rivera Policy Institute survey (1996), but not in older surveys such as the 1990 Latino National Political Survey. Still, the results here point to the possibility that the relationship between party identification and voting may vary across immigrant generations, claims that deserve further testing in future national surveys of Latino participation.

Conclusions

This chapter has offered several findings regarding the relevance of traditional models of voting participation in explaining the participation of first- and second-generation immigrants. First, age and socioeconomic status have a significant effect on participation, even among first-generation immigrants. However, the effects are weaker than those found for second- and third-generation immigrants. Furthermore, the findings provide some support to assimilationist theories of immigrant adaptation, since first-generation immigrants are less likely to be influenced by the legacy of voting participation in their states of residence. Finally, the effects of factors such as residential duration are dependent on whether immigrant groups continue to maintain their ties to ethnic enclaves even after moving out of them. Thus, if residential stability leads to greater participation because individuals have a greater stake in local affairs, the same may not be true for immigrant groups whose primary attachments and concerns are still the enclaves in which they attend religious services and spend their leisure time. Finally, factors such as employment status and marital status do not have a uniform effect on voting across racial groups and immigrant generations, and party identification may not be as important to voting among first-generation Latinos as for those in the third and later generations.

We have seen that some of the traditional factors related to social incorporation and political mobilization that are significant for native-born respondents do not have the same effects among first- and second-generation immigrants. In order to understand immigrant voting, it is therefore necessary to look beyond traditional models of electoral participation. In the next chapter, I shall consider various factors related to immigrant adaptation that have largely been ignored by traditional studies of voting participation and that have not yet been subjected to systematic evaluation across different racial and ethnic groups.

CHAPTER 5

From Newcomers to Settlers

Immigrant Adaptation and Political Participation

> As in other adjustments to the American environment, the
> second generation were the intermediaries. From the start, the
> children of the immigrants were more intimately implicated
> than their parents. The schools had acquainted them with the
> mechanisms of politics and had also imbued them with the
> conviction that government was susceptible to popular con-
> trol and capable of serving popular interests.
>
> Oscar Handlin, *The Uprooted* (1951)

So far, we have explored in considerable detail the extent to which traditional models of political participation account for voting among immigrants of different racial and ethnic groups. We have seen that standard models fare moderately well in explaining participation among
immigrants, although the effects are generally weaker among first-generation immigrants than among those in the third and later generations.
At the same time, other factors related to immigrant incorporation may
also account for differences in voting among immigrants. Factors important to immigrant adaptation include those related to length of stay
in the United States, characteristics of the immigrant's country of origin, and contexts of domestic settlement.[1]

It has been hypothesized that many of these immigrant-related factors have significant effects, but these claims have not yet been systematically tested. For instance, some political theorists have voiced the
concern that access to dual nationality lowers immigrant participation
in U.S. politics. While the effect of dual nationality on citizenship ac-

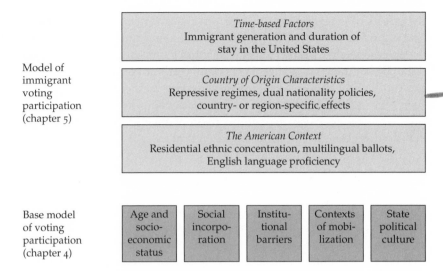

Figure 5.1. An Empirical Model of Immigrant Voting Participation

quisition has been explored in some detail, the effect of such policies on voting participation has received little attention. Similarly, there are those who argue that immigrants coming from communist countries or other repressive regimes are more likely to participate than those coming from nonrepressive regimes. And yet there have been few studies that have examined the effect of coming from a communist regime outside of the particular examples of Cuban and Vietnamese immigrants.

This chapter provides a comprehensive examination of these factors related to immigrant adaptation and their relationship to voting participation. The goal is to generate a new empirical model of immigrant participation, one that builds upon the traditional models of voting participation. Given the various new factors introduced in this analysis, it may be helpful to provide a chart of the various components of the empirical model. As Figure 5.1 indicates, the base model consists of the traditional factors considered in Chapter 4: age and socioeconomic status, social incorporation, institutional barriers to participation, contexts of mobilization, and state political cultures.

To that base model, I add various factors related to immigrant adaptation. The first set of variables are time-based factors, such as generational status and duration of stay in the United States. Next, I consider the effects of various country-of-origin characteristics, such as repressive regime origin, eligibility for dual nationality, and country-specific or region-specific effects. Finally, I turn to factors specific to immigrant life in the United States, such as residential ethnic concentration, access to multilingual ballots, and English language proficiency. As we shall see, some of these factors have strong relationships to voting participation, while others have weak or inconsistent effects that run contrary to expectations based on theories of immigrant assimilation.

Immigrant Incorporation: Time-Based Factors

When considering political participation, as well as other processes of immigrant adaptation, it is useful to think of such processes as having at least two temporal dimensions—across time within the first generation and across immigrant generations. For instance, researchers have generally found that English language ability improves the longer immigrants live in the United States. At the same time, there are also differences in language acquisition across generations. First-generation immigrants frequently do not speak English as well as their children born in the United States, and the second generation often retains some understanding of their parents' native tongue. Those in the third generation and later may have the same level of English language ability as those in the second generation, but they typically lose proficiency in the original migrants' language (Fishman 1972; López 1999). This chapter incorporates both these temporal dimensions—over time and across generations—as predictors of electoral participation.

Traditional theories of immigrant adaptation argued that assimilation is a linear process in both these temporal dimensions, with the economic and social conditions of immigrants improving within the first generation and also across immigrant generations.[2] However, much of the subsequent empirical work in political science has focused only on the first temporal dimension, of differences over time in participation among first-generation immigrants. Thus, for instance, Steven Erie (1988) and Gerald Gamm (1989) use data on naturalization and registration to analyze the pace with which European immigrants participated in electoral politics. However, they pay little attention to what happened to these immigrants after the first generation.

The attention to immigrant political outcomes after the first generation is also found wanting in more recent work on electoral participation among Latinos and Asian Americans. For instance, Carole Uhlaner, Bruce Cain, and Roderick Kiewiet (1989) note in their study of California residents that immigrants are more likely to participate in politics as they spend a greater percentage of their life in the United States. Although this measure does distinguish between the foreign-born and the native-born, it does not consider whether the likelihood of participation continues to increase after the second generation.[3] The lack of differentiation between second-generation immigrants and the rest of the native-born population can also be found in national studies of Latino participation (DeSipio 1996b). As we shall soon see, second-generation immigrants have a likelihood of participation that is different from those in later immigrant generations. Thus, separating out the second generation can offer some important insights on processes of political adaptation among immigrants.

Duration of Stay in the United States

According to standard accounts of immigrant assimilation, those who stay longer in the United States are more likely to participate in politics. Longer duration of stay in the United States can lead to higher participation for several reasons. First, as immigrants live longer in the country, they are more likely to come in contact with mainstream political institutions that are beyond the confines of their ethnic enclaves and institutions (Gordon 1964). They are also more likely to acquire politically relevant information, strengthen their party attachments, and gain experience in dealing with government agencies (Cain, Kiewiet, and Uhlaner 1991; Wong 2000; Jones-Correa 1999). Finally, just as longer stay at a given address gives citizens a greater sense of having a stake in local and state politics, longer stay in the United States can give immigrants a stronger stake in national politics (Handlin 1951).

It is possible that greater experience with the political system can also lead to lower participation as immigrants experience varying levels of distrust or frustration with government agencies. However, most of the empirical evidence so far indicates otherwise—greater exposure to the political system from staying longer in the United States has meant a higher likelihood of electoral participation. These results have been found not only in the earlier scholarship on European immigrants, but also in more recent studies of participation among Latino and Asian immigrants. Thus, for instance, Kevin Hill and Dario Moreno (1996) note in their analysis of the Latino National Political Survey that Cuban immigrants who spend a greater proportion of their lives in the United States are more likely to participate in politics. Similarly, Uhlaner, Cain, and Kiewiet (1989) note in their analysis of a 1984 California survey that Latino and Asian immigrants who spend more time in the United States are more likely to vote. Finally, the effect of duration of stay on voting has not yet been examined with regard to white and black immigrants, a gap which this study seeks to address.

Intergenerational Differences

Temporal processes related to immigrant adaptation do not stop with the first generation. As studies in fields such as sociology and economics have shown, it is also important to examine outcomes across immigrant generations (Borjas 1999; Portes and Zhou 1993). Standard accounts of immigrant assimilation posit that socioeconomic outcomes increase in a linear fashion from the first generation to each succeeding immigrant generation. Over the past decade, several studies have challenged the applicability of "straight-line" theories of immigrant adaptation to second-generation children of post-1965 immigrants (Gans 1992; Rumbaut 1997; Zhou 1997). These studies note that there is no universally linear increase in socioeconomic outcomes from the first generation to later immigrant generations. Instead, they note that different group characteristics and modes of incorporation lead to diverse trajectories that can even include a decline in socioeconomic outcomes between the first generation and second generation.

There have been few studies in political science that have examined the issue of changes in participation across immigrant generations. Some of the early, general treatments of immigrant adaptation paid some attention to the political socialization of the children of immigrants born in the United States. For instance, Marcus Lee Hansen (1938), an early scholar of immigration and ethnic identity, noted that second-generation immigrants were less likely to identify with the country of their parents' birth and more likely to identify with the culture and institutions of the United States. Similarly, historian Oscar Handlin (1951) noted that the children of immigrants were more likely than their parents to be familiar with the mechanisms of democratic politics and confident that government was capable of serving popular interests. Similar analyses of intergenerational patterns are absent in contemporary studies of electoral participation. However, there are studies that note a higher level of participation among the native born when compared to the foreign born. These studies usually explain the lower level of participation among the foreign born by pointing to factors related to immigrant assimilation—such as the absence of language barriers among the native born or the lack of socialization into domestic political institutions among those who immigrate to the United States (Junn 1999; Tam Cho 1999). Still, the question of intergenerational patterns in participation remains unanswered because these studies do not distinguish between the native-born whose parents were born in the United States and those whose parents were born outside the country. The nativity of one's parents could play an important role in shaping political participation—as other studies of political socialization have shown (Jennings and Niemi 1981; Burns, Schlozman, and Verba 2001). The political orientation and participation levels of parents often influence the participation of their children. If immigrant adults are less likely to participate in politics than the native-born, then perhaps the immigrant second generation will be less likely to participate than those whose parents were born in the United States.

In this analysis of electoral participation across immigrant generations, not only do I examine differences between the native born and foreign born; I also separate out the second generation to see if there are any differences in participation between the adult children of immigrants and those in later immigrant generations. Given the separation of the population into three groups (first, second, third and later), we can expect one of several patterns of voter turnout.[4] First, we may expect a pattern of straight-line assimilation in which the likelihood of participation rises with each succeeding immigrant generation (Figure 5.2a). Or we may expect a pattern in which the second generation reaches parity in participation with those in the third generation and later (Figure 5.2b). The difference between these two patterns hinges on whether factors such as disincentives and barriers to participation are eliminated after the first generation or whether they persist in weakened form among second-generation immigrants (as would be the case with straight-line assimilation). In both scenarios, however, first-generation citizens are the least likely to vote. This could be because of linguistic and cultural barriers that make it more difficult for them to obtain political information and vote, or because of persistent ties to the home country that discourage participation in the politics of the United States.

It is also possible, however, that selection effects among those who

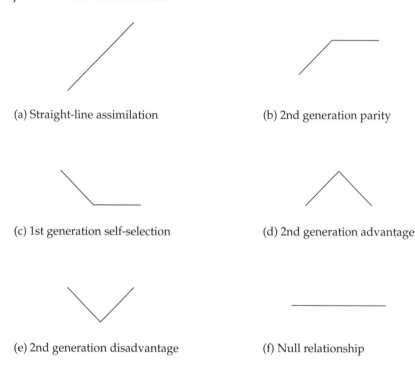

(a) Straight-line assimilation   (b) 2nd generation parity

(c) 1st generation self-selection   (d) 2nd generation advantage

(e) 2nd generation disadvantage   (f) Null relationship

Figure 5.2. Patterns of Intergenerational Differences in Participation

choose citizenship lead to a higher level of participation among the naturalized than among those who are native born (Figure 5.2c). It can be argued that, in contrast to those who are assigned U.S. citizenship by virtue of birth, those who choose to naturalize have an unusually high level of commitment to political participation or have higher levels of political awareness because of preparations for the citizenship exam. In such a scenario, there would be no difference in participation between second-generation immigrants and those in later immigrant generations because the process of self-selection of the more civic-minded would operate only for those who have the choice of acquiring citizenship.

There are two other patterns of possible intergenerational differences in participation, both of which posit an exceptional place for second-generation immigrants. The possibility of a "second-generation advantage" (Figure 5.2d) has already been alluded to by scholars of immigrant incorporation such as Alejandro Portes and Rubén Rumbaut (1996), but the pattern has not yet been found as a result of systematic testing. As Portes and Rumbaut note in their book *Immigrant America*, hostile reactions to first-generation immigrants stirs "ethnic militancy among subsequent generations. . . . Descendants of the first immigrants have gained 'voice' and have used it to reaffirm identities attacked previously with so much impunity" (95). In such a scenario, then, second-generation immigrants are uniquely positioned in that they possess both the motivation and the skills to participate (hereafter referred to as the "motivation/skills hypothesis"). By contrast, those in later generations are more politically apathetic, and those in the first generation lack skills that are relevant to participation.

It should also be noted that another variant of the second-generation exception is one in which the adult children of immigrants have the lowest levels of participation (Figure 5.2e), although there do not seem to be good theoretical reasons to expect this.[5] Finally, it is possible that there is no relationship between generational status and voting, owing to one or more of the following reasons: (1) other factors such as age, race, socioeconomic status, social incorporation, and the like already account for the variation in participation; (2) the effects of self-selection and assimilation operate in opposite directions and cancel each other out.

In analyzing the relationship between immigrant generations and voting, we can also expect to find differences across racial groups. We are likely to find differences because of significant variations in the historical reception given to immigrants from Europe versus those from Asia and Latin America (Gamm 1989; Erie 1988; Espiritu 1992). While mobilization under the New Deal ensured the political incorporation of immigrants from Europe, exclusionary laws and racially discriminatory practices prevented many Asian and Mexican immigrants from exercising their political voice until the 1970s (de la Garza 1996; Espiritu 1992).[6] Even in more recent times, there are racial and ethnic differences in the extent to which immigrants are mobilized into politics. Thus, for instance, party organizations in states such as California and Florida have sought to mobilize Latino voters but have not done the same for first-generation Asian Americans (Wong 2001). Caribbean immigrants in the early twentieth century were incorporated as marginal players in party machines, but they took on several leadership positions in New York City by mid-century. More recently, however, black immigrants from the Caribbean find themselves relatively marginalized from main-

stream political institutions (Kasinitz 1992; Rogers 2000). Thus, by interacting race and generational status, we can expect to find different
patterns of voting participation for white, black, Asian, and Latino immigrants and their descendants.

Results

How does voting participation in recent elections relate to these time-
based aspects of immigrant adaptation? Evidence from the Current
Population Survey indicates that there are considerable generational
differences in the level of voting participation among all racial and ethnic groups (Table 5.1). Looking first at voter turnout within the first
generation, we see a progressive increase in voting participation as immigrants spend more of their lives in the United States. Indeed, as the
figures indicate, the highest levels of participation among all racial
groups can be found among long-term immigrant residents (those who
have lived in the United States for thirty years or more). As we shall
soon see, this gap exists not only because long-term immigrant residents have an older age structure but also because they have spent a
greater proportion of their lives in the United States.

Across immigrant generations, however, there are sizable differences
in voter turnout for members of different racial groups. Among whites,
there is an increase in participation from the first generation to the second generation, followed by a decline among later-generation respondents. This trend conforms to the pattern of a "second-generation
advantage" as outlined in Figure 5.2. Among blacks, generational differences in turnout rates are virtually nonexistent. For Latinos, the likelihood of participation displays a pattern of "first-generation self-selection" noted in Figure 5.2, while for Asian Americans turnout increases
in a linear manner from the first generation to later immigrant generations. Thus, despite the common finding of high participation among
long-term immigrants in the first generation, the bivariate relationships
reveal patterns that vary across racial and ethnic groups. Blacks and
Latinos are similar in that there are no strong generational differences
in participation, whites display a pattern of second-generation advantage, and Asians are the only group for whom the straight-line model of
immigrant assimilation seems to hold.

There are many factors related to individual resources and social incorporation that may account for these generational differences in

TABLE 5.1

Levels of Voting Participation by Race and Immigrant Generation
(adult citizens)

	White (%)	Black (%)	Latino (%)	Asian (%)
First generation				
< 15 years in the U.S.	36	29	26	28
15–29 years in the U.S.	44	50	41	34
30+ years in the U.S.	63	59	55	59
All first generation	56	44	43	36
Second generation	63	46	36	42
Third generation and later	52	46	37	53

SOURCE: Current Population Survey, November 1994 and 1998.
NOTE: Tabulated results are for the midterm elections of 1994 and 1998, since the general
level of turnout in presidential elections is much higher. Generational differences in
turnout are still present among all racial groups in 1996, although the differences are
smaller for all groups other than non-Hispanic whites.

turnout. As we have already seen from Chapter 4, the strongest predictors of participation are age, education, marital status, and residential
stability. As Table 5.2 indicates, there are substantial differences in the
levels of these various factors across race and immigrant generation.
For instance, white immigrants in the third generation and later are, on
average, twelve years younger than their counterparts in the first and
second generation. Similarly, the proportion of college-educated Asian
American citizens decreases from the first generation to later immigrant
generations. Thus, in order to discern the true relationship between
generational status and voting participation, we need to analyze the issue in a multivariate model that controls for such factors.

Even after controlling for individual resources and contexts of social
incorporation and political mobilization, generational differences in
the likelihood of voting remain significant for all racial and ethnic
groups. Figure 5.3 presents the predicted probability of participation
among first-generation immigrants according to the duration of their
stay in the United States. Just as in the case of turnout rates in the bivariate context, the probability of participation in the multivariate

TABLE 5.2

Mean Values of Selected Factors by Race and Immigrant Generation (adult citizens)

	White	Black	Latino	Asian
Age	(years)	(years)	(years)	(years)
First generation	57	44	48	45
Second generation	57	36	38	40
Third generation and later	45	42	38	40
College graduates	(%)	(%)	(%)	(%)
First generation	30	27	14	45
Second generation	25	23	11	32
Third generation and later	25	13	11	36
Long residence[a]	(%)	(%)	(%)	(%)
First generation	67	47	55	54
Second generation	68	40	51	57
Third generation and later	56	49	46	55

SOURCE: Current Population Survey, November 1994–2000.
[a]Fifteen or more years.

model increases as first-generation immigrants stay longer in the United States.

Among white immigrants, for instance, long-term immigrant residents have a 31 percent higher probability of voting than those naturalized citizens who have lived in the United States for less than fifteen years. Latinos display the highest increase in participation—long-term immigrant residents have nearly a 50 percent higher probability of voting than short-term residents. The comparable figures for Asian and black immigrants are increases of 23 percent and 26 percent, respectively. Note that these results hold true even for particular national origin groups. Also, the positive relationship between duration of stay and voting can be found even with an alternative specification of the variable, such as the percent of one's life spent in the United States. This specification captures the number of years an immigrant has lived in the country as well as the age at which the person first immigrated. So, regardless of the measure used, a longer stay in the United States leads

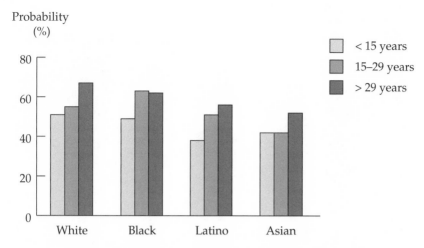

Figure 5.3. Predicted Probabilities of Participation by Length of Stay in the United States Among First-Generation Immigrants. Controlling for all other factors and holding other variables at their group-specific means.
SOURCE: Current Population Survey Voter Supplement 1994–2000.

to a higher likelihood of voting. Thus, the evidence across racial and ethnic groups consistently supports the standard assimilationist model within the first immigrant generation.

The straight-line assimilationist model does not fare as well in accounting for differences in participation across immigrant generations (Figure 5.4). In the multivariate analysis that controls for factors related to age, socioeconomic status, social incorporation, and contexts of mobilization, whites still display a second-generation advantage in voting participation. Second-generation whites have a predicted probability of voting that is 17 percent higher than their first-generation counterparts and 5 percent higher than those in later immigrant generations. For blacks, voting participation increases in a stepwise manner from the first generation to later generations. A similar pattern can be found among Asian Americans, although the increase in participation is not sufficient to bridge the racial gap in participation. Even after being in the United States for three or more generations, Asian Americans are considerably less likely to vote than their black and white counterparts—all when controlling for the effects of socioeconomic status. Note, however, that the higher levels of education and income among

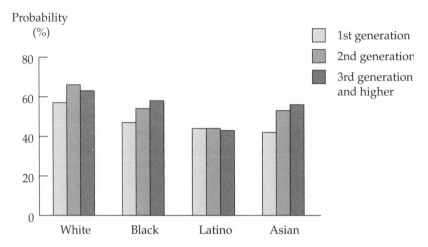

Figure 5.4. Predicted Probabilities of Participation by Immigrant Generation. Controlling for all other factors and holding other variables at their group-specific means.

SOURCE: Current Population Survey Voter Supplement 1994–2000.

Asian Americans serves to bridge most of the gap in participation with blacks and about half the gap in participation with native-born whites. Finally, for Latinos the likelihood of participation remains relatively constant from the first generation to later immigrant generations and is the highest among naturalized citizens who are long-term residents. So we see that generational patterns in participation vary across racial and ethnic groups—a straight-line pattern for blacks and Asian Americans, a second-generation advantage among whites, and a null relationship between immigrant generation and voting for Latinos.

What accounts for these different generational patterns in participation? Looking first at whites, we see that assimilationist accounts of cultural and political adaptation may explain why participation among first-generation citizens is lower than participation among second-generation citizens. First-generation respondents may avoid engagement in American politics because of cultural and linguistic barriers to participation or because of their desire to secure an economic foothold in the United States. However, conventional "straight-line" assimilationist theories cannot account for why second-generation whites are consistently more likely to participate than those in later generations.

Assimilationist accounts are also of limited value in accounting for the generational patterns among nonwhites. For blacks, the high level of participation among those in the third generation and later is due not only to greater integration or assimilation but also to the mobilizing effects of the civil rights movement. Several studies have shown that, even though blacks faced enormous barriers to participation until the 1960s, the civil rights movement was a powerful mobilizer that enhanced citizens' sense of group consciousness and political efficacy (Verba and Nie 1972; Rosenstone and Hansen 1993). So, in addition to facing fewer cultural and linguistic barriers, blacks in the third generation and later are also more likely to have gained high levels of political experience and political efficacy during the civil rights movement. Asian Americans and Latinos also faced several institutional barriers to participation until the 1970s, but they did not experience a social movement on the scale of the civil rights movement. As other scholars have noted, the absence of such broad-scale movements among third- and later-generation Asian Americans and Latinos may be responsible for the continued racial gap in participation for such groups (DeSipio 1996a; Uhlaner, Cain, and Kiewiet 1989).

The results in this study also show racial gaps in participation that exist in the first immigrant generation and that persist through the third generation and beyond. Among white immigrants, the predicted probability of voting among long-term residents is 67 percent, while for Latinos and Asian immigrants the figures are 56 percent and 52 percent, respectively. Even among respondents in the third generation and later, the probability of participation is 63 percent among whites but only 43 percent among Latinos and 56 percent among Asian Americans. The persistence of this racial gap in participation challenges assimilationist accounts of immigrant incorporation that would suggest a convergence in participation by the second or third generation. For instance, Wendy Tam Cho (1999) argues that the lower level of participation among Latinos and Asian Americans can largely be attributed to factors such as English language ability and other aspects of immigrant assimilation. I shall consider the effects of English language proficiency on participation among Latinos later in this chapter. It is important to note here, however, that racial gaps in participation persist even for those respondents least likely to face language barriers (i.e., those in the third generation and later). This points to the possibility that the continued racial gaps in participation are due not to cultural factors such as language proficiency that change with immigrant generation, but rather to sys-

tems of race privilege that endure even among third-generation immigrants (Pulido 2000).

Some may argue that the generational patterns uncovered in this
analysis may not hold when controlling for attitudinal factors such as
political interest, efficacy, and party identification. The Current Population Survey (CPS) does not enable us to test the effects of individual
attitudes because it does not include such measures. However, other
datasets such as the National Election Studies (NES) and the Post/
Kaiser/Harvard (PKH) survey of Latinos do contain measures of
attitudes as well as participation. For white immigrants in the NES,
intergenerational patterns in political participation are reflected to some
extent in political attitudes and party identification. However, adding
attitudinal variables to the model of voting participation does not
diminish the magnitude of the second-generation advantage for whites.
Indeed, the magnitude of the second-generation advantage increases
marginally after controlling for factors such as party identification,
political interest, and efficacy. For Latinos in the PKH survey,
controlling for political attitudes does not change the relationship
between immigrant generation and voting participation.[7] Comparable
data on voter registration among Asian Americans in the Multi-City
Survey of Urban Inequality (MCSUI) reveals that the lower level of
participation among first-generation immigrants persists even after
controlling for factors such as party identification and English language
ability.[8]

So immigrant political incorporation proceeds in a different manner
for members of different racial and ethnic groups. For whites, those in
the second generation are more likely to vote than those in the first generation, as well as those in later generations. This second-generation advantage in participation is not a phenomenon that is limited to the recent past or to a particular dataset. CPS data from the 1990s, as well as
NES data since the 1960s, show a consistently higher likelihood of participation among second-generation whites. This pattern of a "second-
generation advantage" in participation is present in different datasets
and holds true even after controlling for attitudinal factors such as political interest and party identification. The second-generation advantage, while remarkably durable for white respondents, does not apply
to blacks, Asian Americans, and Latinos. For blacks and Asian Americans, participation increases in a linear manner from the first generation
to later immigrant generations. Even with this intergenerational in-

crease, however, voting among Asian Americans in the third and later generations continues to lag behind voting among whites and blacks. Similarly, among Latinos there remains a significant racial gap in participation by the third generation, despite the fact that the likelihood of voting among first-generation immigrants is high relative to immigrants of other racial groups.

It remains to be seen whether the patterns and trends noted in this analysis will continue into the next decade. With record numbers of immigrants applying for naturalization, with the "new" second generation reaching voting age, and with parties and interest groups attempting to mobilize ethnic voters, it is possible that participation among first-generation Asian Americans will increase and that racial gaps in voting will narrow among second-generation immigrants and those in the third and later generations.

Immigrant Incorporation: Country-of-Origin Characteristics

Participation in U.S. elections is not solely a function of how long first-generation immigrants have stayed in the United States, or even of how many generations have passed since a citizen's ancestors first immigrated to the country. There are several other factors related to immigrants' countries of origin and their settlement in the United States that can play an important role in the extent to which they participate in domestic politics. For instance, some may argue, based on the experience of Cuban immigrants, that those who immigrate from communist countries or other repressive regimes are more likely to participate in politics than those who do not come from such countries. These effects may be found not only among first-generation immigrants but also among their adult children in the second generation. Another factor related to the immigrants' country of origin that may be relevant to the extent to which they participate in politics is whether they come from countries that allow dual nationality. Finally, there may be residual country-specific or region-specific effects that have not already been accounted for by factors such as race and ethnicity, repressive regime origin, and dual nationality eligibility.

nigration from a Country Ruled by a
...ressive Regime

For naturalized citizens, coming from communist or other repressive regimes can have a significant impact on the propensity to vote. It is unclear, however, whether repressive regime origins increase or decrease the likelihood of turnout. On the one hand, refugees may be more likely to participate because they have come to the United States primarily for political reasons, while other immigrants primarily come to the United States to improve their economic standing. Having migrated for political reasons, those coming from repressive and communist regimes are likely to possess a keener appreciation of the importance of politics in their daily lives, whether it be from memories of dispossession in the homeland or of an awareness of American foreign policy toward their country of origin. Furthermore, those who qualify for refugee assistance from the U.S. government may have greater skills and experience interacting with government agencies and may have a greater stake in domestic politics as it relates to their continued receipt of such benefits. On the other hand, those who are fleeing regimes with a long history of political repression may be less likely to participate in politics because they are mistrustful of the state. Indeed, abstaining from voting may be a way for communist refugees to exercise their political freedoms, since many of their home country regimes made voting a mandatory act. Finally, immigrants from repressive regimes may not have had the necessary experience with pluralist politics in their young adulthood to participate effectively in American politics. As Handlin (1951) noted in his study of earlier waves of European immigrants from nondemocratic regimes, "To many pursuits of the New World the immigrant was strange upon arrival; to politics he was strangest of all. His European experience had included no participation in government; every question related to these matters would be new to him" (201).

So far, the only comparative studies that have examined the effect of originating from a country having a repressive regime (hereafter "repressive regime origin") on subsequent participation have been those that examine the participation of Cuban and Mexican immigrants. In their 1985 study, Alejandro Portes and Rafael Mozo analyze precinct-level aggregate data from Miami and find that Cuban Americans have higher levels of turnout than those in other Hispanic subgroups. Portes and Mozo attribute much of these national-origin differences in participation to the fact that Cuban immigrants are refugees who immigrated primarily for political reasons. Multivariate analyses of the Latino National Political Survey add further credence to the hypothesis that originating from a communist country (hereafter "communist country origin") serves as a spur to participation. In a 1996 study, John Arvizu and Chris Garcia note that Cuban immigrants are more likely to vote than Mexican immigrants, even after controlling for age, education, income, and length of stay in the United States. However, given the small number of countries of origin in such studies (Cuba and Mexico), the effect of prior political experience on voting participation has not been systematically tested. Indeed, a study of Vietnamese Americans in California reveals that first-generation immigrants express higher levels of distrust of the American political system than do second-generation immigrants (Collett 2000). Thus it remains to be seen whether the voting participation of Cuban Americans is exceptional or whether it is consistent with the electoral participation of immigrants from other communist or repressive regimes.

Finally, just as coming from a repressive regime may influence the likelihood of voting among first-generation immigrants, it may also influence voting participation among those in the second generation. Studies of political socialization have shown that childhood exposure to political activities or discussions by parents has a significant impact on subsequent adult participation (Jennings and Niemi 1981; Verba, Schlozman, and Brady 1995). Thus, if an immigrant family's prior experience with repressive regimes does indeed have a significant impact on political participation in the United States, we may expect the impact to be present among the second generation as well. However, this effect is likely to be weaker among the second generation than the first because the former are influenced not only by the memories and experiences of their parents but also by societal factors that are primarily derived from growing up in the United States.

How well does repressive regime origin account for the voting participation of immigrants and their descendants? Table 5.3 presents the effects of repressive and communist country origins on voting, once controlling for traditional factors related to voting participation (see the Appendix for variable specification). Coming from a repressive regime has virtually no effect on the probability of voting among black immigrants. For Latinos, too, coming from a country ruled by a repressive regime has no significant impact on voting. It is possible, however, that the exceptional case of Cuban immigrants alters the effect for the rest of the Latino population. For instance, the voting participation of Cuban

TABLE 5.3

Repressive and Communist Country Origin and Voting Among First-Generation Immigrants, 1994–2000 (controlling for all other factors and holding other variables at their group-specific means)

	% Yes	% No	Ratio
From Repressive Regime			
White	58.3	64.0	0.91***
Black	58.5	59.0	0.99
Latino	49.2	52.1	0.94
Latino (excluding Cuban)	43.9	50.6	0.87**
Asian American	45.0	41.0	1.10*
From Communist Regime			
White	57.3	63.2	0.91***
Black	21.1	59.2	0.36***
Latino	55.1	48.3	1.14***
Asian American	42.5	44.1	0.96

*** $p < .01$; ** $p < .05$; * $p < .10$
p values indicate the probability of a null relationship or difference.

immigrants is unusually high and may have more to do with the particularities of Miami politics and U.S. foreign policy toward Cuba. Indeed, Dario Moreno (1997) argues that the demographic dominance of Cuban immigrants in Miami, their unique class position, and consensus regarding foreign policy make the Cuban immigrant experience unique among Latinos. If so, then excluding Cuban immigrants will lower the estimates of repressive regime origins among Latinos from other countries. A separate estimation of the effect, after excluding Cuban immigrants from the rest of the Latino population, reveals that this indeed is the case; the probability of voting now actually declines by 13 percent for those who come from repressive regimes (Table 5.3). A similar result holds for white immigrants—the likelihood of voting is 9 percent lower among those who immigrate from repressive regimes than those from democratic countries. Asian immigrants are the only exceptional case here, with repressive regime origin increasing the probability of participation by 10 percent.

Using the more restrictive measure of communist country origin instead of repressive regime origin does not change the nature of the results for immigrants of most racial groups. For white immigrants, the decline in participation associated with a communist country of origin is nearly identical to the decline associated with immigrating from a country with a repressive regime. For blacks, the decline in the likelihood of participation is even steeper than the decline found among whites—those who come from noncommunist countries are nearly three times as likely to vote as those coming from communist countries. However, these results are likely to be unreliable because immigrants from communist countries account for only 1 percent of all black immigrants. Latinos are the only group for whom communist country origin leads to higher participation, a result which is due exclusively to those immigrating from Cuba. Finally, among Asian immigrants, immigrating from a communist country has no significant impact on the probability of voting. So we see that the high level of participation of Cuban immigrants is indeed exceptional when compared to immigrants from other racial groups. Indeed, for white immigrants, coming from a communist country actually lowers the likelihood of voting in the United States. These findings therefore seem to support the contentions of early researchers such as Oscar Handlin, who argued that those coming from nondemocratic regimes did not have the kind of political socialization that was conducive to democratic participation.

Finally, if both repressive regime origins and communist country origins generally lead to a lower likelihood of participation among immigrants, it is possible that these factors also affect the probability of voting among the second generation. The results from the multivariate regressions indicate that this is not the case (see Appendix Table A.4). Having parents who come from a country ruled by a repressive regime leads to slightly lower probabilities of participation, but none of these effects are statistically significant. These weaker effects are likely due to domestic societal influences on the second generation that compete with the attitudes, beliefs, and norms espoused by immigrant parents (Portes and Rumbaut 2001). Thus, while the lack of relevant experiences and skills may be a problem for first-generation immigrants coming from countries ruled by communist or other repressive regimes, it is less of an issue for the children of such immigrants born in the United States.

Dual Nationality

In recent years, there has been a growing interest among scholars of immigrant adaptation on the effects of policies of dual citizenship and
dual nationality on the propensity of immigrants to naturalize and participate in American politics. The terms *dual citizenship* and *dual nationality* are often used interchangeably, even though *citizenship* is the term
that refers to political rights and obligations whereas *nationality* refers
to less formal types of identification with an ethnic or a civic community. In the past three decades, there have been a growing number of
countries that have decided to grant emigrants the right to hold some
form of political membership in their home countries even after they
obtain citizenship in countries such as the United States. In some instances, dual nationality has meant the granting of basic rights or property ownership and unrestricted return to the home country, while in
other instances, it has meant the ability to vote and even run for elected
office in more than one country.[9] In this analysis, I use *dual nationality* as
an umbrella term that involves the guarantee of civic and property
rights in the home country.

Some political theorists have expressed deep misgivings over the
implications of dual nationality to civic participation among immigrants in the United States. They have argued that civic membership in
multiple countries robs American citizenship of its substantive value, as
immigrants continue to retain ties to their home countries and neglect
their obligations as citizens of the United States (Pickus 1998; Rehnson
2001). Others have argued that policies of dual nationality actually help
to hasten the incorporation of immigrants into American politics, citing
evidence from Latino immigrants (Jones-Correa 2001). According to
this latter perspective, many immigrants entertain hopes of returning to
their home country, even if they never actually make a permanent return. For such immigrants, the absence of laws granting dual nationality serves as a barrier to the acquisition of U.S. citizenship because they
fear the loss of rights and privileges in their home countries. Thus, the
granting of dual nationality enables immigrants to simultaneously retain their hopes of return to their home countries as well as their desire
to acquire political membership in the United States. Indeed, evidence
on naturalization among Latino immigrants indicates that those who
come from countries that have recently allowed dual nationality are
more likely to naturalize as citizens of the United States (Jones-Correa
2001).

In addition to questions of naturalization, the issue of multiple state membership also has potentially enormous implications for electoral participation in the United States. However, there have not yet been any systematic analyses of what happens after the acquisition of citizenship. Thus there has been no systematic, cross-racial study of whether those who come from countries that allow for dual nationality are less likely to participate or whether they are just as likely or even more likely to participate than immigrants who come from countries that do not allow for dual citizenship.[10] The former scenario is possible if immigrants from "dual citizenship countries" acquire U.S. citizenship for instrumental reasons, while the latter is possible if such immigrants are more likely to be informed and interested in politics because of a greater awareness of their multiple rights and obligations of citizenship. This study builds on what is currently known about dual nationality and naturalization to provide a more complete picture of the consequences of multiple state membership on participation in the electoral politics of the United States.

In order to test the effects of dual nationality on the likelihood of voting in the United States, we need to analyze datasets such as the Current Population Survey, which includes immigrants from regimes in different regions of the world that vary in policies of dual nationality and citizenship (see Rehnson 2001). The relevant questions to examine with respect to the CPS data are the following: Does the higher likelihood of naturalization among immigrants from countries that allow dual nationality also translate into a higher likelihood of voting participation? Or are immigrants who come from countries with dual nationality policies more likely to choose American citizenship for instrumental reasons and therefore less likely to vote? Table 5.4 presents the effects of such policies on voting in the United States for immigrants of different racial groups.[11]

The results indicate that dual nationality does indeed raise the likelihood of voting among first-generation whites and Asian Americans, but that it has no statistically significant effect on the likelihood of voting among Latinos and blacks. Once again, however, we need to exclude the exceptional case of Cuban immigrants, who are not eligible for dual nationality and whose high level of participation may mask a positive relationship for the variable among other Latino immigrants. From Table 5.4, we can see that this is indeed the case. When Cuban immigrants are excluded from the analysis, Latinos coming from countries that allow dual nationality are 4 percent more likely to vote than

TABLE 5.4

Dual Nationality and Voting Among First-Generation Immigrants, 1994–2000 (controlling for all other factors and holding other variables at their group-specific means)

	Eligible for Dual Nationality		
	% Yes	% No	Ratio
White	63.2	61.3	1.03***
Black	40.6	59.3	0.69
Latino	46.8	50.1	0.93
Latino (excluding Cuban)	45.6	44.0	1.04**
Asian American	57.2	43.4	1.32*

*** $p < .01$; ** $p < .05$; * $p < .10$

those whose countries of origin do not allow dual citizenship. Thus there is no support for the proposition that immigrants who come from countries that allow dual nationality are choosing U.S. citizenship primarily for instrumental reasons. Black and Latino immigrants from such countries are no less likely to vote than their counterparts from countries without dual citizenship provisions. Furthermore, among white and Asian immigrants, those who benefit from policies of dual nationality are actually more likely to vote than those who do not.

Country- or Region-Specific Effects

The countries from which emigrants depart for the United States may be relevant to political participation for reasons other than the ones already articulated here. For instance, immigrants from South Asia often distinguish themselves from immigrants from East Asia and are often treated as such by the larger American society. Part of this difference is due to factors such as racial phenotype, cultural traditions, and English language ability.[12] Part of the perceived difference also stems from variations in the experience of World War II (South Asia was relatively insulated from the war compared to East Asia), and the legacy of colonial rule (China, Japan, and Korea were never formally colonized by European countries while South Asia was under British rule for over a century). Similarly, those coming from Southeast Asia are culturally distinct from immigrants in other parts of Asia and also have a legacy of war and colonial rule different from those of immigrants arriving from South Asia or East Asia. The incorporation of Filipino immigrants may be different still, since the Philippines was the only country in Southeast Asia to be colonized by the United States. Finally, even among immigrants from East Asia, we can expect country-level differences in the incorporation of immigrants into American politics. These differences may stem not only from the recent histories of Japan, China, and South Korea, but also from variations in settlement patterns and reception of immigrants from those countries in the United States.

Country- or region-specific effects may also be found among European immigrants, regardless of whether they come from repressive or democratic regimes, or whether their countries of origin allow dual nationality or forbid it. For instance, some have argued that the Anglo bias in American culture makes it easier for immigrants from the United Kingdom to assimilate into American society than for immigrants from other countries.[13] I shall therefore explore the independent effect of country of origin for the four largest European immigrant groups: those from Germany, Italy, Poland, and Great Britain. One could also examine the effects of being from Eastern Europe and the former Soviet Union on subsequent participation, but these variables are highly correlated with originating from a communist country for white immigrants. A similar problem of collinearity exists for Latino immigrants, with Cuban immigrants the only ones to come from communist countries. However, if one uses the more expansive measure of originating from a country ruled by a repressive regime instead of a communist country, then it is possible that country- and region-specific effects may hold true for immigrants from Mexico, Central America, Cuba, and South America. Finally, in the case of black immigrants, the only sizable countries of origin are Haiti and Jamaica. However, we can also separate out immigrants from other parts of the Caribbean and immigrants from Africa. In the case of Latino and black immigrants, country of origin may have an independent effect on participation even after controlling for repressive regime origin and dual nationality because of factors particular to the histories of migration to the United States, the class composition of the emigrating population, and their reception in the United States.[14]

I turn now to the CPS data to determine whether there are any country-of-origin effects that are independent from the three factors already considered (originating from a country ruled by a repressive regime, originating from a communist country, and dual nationality policies).

Figure 5.5 presents differences in the probability of voting by country of origin or region of origin after controlling for various other factors. Among first-generation white immigrants, Italian immigrants have a probability of voting that is lower than that of all other national origin groups. German immigrants have the highest likelihood of voting, but this difference is not statistically significant at the .10 level. Among black immigrants, Jamaican immigrants have the highest likelihood of voting—higher than participation among immigrants from other Caribbean countries and from Africa. Haitian immigrants also tend to have a higher likelihood of voting than immigrants from Africa, but the difference is not statistically significant.

Controlling for dual nationality policy and originating from a country ruled by a repressive regime does not diminish the Cuban immigrant advantage among Latinos. Even after controlling for such factors, Cuban immigrants have a probability of participation that is 36 percent higher than among first-generation Mexican immigrants. Cuban immigrants also have a higher likelihood of participation than those from Central America and South America, who in turn have a higher likelihood of voting than Mexican immigrants. It is unclear why the latter differences are statistically significant. Some may argue that the higher socioeconomic status among naturalized South American and Central American immigrants is responsible for their higher participation. However, the effects noted here are found after controlling for age, socioeconomic status, and the various other factors listed in Figure 5.1. It is therefore likely that other factors related to country of origin that are not measured in the CPS (such as the frequency of return to the home country or hopes of returning permanently) may be responsible for the persistent gaps in participation between immigrants from Mexico and those from Central and South America.

Finally, among Asian immigrants, there are generally two clusters of groups: those who have probabilities of voting that hover around 50 percent (Filipino, South Asian, and Southeast Asian immigrants) and those whose probability of participation is around 35 percent (Chinese, Japanese, and Korean immigrants). Thus there seems to be a regional difference among Asian immigrants, with those coming from East Asia less likely to vote than those coming from other parts of Asia. Part of these regional differences can be explained by English language ability; since there are many Anglophone countries in South Asia and Southeast Asia, immigrants from these regions are likely to have higher levels of English proficiency than, say, immigrants from China or Japan. A

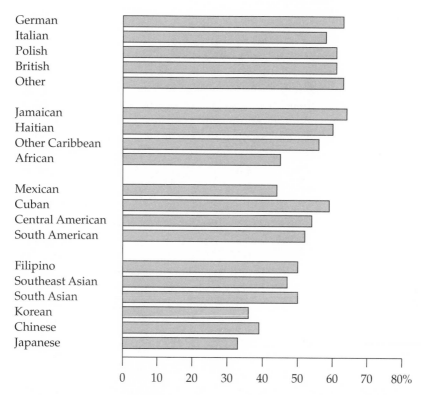

Figure 5.5. Predicted Probability of Voting by Country or Region of Origin Among First-Generation Immigrants. Controlling for all other factors and holding other variables at their group-specific means.
SOURCE: Current Population Survey Voter Supplement 1994–2000.

separate analysis of Anglophone country origin reveals that the variable is indeed positively related to voting among Asian immigrants.[15] Furthermore, controlling for Anglophone origin wipes out the significance of the advantage in participation among South Asian and Southeast Asian immigrants.[16] Finally, controlling for Anglophone origin still leaves intact the significance of the Filipino advantage in participation, although the long history of U.S. intervention in the Philippines can still lead to an advantage in participation beyond those based on English language affinity. Thus the model of Anglo conformity as articulated by Milton Gordon (1964) and others seems to hold true in the case of immigrants from Asia—first-generation immigrants who come from Anglophone countries tend to have a higher level of participation than those who do not.[17]

Finally, just as there may be residual country-of-origin effects among first-generation immigrants that remain after controlling for factors such as dual nationality and originating from a country ruled by a repressive regime, there may also be differences in country-of-origin among second-generation immigrants. However, one would expect the common experience of being born and growing up in the United States among second-generation immigrants to mute the national-origin differences present in their parents' generation. These expectations are largely borne out by the CPS data, which reveal no substantial differences in the probability of voting across national origins for immigrants in the second generation. Even among Latinos, differences are more muted, with Cuban Americans only 16 percent more likely to vote than their Mexican American counterparts. Differences among Asian Americans are also weaker for second-generation respondents. As one may expect, English language proficiency does not seem to play a role in differences among second-generation Asian Americans, since those who trace their roots to Anglophone countries do not have higher probabilities of voting than those who do not. Indeed, the highest levels of participation are among Chinese and Japanese Americans, two Asian immigrant communities that have had the longest history of settlement in the United States. Similarly, controlling for origination from an Anglophone country among second-generation black immigrants still leaves a significant gap in participation between those who trace their roots to the Caribbean and those whose parents came from Africa.

Immigrant Incorporation: The American Context

In addition to country-of-origin characteristics, there are various factors related to the socialization of immigrants in the United States that may also account for whether they vote. For instance, living in an ethnic enclave can increase the likelihood of political mobilization by candidates as well as ethnic organizations. On the other hand, ethnic enclaves may lower participation if such enclaves are also areas with high proportions of noncitizens. The presence or absence of multilingual ballots may also have a significant impact on the participation of immigrants with low levels of English language skills. Finally, English language proficiency may be related to voting participation in ways that have not already been considered. They may weaken the relationship between education and voting, since the skills associated with higher education among non-English dominant speakers may not be helpful for voting in the United States. On the other hand, the presence of Spanish language ballots and living in areas with high proportions of coethnics may serve to mitigate these negative effects associated with the lack of English proficiency.

Residential Ethnic Concentration

Participation in American civic life depends not only on the countries from which immigrants arrive but also on where they settle in the United States. Those who live in states or metropolitan areas with high concentrations of coethnics are more likely to have contacts with or exposure to ethnic media and community organizations. Having higher concentrations of coethnics therefore lowers the per capita cost of ethnic mobilization by interest groups, political parties, and candidate organizations. Among the earlier waves of European immigrants, settlement patterns helped shape the trajectories of immigrant participation in politics. For instance, the concentration of Irish immigrants in a handful of American cities made it possible for them to capture political power at the local level. As Erie (1988) notes, the mobilization of Irish votes represents the classic example of party machines harnessing the demographic concentration of immigrants in urban areas to capture power and distribute rewards such as patronage jobs. Similarly, Jewish immigrants in New York City were able to take advantage of their residential concentration to play a significant role in local politics (Glazer and Moynihan 1963).

At the same time, ethnic concentration is no guarantee of political mobilization and empowerment. For Italians living in cities that were dominated by Irish machines, there was no attempt to naturalize and mobilize immigrant voters. Democratic party bosses in these cities already had constituencies large enough to capture local office and therefore had no incentive to dilute the distribution of patronage by adding Italian immigrants to the winning coalition (Erie 1988; Gamm 1989). Although the viability of party machines has declined considerably since the early 1900s, the logic of minimizing the size of winning coalitions is still operative in cities such as New York. Thus Michael Jones-Correa (1998) finds that local elected officials in Queens make no effort to mobilize or satisfy the needs of immigrants because their electoral security is already guaranteed in a city dominated by the Democratic Party. Even in cities that do not have party machines, ethnic residential concentration may not have a salutary effect on political mobilization and participation. Previous studies of Latino participation have suggested that areas of high ethnic concentrations can be areas of lower mobilization and participation (DeSipio 1996a; de la Garza 1996). This may be due to the effect of other social contextual factors associated with high Latino and immigrant concentrations: higher residential poverty, greater proportions of noncitizens, and peers with low English proficiency (Tam Cho 1999; Espenshade and Fu 1997). More recent work by Jan Leighley (2001) reveals that ethnic mobilization is not related to group size among Latinos even after controlling for the percentage of noncitizens, although the level of electoral participation is indeed higher in areas with larger proportions of Latinos.

While the findings regarding Latinos are certainly suggestive, the effect of residential ethnic concentration on voting has not yet been tested with a national sample that enables differentiation across immigrant generations and racial groups.[18] There is reason to believe that residential concentration may have different effects on participation among first-generation immigrants than among those in later immigrant generations. While first-generation citizens may have deeper ties to their coethnic communities, such ties may not necessarily lead to greater participation in the United States. First, immigrants tend to orient themselves more toward homeland politics than those in later immigrant generations (Collett 2000; Jones-Correa 1998), and so mobilization may not translate into greater participation in domestic politics. Furthermore, first-generation immigrants may be more likely to live in areas where a greater proportion of their coethnics are noncitizens (Gimpel 1999), and so ethnic concentration is less likely to lead to participation and empowerment through the electoral arena. So even if residential ethnic concentration leads to higher electoral mobilization among native-born ethnic and racial minorities, it would have weaker effects among first-generation immigrants.

It is therefore not clear whether proximity to coethnics leads to higher electoral mobilization among contemporary immigrants to the United States. On the one hand, higher levels of ethnic concentration in particular states or metropolitan areas can increase the likelihood of voting, as members of ethnic groups benefit from having a greater chance of affecting electoral outcomes and as political organizations have a greater chance of reaching out to potential voters through ethnic organizations and media. At the same time, the foreign-born may not benefit from the same level of mobilization as those in later immigrant generations if they live in neighborhoods that have higher levels of residential poverty and lower proportions of naturalized citizens.

I turn to the Current Population Survey to discern the effects of ethnic residential concentration on electoral participation. While the CPS does not include information on the neighborhoods of respondents, it is still possible to test the effects of ethnic concentration at the state, county, and metropolitan area levels and to determine whether there are differences in effects across immigrant generations. Since mobilization by political campaigns and party organizations occurs primarily at the state and county levels, we can also expect to find changes in group size at these aggregate levels to make a difference in the likelihood of mobilization and participation. Table 5.5 presents the effect of living in states with low and high levels of ethnic concentration for members of different racial groups and immigrant generations.

As hypothesized, the effect of ethnic concentration is stronger among respondents in the third and later generations than among first-generation and second-generation immigrants. The only case in which state ethnic concentration has a positive effect on voting among first-generation immigrants is among Asian Americans. Even here, however, the effects are weaker than among immigrants in the third generation and later. Finally, note that the effects of state ethnic concentration on Latino voting may be inordinately influenced by California, which not only has the highest number of Latinos in the country but also a unique history of racially charged ballot propositions during the past decade.[19] Excluding California from the analysis does not change the impact of state ethnic concentration on Latino voting; the effects are still weaker among first-generation respondents than among those in later immigrant generations. Finally, it is likely that Hawaii has a disproportionate effect on the variable under consideration because it accounts for about 60 percent of Asian American respondents in the third generation and later. Excluding Hawaii from the analysis does not diminish the impact of state ethnic concentration on Asian American voting. Indeed, it strengthens the effect of the variable among those in the third generation and later, making the difference with respect to first-generation immigrants even more pronounced.

So far, we have examined the effects of ethnic population levels at the state level on political participation. Using state-level measures can capture the mobilization efforts of political organizations on behalf of

TABLE 5.5

State Ethnic Concentration and Probability of Voting by Immigrant Generation, 1994–2000 (controlling for all other factors and holding other variables at their group-specific means)

	% Low	% High	Ratio
Black			
First generation	59.1	58.6	0.99
Second generation	53.8	55.0	1.02
Third generation and later	50.1	59.3	1.18***
Latino			
First generation	48.2	49.6	1.03
Second generation	35.5	39.8	1.12***
Third generation and later	31.2	37.6	1.20***
Asian American			
First generation	40.3	42.8	1.06***
Second generation	42.3	44.3	1.05
Third generation and later	35.9	40.1	1.12
Latino (excluding California)			
First generation	47.9	48.4	1.01
Second generation	35.2	39.3	1.12*
Third generation and later	31.2	37.5	1.20***
Asian American (excluding Hawaii)			
First generation	37.9	45.6	1.20*
Second generation	37.1	44.8	1.21
Third generation and later	37.3	58.0	1.55**

NOTE: Low concentration is one standard deviation below the mean (with a cutoff at 0), while high concentration is one standard deviation above.

*** $p < .01$; ** $p < .05$; * $p < .10$

candidates running statewide (president, senator, governor, attorney general, etc.), as well as statewide ballot initiatives. However, for contests such as U.S. representative and mayor, the relevant locus of mobilization may be at the level of county or metropolitan area. Do the findings of ethnic concentration at the state level also apply at the level of county or metropolitan statistical area (MSA)? Separate analyses at the county and MSA levels indicate that similar findings apply for blacks and Latinos—ethnic concentration has its strongest effects among re-spondents in the third generation and later.[20] For Asian Americans, however, there is no significant relationship between ethnic concentration and voting participation even among those in the third generation and later. It is possible that the reason why the variable is significant at the state level but not at the local level is that Asian American voters are more likely to be interested in statewide issues and candidates than in more local offices. It is also possible that local organizations do not attempt to reach out to Asian American voters in metropolitan areas where they constitute a large proportion of the electorate (Wong 2001).[21] Another likely explanation, however, is the fact that the only counties and MSAs that have Asian American populations over 20 percent are in Hawaii and the San Francisco Bay Area. Outside of these areas, 75 percent of Asian Americans live in MSAs where they constitute less than 4 percent of the electorate.[22] Since there is little variation in the ethnic concentration of Asian Americans at the local level, most of the effects of high residential concentration are dependent on the participation of Asian Americans in Hawaii and the San Francisco Bay Area. The likelihood of Asian American participation in these counties and metropolitan areas is not significantly higher than in areas with lower concentrations of Asian Americans, and so the effect of the variable is not significant. So, with the exception of Asian Americans, findings on ethnic concentration hold at the county and MSA level that are also found statewide—the variable has its strongest impact on voting among immigrants in the third generation and later and demonstrates a weak relationship among first-generation immigrants.

What, then, accounts for the weak link between ethnic concentration and voting among first-generation immigrants? As indicated earlier, some scholars have noted that first-generation immigrants may not benefit from the same level of mobilization that comes with ethnic concentration because of high proportions of noncitizens and high levels of poverty in the areas in which they live. The CPS data confirm the high levels of correlation between Latino ethnic concentration and the proportions of those in poverty (0.82) and those who are noncitizens (0.54). In a separate analysis, I control for the potentially dampening effects of both concentrations of poverty and of noncitizenship while analyzing the effects of county-level ethnic concentration on immigrant participation. I find that, even after controlling for these two factors, ethnic concentration has no significant effect on the likelihood of participation among first-generation immigrants of any race. So there is little evidence which suggests that the null effects of ethnic concentrations on immigrant participation are due to the dampening effects of factors such as residential poverty and low naturalization rates. Assertions regarding the lack of mobilization by parties may explain why larger group size does not lead to higher participation, but they do not explain why ethnic concentration continues to lead to higher participation among those in the third and later generations. There still remains the possibility that first-generation immigrants who are exposed to the same levels of ethnic mobilization as those in later immigrant generations are less likely to be affected by such appeals—if, for instance, their interest in homeland politics serves to weaken the effect of mobilization on domestic political participation. However, since the CPS does not contain data regarding political attitudes, it is not possible to test whether interest in homeland politics is the factor responsible for why ethnic concentrations do not lead to higher participation among first-generation immigrants.

Multilingual Ballots

The traditional literature on barriers to voting participation has focused on absentee ballot restrictions, registration requirements, and racial gerrymandering on voter turnout and racial differences in turnout. When considering the political incorporation of immigrants, linguistic barriers to participation can play just as important a role as some of these other barriers. In 1975, Congress recognized the potential of English ballots to disenfranchise language minorities (those who are "limited-English proficient") and so amended the Voting Rights Act to include provisions on bilingual ballots.[23] According to the provisions, states and political subdivisions are required to provide language assistance to language minority groups who constitute at least 5 percent of their electorate and whose illiteracy rate is higher than the national illiteracy rate (United States General Accounting Office 1997).[24] There are also instances of a handful of jurisdictions that provide language assistance even in cases where they are not required to do so. In a report on ballot language assistance in 1997, the General Accounting Office notes that jurisdictions such as New York City provide language assistance in Korean, and San Francisco County, California, and Sandoval County, New Mexico, provide assistance in Spanish, even though they are not required by law to do so.

The provision of language assistance in Spanish or other languages does not depend on whether the constituencies are made up of natural-ized citizens, second-generation immigrants, and so on. Indeed, the only two states that have Spanish language ballots statewide—Arizona and Texas—have Latino populations of whom only one-half are in the first or second immigrant generations. Still, multilingual ballots are more likely to be of use to first-generation immigrants than to those in later immigrant generations. As I have already noted in this chapter, prior studies of English language acquisition have shown that profi-ciency in English grows stronger as immigrants stay longer in the United States and over immigrant generations. Given that first-genera-tion immigrants are likely to have the strongest need for language as-sistance, their participation should also be the most likely affected by the presence or absence of multilingual ballots. Thus, for example, liv-ing in a Spanish ballot area versus an English-only-ballot area may in-crease turnout for all Latinos, but the difference should be greater for the first-generation immigrants than for later-generation Latinos.

The Current Population Survey is the only data source of individual voting behavior that enables us to test the effects of multilingual ballots on the likelihood of voting among immigrants. Given the national scope of the CPS, it is much more likely to have variation on whether respondents live in areas with multilingual ballots than ethnic-specific ballots such as the Post / Kaiser / Harvard Survey of Latinos or the Latino National Political Survey, which draw their samples primarily from areas that have multilingual ballots.

What does the CPS reveal about the effects of multilingual ballots on voting participation among Asian and Latino immigrants? Table 5.6 presents differences in the likelihood of voting across immigrant gener-ations between Latinos who live in Spanish language ballot areas and those living without access to such ballots. There are four sets of results presented for alternative models that differ on (1) whether they control for the state level of ethnic concentration, and (2) whether the house-hold is a Spanish-dominant household. If the primary impact of Span-ish language ballots were to reduce barriers to participation among those with low levels of English proficiency, then the effects should be most pronounced among those who live in households where Spanish is the only language spoken.

Regardless of the model used, the same picture emerges—the pres-ence of Spanish language ballots has no significant impact on voting among first-generation Latinos. In none of the instances are the coeffi-cients positive and statistically significant. The only instance in which

TABLE 5.6

Access to Spanish Language Ballots and Probability of Voting Among Latinos (controlling for all other factors and holding other variables at their group-specific mean)

	% Yes	% No	Ratio
All households, model 1[a]			
First generation	51.1	52.0	0.98
Second generation	41.8	37.8	1.11
Third generation and later	40.0	36.5	1.10
All households, model 2[b]			
First generation	51.5	51.8	1.00
Second generation	42.3	37.7	1.12
Third generation and later	40.9	35.7	1.15*
Spanish-only household			
First generation	50.2	45.9	1.09
Second generation	33.2	44.8	0.74
Third generation and later	—	—	—
All other households			
First generation	51.8	52.1	0.99
Second generation	42.3	38.2	1.11
Third generation and later	40.4	36.3	1.11*

NOTE: There is an insufficient number of respondents in Spanish-only households in the third and later generation to produce reliable estimates of participation.
[a] Controlling for state-level ethnic concentrations.
[b] Not controlling for state-level ethnic concentrations.
*** $p < .01$; ** $p < .05$; * $p < .10$

the presence of Spanish language ballots has a statistically significant impact on voting is among Latinos in the third and later generations. Thus the results indicate that the introduction of Spanish language ballots is not a cure-all for increasing participation among first-generation Latinos. As I shall demonstrate in Chapter 6, factors related to political threat have played a greater role in shaping Latino immigrant participation during the 1990s than factors related to ethnic mobilization and institutional barriers to participation.

The positive impact of Spanish language ballots on voting among later-generation immigrants points to the possibility that such ballots may not increase turnout directly through the lowering of linguistic barriers to participation but may instead serve as a proxy measure for the likelihood of ethnic mobilization. Since cities and counties that have Spanish language ballots also have large proportions of Latino citizens, ethnic organizations in such jurisdictions are more likely to engage in mobilization because they have a greater potential to affect political outcomes. Furthermore, ethnic mobilization among those in the third and later generations might also have ensured the institution of Spanish language ballots in the first place.[25] The possibility that the presence of Spanish language ballots serves as a proxy for ethnic mobilization is bolstered by the fact that the magnitude of the variable grows stronger when the proportion of Latinos in the county is not controlled for. Also, the fact that such mobilization may not raise participation among first-generation immigrants is consistent with the findings regarding ethnic concentration in this chapter.

There may be other reasons why Spanish language ballots do not have a significant effect on participation among first-generation Latinos. First, the stated existence of multilingual ballots may not be reflected in actual investments and efforts by county registrars to reach out and serve the citizen population with language needs. There are several reported instances of civil rights groups and the Department of Justice in the past few years bringing complaints to counties that are not providing adequate language assistance (Young 2000; U.S. Department of Justice 2002).[26] Indeed, there may be many more instances of inadequate translation and outreach that have not been the target of complaints by institutional actors. Finally, just as in our examination of why ethnic concentration does not lead to higher participation among first-generation immigrants, factors such as residential poverty and concentration of noncitizens may also weaken the effects of Spanish language ballots on voting. Indeed, data from the CPS reveal a high degree of correlation between Latino immigrants living in areas with Spanish language ballots and the level of poverty in the county (0.49), as well as the proportion of noncitizens (0.59).

Just as in the case of ethnic concentration, however, controlling for such factors has no effect on either the magnitude or the significance of the impact of Spanish language ballots on the voting participation of first-generation Latinos.[27] So, as in the case of ethnic concentration, mobilization in areas with Spanish language ballots tends to have a weaker effect on domestic political participation among first-generation immigrants than among those in later immigrant generations. However, this weaker effect does not seem to be due to factors such as residential poverty and concentration of noncitizens. Once again, these results point to the possibility that factors such as the transnational orientation of first-generation immigrants may serve to blunt the impact of ethnic mobilization on voting among foreign-born Latinos.

Finally, in analyzing the effects of multilingual ballots on voting participation among first-generation immigrants, one should also examine the effects of having access to ballots in Chinese, Vietnamese, Korean, Japanese, and Tagalog (for Filipino immigrants). According to the 1997 General Accounting Office report on ballot language assistance, there are seven jurisdictions that have Chinese language ballots (Hawaii, New York City, San Francisco City and County, Alameda County, Los Angeles County, and Santa Clara County), three jurisdictions with Korean language ballots (California, Hawaii, and New York City), three areas with Vietnamese ballots (Santa Clara County, Los Angeles County, and Orange County), and two areas with Tagalog and Japanese (Hawaii and Los Angeles County). Just as in the case of Spanish language ballots, however, there does not seem to be any support for the contention that access to various Asian language ballots increases the likelihood of participation among first-generation immigrants. Even after controlling for factors such as the proportions of those in poverty and those who are not citizens, living in areas with Asian language ballots does not appreciably increase the likelihood of immigrant voting. Thus, just as in the case of Spanish language ballots, the results indicate that the institution of ballot language assistance does not, in and of itself, serve to increase the likelihood of participation among first-generation Asian Americans.

English Language Proficiency

Another important aspect of immigrant incorporation that may be related to electoral participation is the extent to which immigrants are able to communicate in English. English language use is closely related to language proficiency; those with low levels of proficiency are much less likely to communicate in English outside the home than those with high levels of English language proficiency and are much less likely to be able to follow technical instructions in English (PKH Survey of Latinos 1999). Furthermore, both factors depend on the age at which people entered the United States, how long they have lived in the country, their national origin, and the extent of residential segregation in the United States (Espenshade and Fu 1997). The ability of immigrants to communicate effectively in English is often a prerequisite to participation in the democratic politics of the United States. Indeed, rules governing naturalization require that applicants "must be able to read, write, speak, and understand words in ordinary usage in the English language" (Immigration and Naturalization Service 2001). Still, we may find variation in English language ability and use among naturalized citizens. First, the U.S. Citizenship and Immigration Service makes exceptions to the English proficiency requirement for applicants over the age of fifty-five who have been permanent residents for fifteen years and those over the age of fifty who have been permanent residents for twenty years. Furthermore, the level of English proficiency needed to fully participate in the political life of the United States may be considerably higher than those required for naturalization. However, the need to communicate in English may vary according to where immigrants live—whether they live in ethnic enclaves and whether these enclaves are mobilized for participation in U.S. elections.

We can expect English language proficiency to affect the likelihood of immigrant electoral participation in several ways. First, the returns to political skills from education may be weaker for those who lack proficiency in English. Thus someone who has a bachelor's degree but cannot speak English may be less likely to participate in mainstream politics than an English-speaking person with a similar level of educational attainment. English proficiency may also be related to whether immigrants were educated in the United States or abroad. Thus the lack of English proficiency may also reduce the effects of higher education on voting owing to the lack of relevant socialization to participate in U.S. politics (Tam Cho 1999). Language proficiency may also affect the magnitude of other relationships considered in this analysis, most notably those of residential ethnic concentration, dual nationality, and access to bilingual ballots. More specifically, living in ethnic enclaves may mitigate any negative effects associated with the lack of English proficiency; policies of dual nationality may indeed lower U.S.-based political participation among those who are not proficient in English; and access to bilingual ballots should have its strongest effects on those who lack the ability to communicate in English.

The Current Population Survey allows us to address these questions in a limited way. Interviews are conducted either in English or in Spanish based on whether respondents live in Spanish-dominant or English-dominant households. There are no detailed questions on English proficiency in the CPS Voter Supplement, so we are limited to using the rough measure of household language of interview.[28] We have already seen that access to Spanish language ballots does not lead to higher voting among first-generation immigrants in Spanish-dominant households. It remains to be seen, however, if language proficiency is related to voting participation in other ways.

Are the returns to political participation from education lower among Spanish-dominant households than English-dominant households? Table 5.7 presents results from analysis of CPS data when the sample is split into Spanish-dominant and English-dominant households, respectively. First, note that participation is lower in Spanish-dominant households than in English-dominant households across the educational scale among Latinos.[29] As for returns to participation from educational attainment, they are indeed lower among Spanish-dominant Latino households. Among English-dominant households in the first generation, the probability of voting among college graduates is 111 percent greater than among those who are high school dropouts. By contrast, the return to a college degree in terms of electoral participation is only 40 percent among Spanish-dominant households. Differences in the effects of education on voting are also present in the second immigrant generation, once again with the returns lower among Spanish-dominant Latino households. Thus, there does seem to be empirical support for the contention that English language proficiency mitigates the effects of education on voting. However, note that the effects of education on voting are still significant among Spanish-dominant households, indicating once again that factors related to immigrant adaptation are not so strong that they wipe out the positive relationship between education and voting (see Chapter 4).

Language proficiency may also change the patterns of electoral participation associated with policies of dual nationality. Some critics of dual nationality policies may concede that eligibility for dual nationality may not be a problem among those who are already culturally assimilated to the United States. However, they may still worry that access to dual nationality will have a detrimental effect on the voting participation of those who are not English-dominant. The CPS does not allow us to test for the effects of dual nationality policies among those who are dominant in languages other than English or Spanish. Still, it is possible to examine such claims with respect to Latino immigrants. The results from the CPS do not show any reduction in the likelihood of voting among Spanish-dominant Latino immigrants who come from coun-

TABLE 5.7

Household Language and Probability of Voting Among Latinos (controlling for all other factors and holding other variables at their group-specific means)

	Spanish-Dominant (%)	Ratio to Ref. Group	English-Dominant (%)	Ratio to Ref. Group
(a) Education[a]				
First generation				
Less than high school	44.5	—	34.0	—
High school graduate	48.2	1.08	48.7	1.43***
Some college	68.7	1.54***	60.9	1.79***
College graduate	62.5	1.40***	71.8	2.11***
Second generation				
Less than high school	26.4	—	23.1	—
High school graduate	34.8	1.32	36.8	1.59***
Some college	50.4	1.91*	56.6	2.45***
College graduate	53.9	2.04*	71.4	3.09***
(b) Eligibility for Dual Nationality[b]				
First generation[c]				
No	42.6	—	45.5	—
Yes	45.0	1.06	47.3	1.04
(c) Ethnic Concentration[d]				
First generation				
Low	36.2	—	47.8	—
High	44.8	1.24**	50.5	1.06
Second generation				
Low	35.4	—	42.2	—
High	34.8	0.98	41.9	0.99

NOTE: There is an insufficient number of respondents in Spanish-dominant households in the third and later generations to produce reliable estimates of participation. As in Table 5.5, low concentration is one standard deviation below the mean (with a cutoff at 0), while high concentration is one standard deviation above.

[a] Reference group is those with less than high school education.

[b] Reference group is those not eligible for dual nationality.

[c] Excluding Cuban immigrants.

[d] Reference group is those living in counties with low ethnic concentrations.

*** $p < .01$; ** $p < .05$; * $p < .10$

tries that allow dual nationality. Indeed, there is no difference in the effects of dual nationality between those who are Spanish-dominant and those who are English-dominant. When the sample is subdivided by language of interview, the effects remain positive but lose statistical significance.

Finally, I consider the possibility that residence in an ethnic enclave may have a different effect on the participation of Spanish-dominant households than English-dominant households. If parties and candidate organizations mobilize voters living in ethnic enclaves by using Spanish language appeals, then the lack of English use among such residents may not be a liability to participation (Johnson et al. 2003). In such cases, Spanish-dominant households would have a higher rate of participation in ethnic enclaves than in other areas. If, on the other hand, political organizations target Spanish-language messages at Latinos regardless of where they live, then there may not be much advantage associated with living in an ethnic enclave for those who are Spanish-dominant. While the CPS does not contain neighborhood-level measures of ethnic concentration, county-level measures should help to ascertain the interactive effects between language of interview and residential ethnic concentration. As Table 5.7 indicates, those who are Spanish-dominant do indeed have a higher rate of participation when living in areas with high proportions of Latinos than in areas with low proportions of Latinos, a finding that is statistically significant at the .05 level. At the same time, the advantage associated with living in areas of high Latino concentration is considerably weaker for English-dominant households than for Spanish-dominant households and is not statistically significant. So English language proficiency does indeed change the effects of ethnic concentration on voting among Latinos—while the effects may be insignificant for the population as a whole, they are indeed significant among Spanish-dominant households.

Conclusions

In this chapter, we have seen that various factors related to immigrant adaptation bear significant relationships to electoral participation. Time-based factors play the strongest role, as voting increases with duration of stay in the United States for all first-generation immigrants regardless of their racial or ethnic group. There are also significant differences across immigrant generations, but the patterns vary across racial and ethnic groups and provide little support to theories of straight-line assimilation. The relevance of straight-line assimilation to immigrant political incorporation is weakened further by the persistent racial and ethnic gaps in participation even among those in the third immigrant generation and later.

Factors related to immigrants' countries of origin and their settlement in the United States also bear a significant relationship to electoral participation, but not necessarily in ways that may be gleaned from studies of one or two racial or ethnic groups. For instance, the analysis here reveals that originating from a country ruled by a repressive regime is actually associated with a lower probability of participation among white immigrants and non-Cuban Latino immigrants. Using communist country origin produces similar results, indicating that one cannot generalize from the case of Cuban immigrants to argue that those who come from repressive or communist countries are more likely to participate than those who do not. Another significant finding regarding country of origin is that those who come from countries that allow dual nationality are more likely to vote than those who do not. These findings hold not only for white and Asian immigrants but also for non-Cuban Latinos. These results run contrary to the claims of political theorists who warn that those who take on dual nationality do so for instrumental reasons and are less likely to participate in American politics. Finally, there are other country-specific effects among immigrants in all racial groups. Among Latinos, the most significant difference is between Cuban and Mexican immigrants, while for Asian Americans, most of the national-origin differences are accounted for by Anglophone origins. Many of these country-of-origin differences disappear, however, by the second generation. However, this finding does not necessarily support the expectations of assimilationist theories of immigrant adaptation since there are still significant racial gaps in participation in the second generation and beyond (Figure 5.4).[30]

There is one additional aspect to note regarding time-based factors and country-of-origin characteristics: the naturalization stage among first-generation immigrants. Expanding the relevant immigrant population beyond citizens to include all immigrant residents eligible for citizenship (the "eligibles") is important to consider because it may alter the racial disparities, intergenerational differences, and other patterns uncovered in this analysis. Not surprisingly, adding the *eligibles* to the analysis reduces the likelihood of participation among first-generation immigrants of all racial groups. This in turn widens the gaps in participation between the first and later immigrant generations for blacks, whites, and Asian Americans, while for Latinos it creates a new gap in participation where one did not previously exist. Considering group differences in participation with *eligibles* in the denominator also alters the shape of racial disparities in participation within the first immigrant generation. Since Asian and Afro-Caribbean immigrants have a higher propensity to naturalize than European immigrants, including the *eligibles* shows the former two groups as having a higher likelihood of participation than the latter. Furthermore, since Latino immigrants have the lowest propensity to naturalize, including all immigrants eligible for naturalization in the denominator creates a deficit in participation with other groups, one that does not exist when the denominator is confined to naturalized citizens. Looking at participation among citizens and *eligibles* also strengthens the positive relationship between dual citizenship policies and voting participation—again not surprising given the positive relationship between dual citizenship policies and the naturalization stage. Finally, including the eligibles does not change the significance of our findings regarding repressive regime origin and communist country origin—indeed, for Asian Americans and Latinos it strengthens the relationships found among the naturalized population.

This chapter has also shed some light on the effects of a few factors related to immigrant settlement in the United States. The results here confirm the findings of others who show that Latino participation is positively linked to group size (Leighley 2001) and extends such findings to also include Asian American participation. At the same time, it is also evident that increases in the likelihood of participation associated with group size apply primarily to third-generation immigrants and to those first-generation immigrants who have low levels of English proficiency. Finally, the positive effects associated with access to Spanish language ballots are found only among those in the third and later generations. This points to the possibility that Spanish language ballots may serve more as a proxy measure for ethnic mobilization than as an effective tool to induce participation among first-generation immigrants.

The weakness of the relationship among first-generation immigrants with respect to either ethnic concentration or multilingual ballots is not due to factors such as residential poverty or proportion of noncitizens. One reason why participation among first-generation Latinos is not so dependent on factors such as ethnic concentration and Spanish language ballots is that the motivation to participate among immigrants in the 1990s may have largely been based on the extent to which they felt threatened by various legislative issues at the state and national levels. It is likely that political threat served to weaken the effects of these contextual factors since immigrants could experience threat from such legislation regardless of whether they lived in counties with bilingual ballots or with higher proportions of coethnics. It is to these issues of political threat and immigrant-related legislation that I now turn.

CHAPTER 6

Were They Pushed?

*Political Threat, Institutional Mobilization,
and Immigrant Voting*

> A day after the largest demonstration in recent Los Angeles history, enthusiastic organizers and participants exuded optimism Monday about a new political activism that would energize an increasingly diverse Latino community. . . . Reflecting on the historic march, many participants spoke of an updated version of the Chicano movement of the 1960s and 1970s, which resulted in a certain degree of political empowerment for Latinos—but this time with a much stronger immigrant input.
>
> > Patrick McDonnell and Robert Lopez, November 17, 1994

> As a citizenship outreach worker for the Asian Pacific American Legal Center, Catherine Pedroza has been involved in education efforts regarding Proposition 187 within the Asian community since midsummer. Many of those she has approached have been indifferent about the proposition, she said. Some have even said they are in favor.
>
> > Leslie Berestein, September 25, 1994

So far, this book has examined the effects on participation of various immigrant-related variables such as generational status, length of stay in the United States, country of origin characteristics, and factors related to immigrant residential contexts. In this chapter, I consider political contexts that may have a significant and unique impact on the participation of first-generation immigrants. In particular, I examine the extent to which voting in the 1990s was influenced by immigrants' sense of political threat regarding state and national legislation that restricted immigrant access to public benefits.

The mid-1990s were watershed years in the contemporary era of immigration and naturalization, as the United States considered and passed legislation that restricted immigrant access to public benefits. The trend started in California in 1994 with Proposition 187, a measure that denied undocumented immigrants access to public education and continued with national legislation in 1996 that made even legal immigrants ineligible for many welfare benefits. As legislation at the state and national level threatened immigrant access to benefits and their sense of security as residents of the United States, millions decided to seek naturalization. The impact of these measures (hereby termed "anti-immigrant legislation") on naturalization and welfare utilization has already been studied in considerable detail (Fix and Passel 1999; Passel and Clark 1998).

This chapter focuses on the impact of anti-immigrant legislation on electoral participation among naturalized citizens. In doing so, it also addresses a larger theoretical concern over the role of political threat and institutional mobilization in motivating political participation. As the following analysis indicates, the sense of political threat was not felt evenly across ethnic groups and residents of different states. Moreover, the level of ethnic mobilization during this period also varied across groups. In some instances ethnopolitical elites attempted to mobilize groups in the absence of political threat at the mass level, whereas in others the presence of threat was not accompanied by efforts to mobilize the electorate. This chapter therefore seeks to disaggregate the effects of each factor—threat and mobilization—in bringing immigrants to the ballot box during the 1990s.

What happened to immigrant voting after the passage of restrictionist measures in the mid-1990s? Was the sense of political threat sufficient to provoke a voting surge among immigrants, propelling first-generation citizens to the ballot box in angry reaction to various measures that they deemed to be anti-immigrant? Or was mobilization by political and civic institutions also necessary to capitalize on the sense of frustration among many naturalized citizens, prompting them to make themselves heard through the electoral process? Evidence from media and scholarly accounts indicates that immigrant-related legislation in the mid-1990s did indeed produce a voting surge among naturalized citizens (Glastris et al. 1997; McDonnell and Ramos 1996; Pantoja, Ramirez, and Segura 2001). According to news reports of the 1996 and 1998 elections, Republican candidates faced strong opposition from newly registered Latino and Asian American voters, many of them first-generation immigrants (Tobar 1998). Immigrant voters also figured strongly in the 2000 presidential campaign, as George Bush spent several days in California trying to repair the image of the Republican Party among Latino immigrant voters.

While media accounts and the behavior of political candidates indicate a significant voter reaction to anti-immigrant legislation, there have not been many studies that systematically examine the effects of such legislation on the electoral participation of first-generation immigrants. Furthermore, the few studies on this topic have focused only on Latinos in a few states or in particular metropolitan areas such as Los Angeles. For instance, Matt Barreto and Nathan Woods (2000) analyze voter registration and turnout among Latinos in Los Angeles County. Their findings suggest that anti-immigrant legislation prompted a surge in new voter registration and turnout in areas with large immigrant populations. Furthermore, Adrian Pantoja, Ricardo Ramirez, and Gary Segura (2001) analyze data from a three-state Latino survey and find that Latinos who naturalized in California during the period of anti-immigrant legislation had extremely high rates of participation during the 1996 election, but that those who naturalized in Texas and Florida did not have the same high levels of participation. While such findings offer important insights into the effects of immigrant-related legislation on subsequent participation, these studies are limited by the fact that they are confined to the study of Latino participation, often in one state or a single metropolitan area. In this chapter, I analyze the net effects of immigrant-related legislation on subsequent voting participation by examining cross-sectional differences in participation over space, based on the context of political threat and institutional mobilization. I conduct my analysis not only for Latino immigrants but also for white, Asian American, and black immigrants across various states.

Issue Background

In November 1994, voters in California passed Proposition 187, a measure that sought to bar undocumented immigrants from accessing public benefits such as education and health care. The movement to limit immigrant benefits began in 1993 with the small-scale efforts of the

"Save our State" campaign, but it soon gained prominence as the state Republican Party contributed money to its signature-gathering drives and as Republican Governor Pete Wilson made the issue a cornerstone of his reelection campaign (McDonnell 1997). Proponents of the proposition were concerned about the number of undocumented immigrants in California and their impact on the state's spending on public benefits. The ballot measure sparked a series of protests and countermobilizations by civil rights groups and ethnic organizations (Feldman 1994; McDonnell and Lopez 1994). Although Proposition 187 dealt solely with the issue of undocumented immigrants, many Asian American and Latino organizations reacted to the proposition by attempting to frame it as a civil rights issue. Opposition to the proposition was especially strong among Latino organizations, as they mobilized citizens to register and vote in the November 1994 election in order to defeat the measure.

The 1994 election saw not only the passage of Proposition 187 in California but also the Republican takeover of Congress. Within months, legislation targeting immigration and immigrants became viable at the national level. In their attempt to overhaul welfare benefits, the Republican-led Congress passed provisions that made nonnaturalized immigrants ineligible for most means-tested federal benefits and allowed states to exercise discretion in the provision of other welfare benefits. Congress also passed a separate bill that made it more difficult for immigrants and citizens to sponsor relatives for immigration and increased funding for the Immigration and Naturalization Service to crack down on visa overstays and other forms of illegal immigration. In response to the legislation advancing through Congress, many immigrants began to apply for naturalization.[1] Even those permanent residents who had lived in the United States for many years without applying for citizenship decided finally to naturalize. Furthermore, according to media reports of the 1996 election, those who were already naturalized citizens of the United States turned to the ballot box to express their concern and displeasure over the passage of such measures.

The political threat caused by anti-immigrant legislation was felt first in California in 1994 but soon spread to the rest of the country. Thus, for instance, Latino immigrants in Texas were not exposed to the same level of political threat in 1994 as those living in California. As one Texas newspaper noted in October of that year,

In Texas, the situation is different. Aside from increased enforcement by the U.S. Border Patrol at the El Paso–Ciudad Juarez border, the growing "immigrant backlash" fueling efforts in Washington, D.C., to reform federal immigration laws has largely bypassed Texas. There's no proposition on the Texas ballot demanding an end to public services for illegal immigrants. Texas Gov. Ann Richards, a Democrat, and her Republican opponent, George W. Bush, aren't slamming each other in the press or running commercials about illegal immigrants wading across the Rio Grande. (García 1994)

By 1996, however, immigrants throughout the country were exposed to the risk of anti-immigrant legislation as they stood to lose access to benefits, either for themselves or for relatives who were not yet citizens of the United States. The spread of immigration as a politically salient issue from California to the rest of the country was evident not only in terms of legislation passed but also in media coverage near the time of general elections. Table 6.1 presents the number of newspaper stories dealing with immigration one month prior to the general election starting in 1994. The results are presented for California, New York, and Texas—three of the states with the largest immigrant populations in the mid-1990s.

In order to control for factors such as circulation size and the extent of political coverage by newspapers, the amount of news coverage devoted to immigration is normalized by the extent of election coverage in those states for the same one-month period. Thus, I create an index of immigration coverage, which involves dividing the number of immigration-related stories by the number of election-related stories during the same time period. This gives us a good sense of the relative salience of immigration as a politically relevant issue across different state contexts. So, for example, during the month prior to the 1998 election there are roughly equal numbers of stories related to immigration in Texas and California. However, the number of election-related stories from the Texas sources is nearly 85 percent higher than the number of such stories in California. Thus, by using an index that takes into account the level of election coverage in each state, we see that immigration was a more politically salient issue in California than in Texas in 1998.

As the results indicate, coverage of immigration issues in 1994 was exceptionally high in California—the index of immigration coverage for the state was several magnitudes greater than the indexes for Texas and New York. In 1996, when anti-immigrant legislation was no longer confined to California, coverage of immigration issues the month before Election Day was roughly equal for all three states. In the 1998 elec-

TABLE 6.1

Immigration Coverage One Month Prior to Election Day, 1994–2000

	State	Immigration-Related Stories	Election-Related Stories	Index[a]
1994	California	409	568	72.0
	New York	18	366	4.9
	Texas	24	1,267	1.9
1996	California	54	505	10.7
	New York	30	372	8.1
	Texas	94	849	11.1
1998	California	30	394	7.6
	New York	12	426	2.8
	Texas	33	729	4.5
2000	California	22	849	2.6
	New York	18	728	2.5
	Texas	30	1,013	3.0

SOURCE: See Appendix ("Dow Jones Interactive News Coding").
NOTE: Six newspapers were used in each state: California (*Contra Costa Times, Los Angeles Times, Oakland Tribune, San Diego Union-Tribune, San Francisco Chronicle, San Jose Mercury News*), Texas (*Austin American-Statesman, Corpus Christi Caller-Times, Dallas Morning News, El Paso Times, Houston Chronicle, San Antonio Express-News*), and New York (*New York Daily News, New York Observer, New York Post, New York Times, Newsday, Village Voice*). Dow Jones Interactive was used to conduct searches for relevant terms in the headline and lead paragraphs of newspaper stories. Also, news items dealing with immigration and elections exclusive to other states are not included.
 [a] Index of immigration coverage = (immigration-related stories divided by the number of election-related stories) x 100

tion, California had a higher level of immigration-related coverage than Texas and New York, with newspapers printing stories of continued resentment among Latino immigrants toward Pete Wilson and his legacy of racially divisive propositions (Lindlaw 1998). Still, the magnitude of the difference in coverage with Texas and New York is mild when compared to the differences in 1994. Finally, by 2000 there is virtually no difference in the extent of immigration-related coverage in the three states. Furthermore, the salience of the issue reaches its lowest levels, as both Republicans and Democrats showed few differences on immigrant-

ated issues and chose not to broach the topic of immigration restric-
ns (Anderson 2000; Goldsborough 2000).

So, the data from newspaper coverage support the contention that
the salience of immigration and the sense of political threat associated
with anti-immigrant legislation varied between the 1994 election and
subsequent elections—there were considerable state-level differences in
1994, but these differences receded with the passage of immigrant-related legislation at the national level in 1996. The 1998 election featured
some state-level variation once again, primarily because Latino immigrants in California saw the election as a chance to punish the state Republican Party for their earlier support for measures relating to immigration and bilingual education. Given that the 1996 and 2000 elections
do not offer much state-level variation in the level of political threat owing to immigrant-related legislation, this analysis will focus on 1994
and 1998.

Theoretical Background

What happened to political participation among first-generation citizens following the passage of restrictionist legislation? It is instructive
to examine the theoretical literature on political threat and its effect on
participation. Political studies of racial threat go back as far as W. E. B.
DuBois (1935) and V. O. Key Jr. (1949), who argued that electoral strategies and patterns of party control in southern states were shaped in
large part by the threat of political takeover by blacks in areas where
they constituted the majority.[2] In more recent years, scholars have examined the role of racial threat in white opposition to school busing
(Green and Cowden 1992) and in support for David Duke in his run for
governor of Louisiana (Giles and Buckner 1993, 1996; Voss 1996a,
1996b). In the case of white opposition to school busing, Donald Green
and Jonathan Cowden (1992) found that threats to self-interest played
no role in shaping white opinion regarding busing. However, threat did
play a significant role in white behavior as expressed through participation in local politics. In the case of support for David Duke in
Louisiana, perceived threats to group interests were significant, although there is disagreement as to whether the racial threats were ma-
terial or symbolic.[3] In general, then, the theoretical literature indicates
that feelings of political threat can play a significant role in motivating
political participation.

While the literature on political threat may be relevant to anti-immigrant legislation, there are some limitations. First of all, most studies of political threat have been confined to examining the behavior and attitudes of whites who are confronted with political threats involving minorities. It is unclear whether racial threat provokes the same level of mobilization and participation among immigrants and racial minorities as it does among native-born whites.[4] Another limitation to the research tradition on political threat is that it often ignores the role of institutional contexts in framing responses to threat. Partisan and civic institutions often play an important role in mobilizing and channeling responses to threatening actions or legislation (Rosenstone and Hansen 1993). Thus we can expect variation in institutional context to produce variation in the levels of immigrant political participation following the passage of anti-immigrant legislation.

The significance of California residence in shaping immigrant political participation has already been noted by Pantoja, Ramirez, and Segura (2001), and Karthick Ramakrishnan and Thomas Espenshade (2001). As indicated earlier, coverage of the 1996 and 1998 elections in national magazines portrayed a backlash against the Republican Party by first-generation voters (Glastris et al. 1997). While these accounts point to a general increase in voting among naturalized citizens, Pantoja, Ramirez, and Segura (2001) suggest that the mobilization impact on Latino immigrants is stronger in California than in other parts of the country. The authors examine data from the Tomás Rivera Policy Institute (TRPI) on Latino voting participation in California, Texas, and Florida during the 1996 election. Instead of finding that Latino immigrants in all three states were mobilized to register and vote by anti-immigrant legislation at the national level, Pantoja, Ramirez, and Segura (2001) show that recently naturalized immigrants living in California had extremely high rates of registration and turnout, whereas those in Texas and Florida had much lower levels of participation. The authors suggest that immigrant-related legislation leads to greater participation only among those who naturalize in state political contexts that are "politically hostile" and that these state-level effects are sustained even in election years when anti-immigrant legislation is nationalized.

Pantoja, Ramirez, and Segura's (2001) findings stand in contrast to those of Ramakrishnan and Espenshade (2001), who argue that ethnic mobilization in response to immigrant-related legislation is election-specific. Their analysis of Current Population Survey (CPS) data indicates that residence in California led to a disproportionately high increase in voting among first- and second-generation citizens during the

1994 election, but not in subsequent elections. Ramakrishnan and Es-penshade (2001) point out that the "California effect" was absent in the 1996 election because immigrant-related legislation was no longer con-fined to California. Furthermore, they argue that the California effect was weak for naturalized citizens in 1998 because the ballot measure on bilingual education (Proposition 227) was held during the June primary and not the November general election.

Some of the differences in the two sets of findings may be because Ramakrishnan and Espenshade (2001) analyze immigrant generational status without regard to race or ethnicity, whereas Pantoja, Ramirez, and Segura's (2001) analysis of TRPI data is confined to Latinos. Thus, for example, the persistent advantage in participation among natural-ized Latinos in California (found by Pantoja, Ramirez, and Segura) may be consistent with a disappearance of the "California effect" for immi-grants in general if (1) participation among non-Latino immigrants in California had been substantially reduced, or (2) Latino immigrant par-ticipation had increased elsewhere. Differences between the two find-ings may also be because the TRPI dataset is restricted to the 1996 elec-tion year. It is unclear, for example, whether the high participation among California immigrant voters continued into the 1998 midterm election.

The analysis in this chapter seeks to improve upon the findings noted so far. It addresses the generalizability of the findings of Pantoja, Ramirez, and Segura (2001) by including immigrants of all racial and ethnic groups. It also assigns values of political threat for each group separately, thereby avoiding the problem of conflating disparate effects for immigrants of different racial groups (Ramakrishnan and Espen-shade 2001). The analysis here improves upon past findings in another important respect, by taking into account not only the effect of political threat on immigrant voting participation but also the potentially im-portant effects of ethnic mobilization as a way of channeling responses to threat through the electoral process. As I shall indicate shortly, the level of ethnic mobilization varied considerably across racial groups in different states during this period. Introducing both threat and mobi-lization to the analysis of immigrant voting therefore provides a more complete model of the effects of anti-immigrant legislation on electoral participation.

In this analysis, I rely on three sources of information: field inter-views of ethnic leaders; analyses of newspaper coverage of immigra-tion in particular states; and individual-level data on participation from the Current Population Survey Voter Supplements. Information on political threat and ethnic mobilization is derived from the analyses of newspaper coverage and field interviews. This information is subsequently used to create measures of threat and mobilization that are context-specific, varying according to racial group, state of residence, and election year. Finally, these contextual measures are mapped onto CPS data to see if they can explain voter registration and turnout among individual immigrants.

The analysis here relies primarily on data from the 1994 and 1998 midterm elections. The 1994 and 1998 elections serve as appropriate comparisons for the question of anti-immigrant legislation and immigrant participation—most of the surge in naturalizations occurred after 1994, and 1998 was the first election after the implementation of welfare reform and immigration reform at the national level. The 1996 and 2000 presidential elections are less well suited for an analysis of the impact of anti-immigrant legislation on voting. First, voting levels in presidential elections are considerably higher than in midterm elections. As a consequence, the former are often less immune to differences in state-level political contexts than the latter (Rosenstone and Hansen 1993). Furthermore, as has already been discussed in the introduction, the 1996 and 2000 elections do not offer much variation in the degree of state-level threat owing to anti-immigrant legislation. In order to study the effects of different state political contexts on changes in immigrant political participation, I chose the two largest states for each racial or ethnic group's immigrant population: California and Texas for Latinos; and California and New York for whites and Asian Americans.[5] Finally, I chose only New York for blacks because there is no other state in the CPS dataset in which there are sufficient numbers of black immigrants in each election year to produce reliable estimates of participation.

In addition to individual-level information from the CPS, this dataset also includes contextual variables from other sources. I construct measures of political threat and institutional mobilization facing immigrants based on analyses of news reports in the major newspapers of each state. Particular emphasis is placed on stories that reference particular racial or ethnic groups in discussions of the effects of anti-immigrant legislation or the presence or absence of ethnic mobilization. Finally, I also supplement the analysis of threat and mobilization with references to interviews with leaders of ethnopolitical organizations in various metropolitan areas in the states considered. These interviews of Latino and Asian organization leaders are based on my fieldwork during the summer of 2000 in the following metropolitan areas: Orange County, Los Angeles, and San Francisco in California; San Antonio, Houston, and Austin in Texas; and New York City. Names of organizations were obtained using community directories as well as the snowball method. Organizations were chosen for interview if they engaged in any of the following activities: voter registration, voter education, and get-out-the-vote efforts. I interviewed twenty Latino organization leaders or staff members (one per organization)—seven in California and thirteen in Texas—and seventeen Asian American organization leaders—fourteen in California and three in New York. Representatives of two Latino organizations in New York and two Asian American organizations in Texas were also interviewed. A more detailed overview of the interview data and methods can be found in the Appendix.

Threat and Mobilization

Political Threat

How did the level of political threat vary across racial groups and the states in which immigrants lived? Much has already been said in terms of state-level differences in the sense of political threat arising from anti-immigrant legislation. The primary state-level difference in 1994 is between immigrants residing in California and those living in other parts of the country. Not only were the former subject to a daily barrage of media coverage on immigration-related issues,[6] but they were also more likely to participate in protests and demonstrations regarding immigrant rights. At the same time, not all immigrants in California experienced the same sense of threat from Proposition 187. Most of those participating in demonstrations and walkouts over Proposition 187 were Latino immigrants and not Asian or white immigrants (McDonnell and Johnson 1994; Pyle and Hernandez 1994).[7] Part of the disparity in participation is because Latinos make up the largest racial group among first-generation immigrants in California. Furthermore, they constitute a disproportionate share of the undocumented population living in the state. At the same time, the disproportionate impact of Proposition 187 on Latino immigrants is also reflected in the fact that the issue had become racialized during the course of the 1994 election campaign. Many Latino immigrant voters initially remained ambivalent toward Proposition 187, with a sizable proportion in support of the measure. Soon, however, it became apparent that the denial of public education and health care to children of illegal immigrants would be conducted through a policy of racial profiling that would primarily target Latinos. The sense that Latinos were the primary targets of the proposition was reinforced by television ads in favor of the measure. As one article in the *Los Angeles Times* noted,

[Some Latino students] said they decided to act after watching television, both because of news reports of marches from other schools and because of a pro-187 advertisement that students refer to simply as "that commercial." The ad, which shows people scurrying across the California-Mexico border at night, caused Latinos at Leuzinger High School in Lawndale to angrily plan a walk-out last week.

"It's insulting," said sophomore Jorge Higareda. "They show Mexicans, but they don't show Asians coming over in boats or anybody else. It's like we're the only ones coming here." (Pyle and Romero 1994)

Thus, in California there was a racial bifurcation in the sense of threat among first-generation immigrants, with Latinos experiencing higher levels of threat than Asian or white immigrants. Still, all first-generation citizens in California (regardless of Hispanic origin) experienced higher levels of threat than immigrants in other states in 1994, where immigration restriction was not on the political agenda. The former were part of a political climate in which the worth of immigrants was questioned on a daily basis, and so even those who sought to distance themselves from the "problem immigrants" were forced to defend themselves politically in ways that immigrants in other parts of the country did not have to do (Foo 1994).

Finally, there were also racial differences in the sense of political threat among immigrants in New York. While most immigrants in New York were not forced to consider whether they represented a net drain on the state economy, the same was not true for black immigrants in the state. Many blacks in New York, including naturalized immigrants, felt politically threatened and betrayed as the Democratic Party sought to compete with Republicans on who was toughest on issues of welfare reform, crime, and the death penalty—all issues that were framed in a black-white racial context in 1994 (Wilkerson 1994; McCarthy 1994). As we shall see later, this sense of threat did not translate into higher mobilization, as few community organizations urged blacks to go to the polls in 1994. Still, what is relevant in the specification of the threat variable is that the sense of political threat was not uniformly low in New

York during the 1994 election, that black immigrants had a higher sense of political threat than did immigrants of other racial groups living in the state.

In order to systematically assess the effects of threat and mobilization on political participation, it is important to code them before including them in the analysis of individual-level data on participation found in the Current Population Survey. Based on my analyses of newspaper coverage and interviews with leaders of ethnopolitical organizations in the various states, I code the measure of threat on a three-part ordinal scale (representing low, medium, and high levels).[8] A three-part scale is necessary in order to distinguish between California and non-California residents on the one hand and Latino and non-Latino immigrants in California on the other. Thus, since immigrants in California experienced a higher level of threat in 1994 than those living outside of California, the former would receive a threat level of 2 and the latter a threat level of 1. Furthermore, Latino immigrants in California would be assigned a high level of threat (3) because they experienced a higher level of political threat than did their Asian and white counterparts living in the state (Table 6.2a).

Similarly, Asian and white immigrants living in New York would get a low level of threat in 1994 because they were not exposed to an electoral climate in which immigration was a salient issue. However, black immigrants in the state would be assigned a medium level of threat (2) because, as noted earlier, they experienced a higher level of political threat than white and Asian immigrants living in the state. Some might argue that black immigrants' sense of threat in New York was similar to that of Latino immigrants in California and therefore should be assigned a high level of threat instead of the medium-level measure used. While there may be some debate on what level of threat to assign black immigrants in New York in relation to Latino immigrants in California, such uncertainty has little effect on the magnitude or statistical significance of the findings presented in the analysis.[9]

I turn next to specify the levels of threat in 1998 for the groups considered in this analysis. By the 1998 election, the sense of political threat among immigrants had become nationalized owing to the passage of legislation in 1996 that made even legal immigrants ineligible for many public benefits and made it more difficult for naturalized citizens to sponsor relatives to enter the United States. In terms of the coding scheme outlined above, this means that, in contrast to 1994, all immigrant respondents were subject to at least a medium level of threat re-

TABLE 6.2

Political Threat and Mobilization Among Immigrants by Race and State of Residence

		1 = Low	2 = Medium	3 = High
(a) Political Threat				
1994	Latinos	Texas		California
	Asians	New York	California	
	Blacks			New York
	Whites	New York	California	
1998	Latinos		Texas	California
	Asians		California, New York	
	Blacks			New York
	Whites		California, New York	
(b) Electoral Mobilization				
1994	Latinos		Texas	California
	Asians	New York	California	
	Blacks	New York		
	Whites	California	New York	
1998	Latinos		Texas	California
	Asians	California, New York		
	Blacks		New York	
	Whites	California	New York	

gardless of the state in which they lived. Even in 1998, however, there was variation in the level of political threat across racial and ethnic groups within states such as California and New York. Latino immigrants in California continued to experience high levels of political threat because of subsequent propositions regarding affirmative action and bilingual education that were framed in a context of Anglo-Latino tension and competition (Valle, Torres, and Sassen 2000).

Thus, even though there were no racially divisive ballot propositions in California during the November general election,[10] and even though

Pete Wilson could not run again for governor, many Latinos saw the 1998 election as a referendum on the racially divisive legacy of then-governor Wilson. As the *Los Angeles Times* noted on the eve of the general election, "Olivia Hierro, 35, is among those who haven't forgotten Proposition 187. 'We can't let that pass,' Hierro said in an interview recently in a Latino neighborhood of San Francisco. 'The ones that have the power to vote, we can't forget that'" (Lindlaw 1998). The political memories of Latino immigrant voters were reinforced by labor activists and the state Democratic Party, both of whom framed the Republican gubernatorial candidate, Dan Lungren, as someone who was cut from the same mold as Pete Wilson. The same article in the *Los Angeles Times* noted, "Democrats continue to see their party as the natural home for Latinos and are working hard to make sure Latinos don't forget Wilson's embrace of Proposition 187. Davis is airing a Spanish-language television ad showing Lungren and Wilson together" (Lindlaw 1998).

In my field interviews with coordinators of Latino outreach in the state Democratic and Republican parties, members of both parties acknowledged the Democratic Party's successful exploitation of Wilson's legacy during the 1998 election. As one Latino Republican activist in California noted, "[Proposition] 187 was definitely a turnoff. The Democrats realized it was a wedge issue and have hammered it home ever since. . . . Wilson was shown the door after that, but Democrats still use him to remind Latinos."[11] Thus, thanks to the framing efforts of the state Democratic Party and the cumulative effect of various ballot propositions that Latinos deemed to be targeted against them, Latino immigrants in California continued to experience a higher sense of political threat during the 1998 election.

By contrast, Asian immigrants in California did not sense the same degree of threat over the legacy of Pete Wilson. Indeed, some Asian American business leaders and professional groups actually endorsed Pete Wilson and Proposition 187. For instance, in one fund-raiser in Southern California, "Wilson's call for changes in immigration law and tougher laws against crime drew repeated applause and chants of 'four more years' from the crowd of about 150 Asian American leaders and Wilson supporters" (Eljera 1994). Furthermore, exit polls by the *Los Angeles Times* reveal that Asian American voters were more split on the issue of Proposition 187 (47 percent in favor, 53 percent against) than were whites (63 percent for, 37 percent against) or Latinos (23 percent for, 77 percent against). The absence of a sense of threat among Asian immigrants in California was also evident in Public Policy Institute of

California surveys from the spring of 1998, in which Asian immigrants were considerably more likely than Latino immigrants to say that they trusted Pete Wilson to solve the state's problems (Baldassare 1998). Tellingly, the level of trust in Pete Wilson among Asian immigrants was similar to that among white immigrants in California. Finally, even on issues such as affirmative action and Proposition 227, Asian Americans seemed to have been less threatened by restrictionist legislation and were the group most likely to be divided on the issue in California (Tam Cho and Cain 2001). Thus the racial bifurcation in the sense of political threat among California immigrants was present in 1994 and continued in 1998, with Latino immigrants experiencing higher levels of political threat than other immigrants living in the state.

Latino immigrants in Texas did not face the same level of political threat as their counterparts in California because the Republican Party under Governor George W. Bush was able to keep divisive issues such as affirmative action and immigrant restriction off the state's political agenda. So Latinos in Texas encountered medium levels of political threat in 1998—even though they were negatively affected by national legislation in 1996, their sense of threat was not compounded by state-level measures that exacerbated tensions and competition between Anglos and Latinos. Finally, black immigrants in New York experienced levels of threat that were higher than their Asian and white counterparts in the state. Just as other immigrants in the state, many had been adversely affected by the welfare reform provisions passed at the national level in 1996 and at the state level in 1997. However, blacks in the city, including black immigrants, were also deeply angered over the issue of police brutality. Anger over police brutality was particularly high in the black immigrant community following the police assault on Abner Louima in the preceding year. Indeed, Police Commissioner Howard Safir had transferred several African American officers, particularly of Haitian descent, into the Flatbush neighborhood of Brooklyn in 1998 in order to mend relations with the Caribbean community living in the area (Roane 1998). Still, community members voiced their frustration and dissatisfaction at a rally in Flatbush on August 9, 1998— the one-year anniversary of Abner Louima's torture (Cauvin 1998).

Concerns over police brutality were sustained and heightened just two months before Election Day, as city police abruptly ended the Million Youth March, an action which led to violence and confrontation between protesters and police officers. As the *New York Times* reported, "As Saturday's ralliers began to disband, a police helicopter began making passes over the crowd and officers in riot helmets stormed the stage from behind. Soon bottles, barricades and trash baskets were fly-ing" (Allen 1998). In a subsequent editorial on September 9, the *New York Times* noted, "the massive deployment of police and military-look-ing equipment focused the community's anger on City Hall rather than Mr. Muhammad. Harlem's officials said their constituents felt the Police Department's tactics were aimed more at intimidating the community than protecting it." Thus concerns over police brutality gave black im-migrant voters a larger sense of threat than they would have felt with the passage of anti-immigrant legislation alone.

Electoral Mobilization

Just as the level of political threat varies by racial group and state of res-idence, so too does the extent of institutional mobilization (Table 6.2b). As we shall soon see, however, levels of institutional mobilization do not necessarily correspond to levels of threat. By institutional mobiliza-tion, I mean the electoral mobilization of members of an ethnic group by candidate organizations, ethnic party organizations such as Tejano Democrats, or civic organizations such as the Chinese American Politi-cal Association and Southwest Voter Research and Education Project (Southwest Voter).[12] In both 1994 and 1998, electoral mobilization among Latino immigrants in California was high. In 1994, several Latino organizations in California mobilized against Proposition 187 through campaigns for voter education, registration, and get-out-the-vote efforts (King 1994). Even in 1998, mobilization in response to po-litical threat was high among Latino immigrants in California. Partisan groups such as the Chicano / Latino Caucus of the California Demo-cratic Party (CLC) found it relatively easy to mobilize voters by framing the election as a referendum on the legacy of the outgoing governor, Pete Wilson. They pointed out the various threats for which Pete Wil-son and the GOP were responsible: anti-immigrant legislation as well as curbs on affirmative action and bilingual education. The CLC was also innovative in the way it targeted Latino immigrants: it left regis-tration activities to organizations such as Southwest Voter and focused instead on mobilizing absentee ballots during the month before the general election, in addition to get-out-the-vote (GOTV) efforts on Elec-tion Day (Ybarra 2000). Along with the CLC, civic groups such as Southwest Voter, Mexican American Legal Defense and Education Fund, and the Salvadoran American Legal and Education Fund

(SALEF) conducted massive registration and get-out-the-vote efforts. Many of those targeted for mobilization by Southwest Voter and SALEF were newly registered voters, many of whom were first-generation citizens.[13]

Electoral mobilization among Latino immigrants in Texas was significantly lower than the corresponding level of mobilization in California. In 1994, Latino organizations in Texas did not engage in the kind of mobilization efforts found in California (Villareal 2000). And, unlike the Democratic Party in California, Democrats in Texas were not successful in mobilizing Latinos to vote in 1998, either because of the lack of a viable candidate against Governor George W. Bush or because of factional divisions within county Democratic organizations (Quintanilla 2000).[14] Even Republican outreach efforts to Latino voters in Texas were low on the scale of mobilization. Bush's strategy to draw Latino support in 1998 was aimed more at converting those who were already likely to vote through the use of television and radio advertisements than at grassroots efforts to mobilize new voters.[15] Finally, even civic organizations in Texas did less to mobilize Latino immigrant voters in 1998 than their counterparts did in California. Given the large native-born Latino population in Texas, community organizations spent less time registering newly naturalized citizens and focused more on GOTV among already-registered voters.[16]

Mobilization among blacks in New York, regardless of immigrant generation, was low in 1994. As indicated earlier, many blacks felt that the election centered around which gubernatorial candidate was tougher on crime and welfare, both issues that were framed as black problems. Latino organizations in California in that same election year reacted to a similar form of political scapegoating by mobilizing in high numbers. Black organizations in New York, however, did not mobilize their bases (Wilkerson 1994). There are a couple of possible reasons why the reactions differed so starkly. First, in California the stakes were not only the gubernatorial and Senate elections but also a statewide ballot proposition. Thus, even if Latinos were dissatisfied with the candidates, they could still be convinced that high turnout would help to defeat Proposition 187.

By contrast, blacks in the 1994 New York election felt like the candidates did not really offer a meaningful choice at all. As one black member of Mario Cuomo's reelection effort noted, "Cuomo just wasn't able to galvanize the numbers as he did four years ago or the first time he ran. . . . I think that more than ever, you had Democratic candidates not talking to their base, not addressing their issues, and acting more like Republicans than Republicans" (McCarthy 1994). Another reason why mobilization among Latino immigrants was higher in California may have been that Latino political leaders and Democrats saw the election as an opportunity to draw upon the growing Latino population for future electoral battles. By contrast, the black immigrant population in New York had not grown so large as to merit large-scale registration and GOTV efforts by ethnopolitical organizations. Whatever the reason, the low level of mobilization among black immigrants in New York was reflective of the generally low level of mobilization among all blacks that election year.

Mobilization among black immigrants in New York seems to have increased between 1994 and 1998. In previous election years with higher levels of turnout among blacks in New York, mobilization among native-born blacks did not necessarily mean mobilization of black immigrants as well. Indeed, research by Reuel Rogers (2000) reveals that party organizations in New York City have had few incentives to mobilize Caribbean immigrants.[17] However, following the passage of immigration restriction and welfare reform in 1996, black immigrants in metropolitan areas such as New York City were able to access political and immigrant advocacy organizations to assist with the process of naturalization and voter registration. Furthermore, the organization for Charles Schumer for Senate in 1998 made efforts to mobilize black immigrant voters in an extremely close race with incumbent Alfonse D'Amato (Gonzalez 1998). Finally, by 1998, Caribbean American candidates in the Flatbush neighborhood of Brooklyn were beginning to mount strong challenges in contests for Assembly seats. For instance, Assembly District 42 had two Caribbean candidates challenging the incumbent representative, one of whom was Samuel Nicolas, cousin of Abner Louima, who had raised substantial sums of money and even received the endorsement of the *New York Times*.[18] Thus, electoral mobilization among black immigrants in New York was low in 1994 and moderate in 1998—despite the traditional exclusion of Caribbean immigrants from Democratic Party structures, the closeness of the 1998 Senate race and the rise of black immigrant candidates led to levels of mobilization that were higher than normal.

For Asian immigrants in California, there were several ethnic organizations that engaged in campaigns of voter education, registration, and GOTV prior to and during the 1994 election. In the Los Angeles metropolitan area, for instance, organizations such as Chinese Americans United for Self-Empowerment and Asian Pacific Americans for a New L.A. engaged in voter registration and voter education drives to defeat Proposition 187 (Nguyen 1994).[19] However, this mobilization was not as large as it was for Latinos in the state, nor did it sustain itself through the 1998 election. First, as has already been indicated, Asian immigrants felt less threatened by Proposition 187 than Latino immigrants did. Furthermore, Asian American organizations found it difficult to get their constituencies to be interested in the issues of affirmative action and bilingual education. Finally, there was a substantial decline in party outreach efforts to Asian Americans following the campaign fund-raising scandals of 1996. In my interviews with members of Asian American organizations in New York, Los Angeles, and the San Francisco Bay Area, none of the leaders mentioned the limitations on campaign finance as a significant issue affecting their community's rank-and-file population. They did note, however, that because of the fallout from the scandals, Asian immigrants were less likely to be party activists and that party and candidate outreach by statewide and national organizations had declined considerably since 1996.[20] This decrease in party and candidate mobilization affected Asian immigrants not only in California but also in other parts of the country. Thus Asian immigrants in the 1998 election generally experienced low levels of electoral mobilization by party and ethnic organizations.

Finally, white immigrants also experienced relatively low levels of mobilization when compared to their Latino counterparts. There were few party or civic organizations that made explicit attempts to mobilize white immigrant voters. For instance, white immigrants in California were not a politically active community or even recognized as a political community per se. Most of the immigrant organizations in the Los Angeles and San Francisco Bay Area were oriented toward the needs of immigrants from Latin America and Asia.[21] By contrast, white immigrants in New York had access to a large network of immigrant advocacy and service organizations that either were cross-racial in their orientation or explicitly served the needs of immigrants from Russia, Armenia, Italy, and so on. Thus, for instance, the *Directory of Services to Immigrants* (2000), a guide to community-based organizations put out by the New York City Mayor's Office of Immigrant Affairs and Language Services lists twenty-nine organizations in Brooklyn and thirty-five in Manhattan that offer immigrant-related services with language assistance in European languages such as Russian, Armenian, Ukrainian, Estonian, and the like. So for both 1994 and 1998, we would expect white immigrants in New York to have had a higher level of mobilization than white immigrants living in California and other parts of the country.[22]

Combining the two measures of political threat and institutional mobilization, we get the frameworks for the 1994 and 1998 elections shown in Table 6.3. Note that the measures of threat and mobilization are not collinear; higher threat does not always mean higher levels of mobilization. Among Asian immigrants in California, for instance, medium threat was combined with low mobilization in 1998. Similarly, Latino immigrants in Texas experienced low levels of threat but medium levels of mobilization in the 1994 election. Finally, in the same election year, immigrant whites in New York faced relatively low levels of threat and medium levels of mobilization.

Using the variable specification outlined above, I analyze whether institutional contexts of mobilization and variations in political threat explain differences in participation across states and racial/ethnic groups. The most rudimentary way of modeling cross-sectional differences in participation owing to threat and mobilization is the following:

$$\text{logit}(y_1) = \beta_1 * \text{resources} + \beta_2 * \text{social incorporation}$$
$$+ \beta_3 * \text{threat} + \beta_4 * \text{mobilization} \qquad (1)$$

where y_1 is the measure of political participation (voting, registration or turnout); *resources* include individual-level factors such as age, income, and education; and *social incorporation* refers to measures of "social connectedness" such as marital status, residential duration, and employment status. Finally, *threat* and *mobilization* will be allocated on a scale of 1 to 3, with 3 signifying high levels of threat and mobilization, respectively.

If only the level of political threat were important, then we would expect the coefficient for the mobilization variable (β_4) to be insignificant in Equation 1. In concrete terms, this means that during the 1998 election in New York there would be little variation in the voting patterns of black immigrants and Asian immigrants, both of whom were exposed to medium levels of political threat but to medium and low levels of mobilization, respectively. If, on the other hand, institutional mobilization were the only important variable, then we would expect the coefficient for the threat variable (β_3) to be insignificant. In other words, there would be little variation in the voting patterns of Asian and black immigrants in New York, both of whom faced similar levels of mobilization in the 1994 election but varying degrees of threat. Finally, if

TABLE 6.3

Electoral Mobilization and Political Threat Among Immigrants, 1994 and 1998

Political Threat		Electoral Mobilization		
		1 = Low	2 = Medium	3 = High
1994	1 = Low	New York Asians	Texas Latinos, New York whites	
	2 = Medium	California whites	California Asians	
	3 = High	New York blacks		California Latinos
1998	1 = Low			
	2 = Medium	California and New York Asians; California whites	Texas Latinos; New York whites	
	3 = High		New York blacks	California Latinos

both factors were important, then we would expect both β_3 and β_4 to be significant and positive. In this scenario, participation in contexts of high political threat as well as high mobilization would be higher than participation in contexts with only high levels of mobilization or high levels of threat, respectively. Of course, there may also be some interactive effects between the two variables, in which mobilization leads to even larger increases in participation in situations of high threat. However, subsequent analyses of the CPS data reveal no significant interactive effects.

One limitation of the model as presented in Equation 1 is that it does not control for other state-level factors that may be relevant for voting—factors such as the history of voting participation in the state and whether there was a close senate or gubernatorial race in the state that year. While controlling for such factors may be important, it also causes some of the variables such as race to drop out of the estimation because we have coded for immigrant groups in only three states. One solution, therefore, is to assign values of threat and mobilization on a national scale for the rest of the states. Equation 2 indicates the model for an estimation based on data from across the United States:

$$logit(y1) = \beta_1 * \text{resources} + \beta_2 * \text{social incorporation}$$
$$+ \beta_3 * \text{state voting history}$$
$$+ \beta_4 * \text{close senate/gubernatorial race}$$
$$+ \beta_5 * \text{threat} + \beta_6 * \text{mobilization} \tag{2}$$

Based on some of the analysis already presented, it is possible to assign values for threat and mobilization for the rest of the country. For instance, blacks in 1994, regardless of immigrant generation, experienced high levels of political threat and low levels of mobilization, with black organizations nationwide having little incentive to mobilize on behalf of Democratic candidates who sought to compete with Republicans on who was tougher on issues such as crime and welfare (Wilkerson 1994). Similarly, first-generation immigrants across the country, regardless of racial group, experienced higher levels of political threat after the passage of restrictionist legislation on immigration and welfare in 1996. However, one drawback to assigning values for other states is greater imprecision in the way that threat and mobilization are specified. Still, these may be offset by the benefits of such a strategy, namely the ability to control for other state-level factors and to get estimates for the effects of threat and mobilization that are not entirely dependent on immigrants in the three states considered.

Now that we have established the categories of threat and mobilization for various groups in 1994 and 1998, as well as the analytical framework, we can proceed to examine the relative effects of the two variables on the likelihood of voting among immigrants. Tabulated data from the 1994 election indicate that there are sizable differences in rates of electoral participation among first-generation respondents in the different categories. However, the patterns in voting rates do not match our expectations regarding threat or mobilization. It is true that experiencing low levels of threat and low levels of mobilization also had the lowest rates of voting participation. However, the rates of participation actually decrease when moving from a situation of low mobilization to medium mobilization for those experiencing medium levels of threat. Furthermore, among those whose communities were subject to medium levels of mobilization in 1994, those who faced high levels of threat had lower rates of participation than those with medium levels of threat. Similar inconsistencies in voting rates can be

TABLE 6.4

Threat, Mobilization, and Change in Participation Across Space

		Voting	Registration	Turnout
(a) California, Texas, and New York[a]				
1994	Threat	0.423***	0.046	0.811***
	Mobilization	0.031	-0.221	0.435*
1998	Threat	1.685***	0.705**	2.379***
	Mobilization	-0.339	-0.465*	-0.104
(b) National Sample[b]				
1994	Threat	0.429***	0.110	0.788***
	Mobilization	-0.293***	-0.276**	-0.180
1998	Threat	0.635***	0.591**	0.566*
	Mobilization	-0.132	-0.330***	0.242

SOURCE: Current Population Survey Voter Supplement.
For detailed regression results, see Appendix Tables A8 and A9.
NOTE: "Turnout" is voting among registered voters; "Voting" includes registration as well as turnout among adult citizens.
[a]Controlling for individual resources, social incorporation, and race.
[b]Controlling for individual resources, social incorporation, race, immigrant characteristics, and state-level factors.
*** $p < 0.01$; ** $p < 0.05$; * $p < 0.1$

found in the 1998 election, as higher mobilization does not lead to higher voting rates among those experiencing medium levels of threat.

Of course, there are several factors other than threat or mobilization noted in Equation 1 that can account for these seemingly inconsistent differences in participation. Table 6.4 shows the results of logit regressions of registration, voting, and turnout that controls for such factors.[23] Note that the relative magnitudes and statistical significance of institutional mobilization and political threat remain the same regardless of whether one controls for race and ethnicity. Also, in results not reported here, adding an interaction term of threat and mobilization does not improve the explanatory power of any model of participation in either 1994 or 1998.

In both election years, the likelihood of voting was positively and strongly associated with higher levels of threat. Looking at the components of voting participation—registration and turnout—it is interesting to note that, in 1994, when immigrant-related issues had just begun to appear on the political agenda in California, political threat had a stronger effect on turnout than on registration. Indeed, during that year, there was no significant relationship between threat and registration. This finding is not surprising. Since Proposition 187 gained prominence among mass publics only in the fall of 1994, the message of impending threat may not have reached naturalized citizens in time for them to register for the November election.

By 1998, however, political threat had a strong and significant relationship to both registration and turnout. Increases in the likelihood of voting were also associated with higher levels of mobilization, although the coefficient was not statistically significant in either election year. An examination of the two components of voting participation (registration and turnout) reveals null or inconsistent effects for the mobilization variable. Thus, threat seems to be a stronger and more consistent predictor of voting participation than mobilization among first-generation immigrants during this period.

As Table 6.4 indicates, the findings regarding the explanatory value of threat and mobilization also hold when the analysis is extended to the national sample. Thus, even after controlling for various state-level factors and immigrant characteristics, political threat is a stronger and more consistent predictor of participation than is institutional mobilization. Furthermore, just as in the analysis of the limited state sample, threat has a stronger effect on turnout in 1994 and affects both registration and turnout in 1998. In sum, the results indicate that political threat is a consistent and strong predictor of electoral participation, with the immediate effects manifest in the area of turnout and lagged effects also being felt in the process of voter registration. By contrast, contexts of mobilization have weaker and more inconsistent relationships to electoral participation.

Before concluding this chapter on threat and mobilization, I address two additional concerns regarding the analysis and the results presented here. First, some may argue that the variables of threat and mobilization, as they are coded here, can explain voting participation not only among first-generation immigrants but also among those in the second generation and perhaps even those in later immigrant generations. The first possibility is noted by Ramakrishnan and Espenshade (2001), who argue that second-generation immigrants are also affected by immigrant-related legislation because such legislation affects the welfare of their living parents. We might also expect consistent results for the third and later generations if the hypothesized effects of threat are likely to be based more on race or ethnicity than on immigrant generation. In order to test for this possibility, I use the same model and variable specification to analyze the voting participation of those in other immigrant generations. I find that the threat variable is indeed significant for those in later immigrant generations in most cases.[24] However, the magnitude of the threat variable is stronger for first-generation respondents than for those in the third and later generations. In 1998 the coefficient for the threat variable is over twice as large (0.635) among first-generation respondents as among those in the third and later generations (0.307). In 1994, the threat coefficient is 0.429 for first-generation respondents versus 0.351 for those in the third and later generations. Both of these differences in the magnitude of the threat coefficient are statistically significant at the .10 level.

Among second-generation respondents, threat from anti-immigrant legislation displays a less consistent relationship in the two election years considered. In 1994, the variable has a strong relationship to voting participation, echoing the findings of Ramakrishnan and Espenshade (2001) indicating that second-generation citizens are more responsive to immigration restriction than those in the third and later generations.[25] In 1998, however, the threat coefficient is very small (0.085) and fails tests of statistical significance. Perhaps this is an indication that second-generation immigrants are similar to first-generation immigrants in their short-term responses to anti-immigrant legislation but differ in their responsiveness over the longer term.

Finally, some may argue that these results concerning threat and mobilization may be influenced by the inclusion of white or black immigrants in the sample. The inclusion of white and black immigrants may be seen as faulty, either because they represent a smaller proportion of contemporary immigrants or because the variables of threat and mobilization are less accurately defined for those groups. Thus even controlling for race in the estimation of threat and mobilization may mask the true effects of the variables for Latino and Asian immigrants. A separate analysis of threat and mobilization at the national level after excluding white and black respondents produces results that are similar to the ones presented here. Indeed, the effect of threat on participation grows even stronger in the two elections when the sample is restricted to Latino and Asian immigrants, with a doubling in the size of the coefficient values.[26] Finally, mobilization continues to fail to predict higher participation among Latino and Asian immigrants. So the findings regarding threat and mobilization as they are presented in this chapter hold even if white and black immigrants are excluded from the analysis.

Conclusions

The analysis in this chapter has shown that certain types of political contexts can indeed play a significant role in motivating electoral participation. Specifically, the political threat represented by various immigrant-related measures played a significant part in increasing voting participation in the 1994 and 1998 elections. These findings echo the those of Pantoja, Ramirez, and Segura (2001) regarding Latino immigrants. Those authors noted that Latinos who naturalize in contexts of political threat are more likely to participate in electoral politics than those who naturalize in more neutral contexts. This study goes beyond the experiences of Latino immigrants and tests for the effects of political threat as it varies across racial groups and state boundaries.

Another significant finding regarding political threat is that its immediate effects are to increase turnout among already registered voters, but over the long term, its effects are felt more strongly in the component of voter registration. Thus, when the wave of anti-immigrant legislation first hit California in 1994, the impact was felt among those who were already registered. Those who were not registered but who were affected by such legislation could turn to the ballot box only in the longer term by registering to vote. Another finding that echoes the results found in Chapter 5 is that the effects of mobilization contexts on electoral participation are weak and inconsistent for first-generation immigrants. The evidence here suggests that mobilization efforts in the absence of threat have limited effects on participation among low-propensity voters such as first-generation immigrants who have limited political knowledge and relatively weak feelings of party identification. Another reason for the relative weakness of the mobilization variable is the likelihood of a respondent being targeted for mobilization may be smaller than the likelihood of that respondent feeling threatened by the effects of such legislation. Such a scenario is likely because the pool of those being affected by a piece of legislation is always larger than the pool of those who are mobilized in response to such legislation. Whatever the reason, ethnopolitical organizations face considerable limits in trying to mobilize first-generation immigrants to vote in elections in th absence of any credible electoral threat.

This is not to say, however, that such organizations do not matter in terms of immigrant participation. Indeed, successfully portraying an issue as "anti-immigrant," "anti-Latino," or "anti–Asian American," for example, often depends on the ability of social movement actors to create an issue frame that resonates with their constituent populations and to have the resources necessary to spread their message (McAdam 1982; Benford and Snow 2000). Still, attempts to encourage participation among first- and second-generation immigrants with general references to civic duty and community empowerment face limited success at the ballot box.[27]

Finally, it is debatable whether the effects of threat noted here are just as relevant in presidential elections as in midterm elections. Since voting in presidential elections is considerably higher than in midterm elections, contextual factors at the state level such as political threat may not make much of a difference in participation in presidential contests. The data here do not enable us to test this hypothesis because there is little state-level variation or ethnic differences in the effects of immigrant-related legislation in the presidential contests during this period.[28] With the Republican Party in California and nationwide eager to mend fences with immigrant voters, it may be some time before legislation provokes a differential sense of threat among immigrants in order to provide a test of the threat hypothesis in presidential elections. However, concerns over the "war on terrorism" and the backlash against Arab Americans and South Asian Americans following the September 11 attacks may once again produce differences in the sense of threat among immigrants of different racial groups, religious affiliations, and national origins. Indeed, there have been reports of sharp increases in applications for naturalizations among immigrants of Middle Eastern descent following the domestic repercussions of the present war on terrorism (Sheridan 2002).[29] Whether this sense of threat can translate into higher participation in the 2004 election and beyond still remains to be seen.

CHAPTER 7

Beyond the Ballot Box

*Nonvoting Political Behavior Across
Immigrant Generations*

There's a whole new class of new immigrants that's entrepre-
neurial that hasn't participated in government.... As campaign finance [reform] takes hold, as there's less land to develop, politicians have to find new sources of money. Where's
the money going to come from? Why not organize those who
are unorganized?

Hank Sheinkopf, a New York–based
political consultant

The greatest obstacle Hispanic political hopefuls are facing is
their difficulty in raising campaign contributions . . . The
Latino community—because it has less disposable income
and little tradition of political giving—usually fails to contribute much to Latinos on the campaign trail.

Ana Radelat

So far, we have seen that there are significant differences in voting
across racial groups and immigrant generations in America. And, even
though traditional theories of political participation can explain who
votes and who does not participate in immigrant America, many factors related to immigrant adaptation also play a significant role in explaining voting participation. Of course, democratic participation extends well beyond the ballot box, with several other ways for citizens
to engage in the civic life of the state. These include not only voting
but also other activities such as attending local meetings, writing to
elected officials, contributing money to politics, and attending protests

and rallies. As in the case of voting, involvement in these forms of political engagement may be distributed unevenly across members of different racial groups and immigrant generations. Some activities, such as giving money to politics or working in political campaigns, may exacerbate inequalities associated with race and immigrant generation. At the same time, other political activities such as attending local meetings may serve to dampen participation inequalities found at the ballot box.

In this chapter, I examine immigrant political participation in California from the 2002 election cycle, using data from the Public Policy Institute of California (PPIC) Statewide Survey. The analysis is based on three statewide surveys of California residents conducted by the Public Policy Institute of California between August and October 2002. The PPIC Statewide Survey is a telephone survey of approximately two thousand adult residents in California, with interviewees derived from a computer-generated random sample of telephone numbers (Baldassare 2002b). The survey questionnaire is conducted in either English or Spanish. The PPIC surveys are one of the few surveys of public opinion and political participation that contain sufficient numbers of Latinos, Asians, whites, and blacks to provide precise estimates of participation. Pooling the three monthly surveys allows for more reliable comparisons across racial groups and immigrant generations, with controls for factors such as age, education, home ownership, and immigrant generation.

However, there are a few important limitations to the PPIC survey data. While the data are derived from recent elections, they may have limited utility in explaining immigrant political participation in other states, especially those where immigrants constitute a smaller share of the adult citizen population. Also, the California immigrant population does not have a sufficient number of Afro-Caribbean immigrants to provide reliable estimates of participation or to allow for comparisons across immigrant generations for black citizens in the electorate. Still, the PPIC surveys are useful because they allow for comparisons across racial groups and immigrant generations from the same data source. Many other recent surveys—whether they be cross-racial data collections such as the General Social Survey and the National Election Studies or ethnic-specific surveys such as the Post / Kaiser / Harvard survey of Latinos—lack important measures of political activities and do not have sufficient numbers of respondents from different racial groups and immigrant generations. So, by using recent data on various forms of political participation, we are able to provide a more detailed answer to the question of whether members of some groups are consistently more organized into politics than others. However, the findings from this analysis can only be suggestive of what might be expected at the national level. To get a truer understanding of national-level patterns in various political activities, future surveys of political participation need to incorporate variables related to immigrant adaptation, contain sizable samples of Latinos and Asian Americans, and include measures of political participation beyond voting.

Group Differences in Political Participation

Table 7.1 presents participation rates for members of different racial groups and immigrant generations in California from the 2002 election cycle. As the results indicate, there are several activities with differences in participation across immigrant generations. Before starting to examine these differences, however, note that there is one remarkable degree of similarity across the various groups: the rank ordering of political activities. For instance, voting ranks as the most widespread form of political activity across racial groups and immigrant generations. As Table 7.1 reveals, however, there is a notable exception to this pattern among Latinos. Among first-generation Latinos, the most prominent form of political participation is not voting but attendance at local meetings where issues such as education and other local policies are discussed. The same holds true for third-generation Latinos, while for second-generation Latinos the rate of attendance at local meetings is equal to that of voting. The only other group for whom attendance at local meetings ranks higher than voting is among second-generation Asian Americans. Among whites, by contrast, attendance at local meetings is 28 percent to 47 percent lower than the rate of participation in elections, depending on the immigrant generation. The figures are similar for blacks in the third and later generations and for the rest of the Asian American population in California. So, the relatively high levels of participation in local affairs among Latinos and second-generation Asian immigrants are exceptions to the more general rule, in which voting is the most widespread form of political participation. Those exceptions aside, however, it is remarkable to note that there is a strong similarity in the rank ordering of political activities across racial groups and immigrant generations in California. After voting, signing petitions is the next

TABLE 7.1

Participation in Various Types of Political Activities, by Race and
Immigrant Generation

	Vote Regularly (%)	Sign Petitions (%)	Attend Local Meetings (%)	Write to Elected Officials (%)	Contribute to Political Causes (%)	Attend Rallies (%)	Do Party Work (%)
First generation							
Latino	38	23	45	15	9	12	4
Asian	39	33	31	22	16	15	5
White	54	40	39	30	22	16	7
Black	—	—	—	—	—	—	—
Second generation							
Latino	35	30	37	14	7	14	4
Asian	32	47	38	28	19	13	8
White	66	43	35	37	35	18	9
Black	—	—	—	—	—	—	—
Third generation and later							
Latino	41	35	47	23	15	12	5
Asian	48	37	39	20	20	8	9
White	59	45	38	35	25	17	8
Black	53	39	44	20	18	19	7

SOURCE: PPIC Statewide Surveys, August–October 2002.

most pervasive form of participation, followed by attendance at local meetings and writing to elected officials. Finally, the lowest levels of participation can be found in activities such as giving money to politicians and political causes, attending political rallies, and working on behalf of parties and political campaigns.

Of course, the presence of a strong similarity in the ordering of political activities across racial groups and immigrant generations does not mean the absence of significant group differences for each type of activity. Indeed, as we shall soon see, there are significant differences across immigrant generations within each racial group and across racial groups for each immigrant generation. Disparities in political participation can be measured either as tabulated differences in a bivariate model or as regression coefficients in a multivariate model. In this section, I present tabulated differences in participation which indicate the extent to which members of each group are overrepresented or underrepresented in their share of the participating population. Later, I shall focus on group differences in a multivariate regression, which indicates the extent to which generational patterns in voting apply to other types of political activity.

Voting Regularly

As noted in the previous chapter, media reports during the late 1990s in California pointed to the rise in numbers of immigrant and ethnic voters as the awakening of a sleeping giant. According to these reports, first-generation immigrants went to the ballot box in droves to register their anger and opposition to various statewide initiatives targeting issues ranging from illegal immigration to affirmative action and bilingual education. Thus legislation that targeted immigrant issues enabled Latino citizens in California to finally reach the same levels of voter turnout as those of other groups in the state. Scholarly work on voting during the 1990s has generally confirmed the rising level of political participation among Latino immigrants, although there does not seem to have been a similar spike in participation among Asian immigrants. Furthermore, it is unclear whether the equalization of turnout among ethnic groups in 1998 is still present today or whether the ranks of regular voters are still disproportionately white.

Recent data from the PPIC surveys enable us to answer this question on group disparities in the ranks of those who vote regularly in elections. It should be noted that the 2002 election in California was marked by high levels of citizen apathy in the gubernatorial campaigns and other statewide campaigns. Although a few ballot measures, such as the measure on after-school programs (Proposition 49—the "Arnold Schwarzenegger proposition"), received voter attention and interest, the overall election was a typical midterm election with significantly lower levels of citizen engagement and interest than a presidential election. Data from the 2002 election cycle can therefore give us an updated picture of whether group disparities in voting are present in California in the "post-187" and "post-209" eras.

As Table 7.1 indicates, about one-half of California's citizens can be considered regular voters, but there are significant differences across racial groups and immigrant generations. Just as in the national CPS data, the highest level of voting in the PPIC dataset is among second-generation whites, with 66 percent saying that they vote regularly in state and local elections. And, even though first- and third-generation whites display lower rates of participation than their second-generation counterparts, they still have among the highest rates of voting in California. By contrast, Latinos and Asian immigrants in the first and second generation display the lowest rate of participation, with less than 40 percent of respondents saying that they vote regularly in elections. Finally, Asians, Latinos, and blacks in the third and later generations display rates of voting participation that are closer to the state mean of 53 percent.

It is possible that these differences in participation are due primarily to differences in the age structure of the various populations. In the PPIC survey, for instance, the oldest respondents tend to be white, followed by blacks, Asians, and Latinos. Controlling for the age of respondents does little, however, to diminish group disparities among the ranks of those who vote regularly in elections. Finally, other factors such as socioeconomic status may also account for these gaps in participation, issues that are addressed later in this chapter. Note that there are sizable gaps in voting across racial groups and immigrant generations, differences that belie the optimism of increased turnout among Latino immigrants in the mid-1990s.

Signing Petitions

Petitions for state and local ballot propositions are important to the study of racial and immigrant politics for two reasons. First, ballot propositions have the potential to be less protective of minority interests than decisions made by representative institutions such as state legislatures and city councils. Legislative bodies allow for deliberation and trade-offs across issues, allow for some issues to be insulated from public contestation, and in some cases require supermajorities in order for a particular issue to prevail. In such a system, groups that are in the minority on a particular issue do not necessarily lose out on that issue. Propositions, on the other hand, allow for the majority to consistently prevail over the minority and do not allow for deliberations or trade-offs once measures reach the ballot. Thus the potential for minority interests to be overruled is significantly greater in ballot propositions than in the rule-making bodies of state and local government.

Ballot propositions have also been related to race and immigration through their content—some of the most highly publicized and contested measures at the statewide level during the 1990s dealt with race and immigration. In propositions related to illegal immigration, bilingual education, and affirmative action, the policy preferences of the California electorate were generally divided between whites and nonwhites, as well as between first- and second-generation immigrants and those in later immigrant generations. Furthermore, on such issues, nonwhites were consistently on the losing side of the issue. However, as a recent study by the Public Policy Institute of California has pointed out, most of the state and local propositions in California do not explicitly deal with issues relating to race, language use, or immigration (Hajnal and Louch 2001). The study shows that for these propositions Latinos and blacks are just as likely as whites to be on the winning side of an issue. The authors conclude that race is not a significant factor in determining preferences over most ballot propositions in California.

One issue that remains unexplored, however, is whether there are group differences in the process of signing petitions and getting propositions on ballots. These activities are arguably just as important as the act of voting because they help set the agenda of which questions make it on state and local ballots and which do not. Thus the race and immigrant generation of citizens may not be significant in terms of vote choice in many ballot propositions, but they may still be significant in terms of the power to set the issue agenda of such measures. As Table 7.1 indicates, there are sizable differences in the rates of petition signing across various groups. Just as in the case of voting, whites tend to have the highest rates of participation: 40 percent among first-generation whites, 43 percent in the second generation, and 45 percent in the third and later generations. By contrast, the lowest rates of participation in petition signing are among first-generation Asian immigrants (33 percent), second-generation Latinos (30 percent), and first-generation Latinos (23 percent). Finally, just as in the case of voting, these group differences in signing petitions are not due solely to variations in the age structure of the various populations. Controlling for the effects of age still leaves intact most of these gaps in participation.

There may be different reasons for these racial gaps in participation. Rates of petition signing among Asian Americans and Latinos may be lower because petition gatherers are less likely to target areas with high proportions of noncitizens. To the extent that whites, blacks, Asian Americans, and Latinos share the same policy priorities, this difference in petition gathering may not lead to any racial differences in policy influence. However, petition gatherers may be less likely to target nonwhites precisely because they do not share the same policy priorities as whites. Also, even if nonwhites are asked to sign petitions, they may be more likely than whites to feel that such petitions are tangential to their concerns or run contrary to their interests. Thus, to the extent that first-generation Latinos and Asian immigrants have policy preferences that are significantly different from those of native-born whites, their lower rates of participation in signing petitions means less power in setting the legislative agenda of ballot propositions.

Local Meetings

In addition to voting and signing petitions, citizens also have the opportunity to participate in politics by attending meetings that relate to public policy issues at the local level, including schools, land use, and government services. The PPIC surveys' measure of participation in local meetings includes hearings called by elected or appointed officials or institutions; official meetings of councils, boards, and commissions; and also attempts by nongovernmental actors to organize and mobilize on local issues.

Given the consistent group disparities in participation found in voting and signing petitions, we may expect to find the same set of disparities for attendance at local meetings. Data from the PPIC surveys indicate that this is not the case (Table 7.1). Instead of having the lowest rates of political participation, Latino citizens rank highest in their attendance at meetings that involve local issues: 47 percent among third-generation Latinos and 45 percent among the first generation. The relatively high level of participation in local meetings is also found among third-generation blacks in the PPIC survey, with participation rates of 44 percent. By contrast, first-generation Asian American citizens have the lowest rate of attendance at local meetings (31 percent), a difference of more than 30 percent when compared to first-generation Latinos.

What accounts for this high level of participation among native-born blacks and first-generation Latinos? First, the higher levels of attendance at local meetings may be a function of the greater presence of blacks and Latinos in school boards and city councils than of Asian Americans. On the other hand, these racial differences may simply be based on the demographic profiles of the various populations, most notably the proportion of respondents with school-age children. Latinos and blacks are more likely to have children of school age than whites or Asian Americans and so may be expected to have a greater proportion interested in education and related issues. Indeed, controlling for the presence of children under eighteen years of age reduces the statistical significance of these group differences in participation. Even with this caveat, however, group differences in attendance at local meetings are an important exception to the general pattern we have found so far, of high participation among whites of all immigrant generations and low participation among first-generation Latinos and Asian Americans.

Writing to Elected Officials

Elected officials pay attention not only to who attends local meetings or gives money to their campaigns but also to those who write to them with various concerns. Some of these concerns may be opinions on policy, whereas others may be requests for assistance with navigating federal, state, or local bureaucracies. As other studies have shown (Verba, Schlozman, and Brady 1995), requests for assistance are most common among those writing their local and state representatives, while expressions of policy opinion are more common among those writing elected officials at the national level. Both these types of requests have implications for influence over public policy. If some groups are more likely than others to write their elected officials for assistance, they are also likely to enjoy a greater ability to navigate government bureaucracy in ways that benefit their interests.[1] Group disparities in writing letters on policy issues also have significant implications for the relative ability of each group to influence legislative agendas and bill passage.

As data from the PPIC surveys indicate, there are enormous group disparities in the rate of citizen contact with elected officials (Table 7.1). As in most other forms of participation, first-generation immigrants have the lowest rates of participation and those in the third generation have the highest. There are also significant disparities by race. Indeed, the differences are among the strongest we have considered so far. Whites in California have the highest rate of contacting elected officials, ranging from 30 percent to 37 percent depending on the immigrant generation. These rates of participation are more than twice as high as the rate of contact among Latino immigrants in the first generation (15 percent) and second generation (14 percent). It is possible that much of the disparity is due to the lower ability of many Latino immigrants to communicate effectively in English. I allow for this possibility by separating out those Latinos who were interviewed in Spanish versus those interviewed in English. I find that those who were interviewed in Spanish have a rate of contact with elected officials that is 35 percent lower than those interviewed in English.[2] Still, even among English-proficient Latinos the gap in participation with whites is large, with participation rates ranging from 15 percent to 23 percent across immigrant generations. Higher rates of citizen contact with elected officials are found among first-generation Asian immigrants (22 percent) and among third-generation blacks (20 percent), but these are still lower than the rate of participation among whites of all immigrant generations. So English language ability does not adequately account for the wide gap between whites and Latinos in the rate of contact with elected officials. Thus, whatever relative advantage Latino immigrants may enjoy in terms of attendance at local meetings, such patterns are rare when compared to other types of political participation such as writing to elected officials.

Giving Money to Political Causes

In considering group differences in political participation, it is important to also pay attention to contributions to parties and campaigns. Giving money to political causes may rank lower than other forms of political engagement in terms of participation among the general populace. Nevertheless, political contributions bear significant relationships to access and influence in politics. Giving money to political causes may affect policy outcomes directly by improving the margin of victory of favored ballot propositions. Money can also influence policy outcomes indirectly, both by shaping access to elected officials and by affecting the margin of victory of candidates who are friendly to a group's issues.

The question naturally arises as to whether members of certain groups have greater access or influence than others when it comes to campaign finance. Results from the PPIC surveys indicate that there are indeed significant gaps in the rates of political giving across racial groups and immigrant generations in California. Just as in the case of voting and signing petitions, whites are most likely to give to political campaigns and organizations. The highest rates of political giving are found among second-generation whites (35 percent), but even first-generation whites have rates of political giving that surpass those of native-born Latinos or Asian Americans. Also, just as in the case of citizen contact with elected officials, political giving is low among first-generation Asian immigrants (16 percent) and is lowest among Latinos in the first and second immigrant generations (9 percent and 7 percent, respectively).

The lower level of campaign contributions among first- and second-generation Latinos may not be surprising, given the income disparities between whites and Asians, on the one hand, and Latinos on the other. Still, group differences in income do not mirror differences in campaign contributions. In the PPIC survey, Asian citizens have income levels that are similar to those of whites, yet their rate of campaign giving is only two-thirds of that of whites. Similarly, even though Latinos have levels of income similar to those blacks, they display a rate of campaign giving that is only half that of their black counterparts. Finally, even though income levels among Asian Americans are similar across immigrant generations, the rate of giving increases from the first generation to later immigrant generations. Later in this chapter, we shall explore whether group differences in campaign giving would persist if all groups had the same levels of education and home ownership. In the absence of such equalization, however, the results presented here indicate that there are sizable differences in the extent to which members of different racial groups and immigrant generations are represented among those who give money to political campaigns. These differences in campaign contributions reinforce group disparities in other types of political activities, leaving Latino and Asian immigrants with a lessened ability to gain access to elected officials and to influence policy decisions.

Attending Rallies

Attending rallies and speeches may have a less direct impact on public policy than many of the other activities considered so far. Protest rallies can have modest impacts on setting the legislative agenda by forcing political candidates to take positions on particular issues during election years. During election years, however, the most common forms of rallies are those organized by political parties and campaigns that enjoy substantial control over the themes and issues addressed in such events. Attendance at campaign rallies is likely to have only a small impact on electoral outcomes when compared to campaign contributions and voting. Still, rallies provide an avenue for participation and political expression for those who lack the monetary resources to contribute to campaigns or the political knowledge necessary to participate in local meetings. Indeed, attendance at local rallies is also open to those who are not citizens of the United States, a fact that could influence the relative level of participation among members of different racial and ethnic groups in California.

Just as media reports of the 1994 and 1998 election campaigns in California noted a rise in voter participation and mobilization among first-generation Latinos, they also pointed to a heightened incidence and level of attendance at political rallies (Bustillo and Davis 1994; McDonnell and Johnson 1994). As in the case of voting, however, it is unclear whether the higher level of participation among Latino immigrants carried through to 2002, a midterm election that was characterized by high levels of citizen disinterest and disengagement. Table 7.1 presents the rate of attendance at political rallies and speeches among citizens of different racial groups and immigrant generations. Far from serving as an equalizer, participation in political rallies follows patterns similar to those found in other political activities, with low levels of participation among Latinos and Asian Americans of different immigrant generations and the highest levels of participation among native-born whites and blacks.

Does the inclusion of noncitizens change these group differences in participation? Including noncitizens does raise the *level* of participation among first-generation Asian Americans and Latinos by 20 percent and 45 percent, respectively. However, including noncitizens does not improve the *rate* of participation. For both groups, adding noncitizens has no effect on the rate of participation because there is no appreciable difference in the rate of attendance among citizens and noncitizens in the first immigrant generation. Finally, even with the inclusion of noncitizens, the fundamental racial differences in attending political rallies still remain, with first-generation Latinos and Asians accounting for a disproportionately smaller share of participants than members of other racial groups and immigrant generations.

Party Work

Finally, are there significant differences across racial groups and immigrant generations for those who work for party organizations and political campaigns? As other studies have shown, party activists can play a significant role in shaping legislative agendas in the short term and the directions of party platforms and political strategies in the longer term. As Table 7.1 indicates, participation in party and campaign organizations constitutes the least widespread form of political activity in California, with only 7 percent of adult citizens reporting participating in such activities in the past year.

Given the low levels of participation in the general population, it becomes more difficult to ascertain differences in involvement across racial groups because of the small baseline for comparison. Still, data from the PPIC surveys indicate that first- and second-generation Latinos have the lowest rates of engagement in party work, significantly lower than their Asian American and white counterparts. This low level of participation among Latinos is surprising, given the rise of Latino leaders within the state Democratic Party, as well as efforts by political candidates, party caucuses, and unions to mobilize Latino immigrants. Indeed, many have remarked that party organizations in California are more likely to target Latinos for mobilization than Asian Americans (Wong 2001).[3] Here, the PPIC data indicate that even if first- and second-generation Latinos are more likely to be the targets of voter mobilization efforts, they are not more likely than Asian immigrants to work for political parties and campaigns.

Group Differences After Demographic Controls

So far we have examined tabulated differences across racial groups and immigrant generations for various forms of political participation. These bivariate differences are important to consider because they indicate the extent to which members of certain groups are overrepresented or underrepresented in their share of the overall citizenry. To explain these disparities, however, we need to analyze the effects of race and immigrant generation in a multivariate context that controls for other factors such as age, education, income, gender, and home ownership. Analyzing group differences in a multivariate context enables us to explain not only why some groups are more likely to be organized into politics than others but also what kinds of policies may reduce inequalities in political participation across racial groups and immigrant generations.

Controlling for these various demographic factors does indeed re-

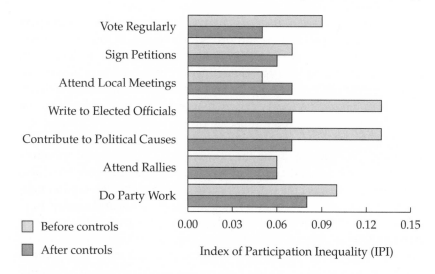

Figure 7.1. Participation Inequalities Based on Race and Immigrant Generation, Before and After Demographic Controls
SOURCE: PPIC Statewide Surveys, August–October 2002.

duce the size of many of the group differences noted in the previous
section. Age and education have the strongest effects on reducing inequalities in participation, followed by home ownership, income, and
gender.[4] At the same time, significant differences across racial groups
and immigrant generations still remain. Figure 7.1 presents group differences in participation for several political activities after controlling
for the various demographic factors noted above. Given the number of
groups and outcomes being considered, the results are presented in
summary form as the Index of Participation Inequality (IPI). The IPI is
a standardized measure of group disparities based on the Hoover coefficient of inequality. The Hoover coefficient is preferable to the Gini coefficient of inequality because the latter treats groups differently based
on whether they are associated with high or low outcomes. Thus, for instance, in measures of income inequality, the Gini coefficient performs
poorly in aggregating the incomes of top income groups. A similar limitation is found for the Gini coefficient for political and civic participation measures.

The IPI is calculated in the following manner: It takes the deviation of each group's share of the participating population from its share of the adult citizen population and provides a summary measure of participation inequality based on the sum of these absolute deviations. In this case, the relevant groups are defined by race, ethnicity, and immigrant generation. The IPI is standardized to a "0 to 1" scale, with the maximum theoretical level of participation inequality set to 1 and the minimum set to 0. So, if a minuscule proportion of the population accounted for everyone who gave money to politics, then the IPI level would be close to one. If, on the other hand, all groups had the same level of participation, then the IPI level would be zero.

Figure 7.1 presents the extent of participation inequality by race, ethnicity, and immigrant generation in both the bivariate and multivariate contexts. As we saw in Table 7.1, the greatest bivariate differences in participation are associated with writing letters to elected officials and contributing to political parties and campaigns, and the smallest differences are associated with attending meetings on local issues. Controlling for age, education, income, gender, and home ownership reduces the Index of Participation Inequality for most of the activities considered. For voting, writing to elected officials, and contributing to political causes, the IPI levels are reduced by about 50 percent. However, controlling for age, gender, and socioeconomic status does little to change the levels of participation inequality associated with signing petitions, attending rallies, and doing work for political parties and campaigns. Finally, controlling for various demographic factors actually increases the IPI level associated with attending local meetings because of the higher-than-average participation among blacks and first-generation Latinos.

The biggest reductions in participation inequality are associated with age, educational attainment, and home ownership. Thus, we can expect the aging of the first- and second-generation immigrant population to have salutary effects on participation inequality. Policies aimed at reducing group disparities in education and home ownership can reduce these disparities even further, although it is debatable whether such policies are likely to succeed in the near future. However, even if disparities in educational attainment, income, and home ownership were equalized, significant group differences in participation would remain. In particular, first-generation Asian immigrants would remain significantly less likely to vote, sign petitions, attend local meetings, write to elected officials, and contribute money to political causes. Similarly, second-generation Latino immigrants would continue to lag behind other groups in terms of signing petitions, writing to elected officials, and contributing to political causes. Interestingly, however, first-generation Latino immigrants would participate at levels comparable to third-generation whites and blacks for all activities other than signing ballot petitions.

So far we have seen that there are significant inequalities in participation across members of different racial groups and immigrant generations. Furthermore, even though factors such as age, education, income, and home ownership account for some of these differences, significant disparities remain for all of the various political activities considered. There are other aspects of immigrant incorporation such as language use, country of origin, duration of stay in the United States, and residence in ethnic enclaves that may account for some of these residual differences in participation. The PPIC surveys do not contain relevant measures for most of these other measures of immigrant incorporation in the United States.

One notable exception is the ability to differentiate between those who answered the survey in English versus Spanish, which in turn can serve as a rough measure of English proficiency. As in the case of voting participation, we may expect English-proficient Latinos to be more likely to participate in other forms of political participation than those who are unable to communicate effectively in English. Results from the PPIC data indicate, however, that the relationships between language use and participation are mixed (Table 7.2). For certain types of political activities, such as writing to elected officials, signing ballot petitions, and contributing money to political causes, English-speaking respondents demonstrate a higher level of participation than those answering the surveys in Spanish. On the other hand, Spanish-speaking respondents are just as likely as their English-proficient counterparts to attend local meetings and political rallies, as well as to engage in work for parties and political campaigns. Indeed, there is a slight advantage associated with Spanish language use, although these differences are not statistically significant.

This divergence in results for language use by the type of political activity is understandable given that Spanish-speaking respondents participate less in activities that involve money (given their lower levels of income) or that generally require the ability to communicate effectively in English (writing to elected officials). On the other hand, attending local meetings or rallies does not require English proficiency for those Latinos who live in cities or neighborhoods with large con-

TABLE 7.2

Participation in Various Types of Political Activities Among Latinos by Language of Interview

	English (%)	Spanish (%)
Vote regularly	40	38
Sign petitions	33	25
Attend local meetings	42	49
Write to elected officials	19	13
Contribute to political causes	12	6
Attend rallies	12	14
Do party work	4	5

SOURCE: PPIC Statewide Surveys, August–October 2002.

centrations of Latinos and who communicate primarily in Spanish. These differences in the importance of English proficiency merit further analysis using national data that contain more detailed measures of the contexts of immigrant incorporation and political mobilization. Still, from what we can glean from the PPIC surveys, language use bears a significant relationship to political participation among Latinos for those political activities that require high levels of English proficiency. Finally, even with controls for English proficiency among Latinos, the general point remains: first-generation Latinos lag behind native-born whites in many forms of political participation. These inequalities, when combined with the lower level of participation among English-speaking Asian immigrants, point to a situation in which group inequalities at the ballot box are reinforced by inequalities for most other types of political activities. Far from serving to bridge the gap in participation between members of different ethnic groups and immigrant generations, the ability to participate in various political activities leads to a greater division in participation between native-born whites, on the one hand, and first- and second-generation immigrant Latinos and Asians, on the other.

CHAPTER 8

The Future of Immigrant Political Participation

Directions in Policy and Research

THE FINDINGS IN this book demonstrate that the acquisition of citizenship does not easily lead to political participation among first-generation immigrants. Naturalization is not enough; there are still substantial gaps between naturalization and voting, and these gaps are even wider for other types of political activities such as writing to elected officials and contributing to political causes. Thus organizations seeking to empower first-generation immigrants to participate cannot achieve their ends by simply getting the foreign-born to naturalize, nor can they do so by simply encouraging citizens to register to vote.[1] They have to make candidates and elections compelling to first-generation immigrants, perhaps by calling attention to political threats facing their various communities. However, as the recent experience of the 2002 California election has shown, there may be limits to how long ethnopolitical organizations can rely on a sense of threat to motivate political participation. In general, Latino organizations found it difficult to motivate their constituencies; they could no longer rely on the memories of Pete Wilson to activate a sense of threat among Latino citizens and compel them to return to the ballot box. Consequently, voting rates among Latinos dropped considerably between the 1998 and 2002 elections (García 2002). The share of Latinos in the state electorate also dropped because, although turnout was low among all Californians, the drop was steeper for Latinos than for whites.

What can be done to reduce these disparities in participation across racial groups and immigrant generations? As we saw in Chapter 6, the successful framing of an issue as a political threat can propel many first-generation immigrants to the ballot box. However, relying on political threat to increase long-term participation has several limitations. First, policies may primarily target immigrants from particular socio-economic classes or from specific countries or regions of origin (such as Latino immigrants and Proposition 187 or Arab immigrants in the post-9 / 11 era). Such disparate effects make it difficult for ethnopolitical organizations to frame an issue as threatening to all immigrants, as seen in the divergence of opinion between Asian and Latino immigrants in California over Proposition 187. Furthermore, ethnopolitical organizations may not always succeed in framing an issue affecting their communities as politically threatening or requiring activism at the ballot box and beyond. Finally, political parties and candidates may learn from previous immigrant activism and scale back their anti-immigrant rhetoric in future legislative measures, thereby making it more difficult for immigrant advocates to frame an issue as politically threatening. Thus, for various reasons, the reliance on political threat is not a viable long-term strategy to increase participation among first-generation immigrants.

As far as long-term solutions are concerned, some may argue that all we need is the passage of time. With participation higher among long-term residents and among the immigrant second generation, it is tempting to conclude that a laissez-faire policy will solve the problem of participation inequalities across racial and ethnic groups, with a system of political pluralism once assimilation has taken hold. While this study does show that political participation generally increases with time and generations spent in the United States, there are still sizable racial disparities in participation in the immigrant second generation and even among those in the third and later generations. Thus the passage of time may lead to reductions in race-based disparities in participation, but it is certainly not sufficient to produce participation equality.

One possible long-term strategy to increase political participation among immigrants is to help them upgrade their civic skills and English proficiency. Those in the first and second generation who are proficient in English generally have a higher rate of participation than those who are not. Ethnic and civic organizations already provide language support for those immigrants wishing to naturalize by providing them the language skills and civic knowledge needed to pass the citizenship exam. Such organizations can help increase the level of political participation after the acquisition of citizenship by providing even more training in skills necessary to participate effectively in politics. These skills include knowing whom to contact in state and local government and learning how to compose a formal letter to an elected official or newspaper editor. Such skills can increase the participation of naturalized citizens in activities such as writing letters to elected officials, working for political parties, and running for elected office.

Finally, policies aimed at improving the socioeconomic standing of Latinos and blacks also hold the promise of reducing group disparities in political participation. As indicated in Chapter 7, many of the gaps in political participation (for activities such as signing petitions and writing to elected officials) can be substantially remedied by equalizing factors such as educational attainment and income across racial groups and immigrant generations. However, it is far easier to call for the equalization of such outcomes than to expect their actual occurrence. Not only is there limited political will to enact redistributionist policies; there are also enormous structural constraints in the form of race-based patterns of residential poverty and fiscal pressures on many state and local governments. Furthermore, even if successful redistributionist policies were considered and successfully enacted, many group differences in participation would persist (Chapters 5 and 7).

There are other aspects of institutional behavior that may play important roles in encouraging greater participation among immigrant nonwhites—such as the promotion of ethnic candidates in political primaries, recruitment in immigrant-heavy areas for party and campaign work, changes in party platforms and institutional agendas, the political activation of ethnic associations, and greater outreach efforts by organized labor to advocate for the rights and interests of immigrant labor. Even policies related to immigrants' countries of origin, such as the provision of dual nationality, can lead to greater participation in U.S. politics, not only through higher rates of naturalization in the United States but also through higher rates of participation among the naturalized. Finally, national policies aimed at legalizing the undocumented population and making them eligible for eventual citizenship should go far in bridging the gap between immigrants' share of the resident population and their share of the American electorate. Clearly, the passage of time is not, by itself, sufficient to bridge these gaps in participation across racial groups and immigrant generations. With the ranks of naturalized citizens growing each year, and with Latinos, Asian Americans, and Afro-Caribbeans accounting for an increasing share of the immigrant second generation, policy experimentations and interventions are necessary to reduce the gaps in participation across racial groups and immigrant generations.

In addition to considering policies aimed at equalizing rates of political participation, it is also worth thinking about the effects of immigration on the American political party system. As the California Republican Party learned in 1996 and afterward, targeting immigrants may reap political rewards in the short term, but it risks provoking a prolonged electoral backlash among immigrants. Indeed, the long-term effects of anti-immigrant legislation in California were more evident in patterns of party identification than in any sustained increase in immigrant voter turnout. For instance, turnout among Latino immigrants declined between the 1998 and 2002 statewide elections because the political threat from prior ballot propositions had begun to fade, and because Gray Davis ran a lackluster campaign and showed only lukewarm support for various immigrant-friendly bills. Despite the low turnout, however, Latinos in California were still loath to vote for Republican Bill Simon. George W. Bush and other Republicans have sought to change the image of the Republican Party in the minds of many immigrants through various policy pronouncements and gestures of good will, but results from recent elections still show a significant level of resistance to Republican candidates among immigrants in California and elsewhere.[2] Thus, while the turnout effects from anti-immigrant legislation lasted only a few electoral cycles, the effects on party identification and candidate choice have endured and are largely disadvantageous to the Republican Party.

The partisan advantage of the Democratic Party over the GOP is not something that is confined to first-generation immigrants. Indeed, data from the National Election Studies show that there is a second-generation shift toward the Democratic Party among white immigrants before regressing back to a Democratic / Republican split by the third generation. Furthermore, this second-generation bias toward the Democratic Party holds true across political cohorts (pre–New Deal, New Deal, and post–New Deal cohorts) and is not explained away by demographic factors or differences in national origins. Existing surveys of Asian Americans in California and elsewhere also indicate a Democratic Party advantage in the second immigrant generation and show that it even extends to the third generation (Baldassare 2002b; Lien 2004). Data from Latino surveys also show that there is a persistent advantage to the Democratic Party among second-generation immigrants and those in later immigrant generations (with the notable exception of Cuban immigrants). If the future political incorporation of immigrants is similar to that of the past, then the Republican Party may face a significant disadvantage in party identification among the descendants of the present waves of immigrants. However, it is also possible that the future generational trajectory of party identification and electoral participation will change based on political issues such as affirmative action and abortion, as well as sociological trends such as intermarriage and residential assimilation.

In the meantime, scholarly research on political participation among immigrants needs to bridge the disciplinary gap between economic and sociological studies of immigrant adaptation, on the one hand, and political science analyses of race and ethnicity, on the other. This study is very much at the intersections of these disciplines, as the findings on political participation inform sociological theories of immigrant adaptation and the findings on immigrant politics prompt a reformulation of existing models of political participation. This study has shown some support for standard theories of immigrant assimilation, as political participation increases with the number of years that immigrants stay in the United States and as country-of-origin characteristics matter less for second-generation immigrants than for the first generation. At the same time, there are limits to the straight-line assimilation story. Even as country-of-origin characteristics become less salient over time, racial and ethnic gaps in participation persist into the third generation and beyond. Thus, in the political sphere there continues to be a differentiation along racial and ethnic lines despite convergence in other outcomes such as language use and educational attainment.

There are other ways in which studies of political participation can inform our understandings of immigrant adaptation. For instance, there is an ongoing debate among scholars of immigrant adaptation over whether first- and second-generation immigrants fare better in ethnic enclaves than in more racially integrated settings. Critical measures of outcomes in this debate include earnings, successful self-employment, occupational mobility, educational attainment, and the ability of parents to maintain discipline and control over their children. This study shows that there are political consequences to residential ethnic concentration as well, with higher political participation in ethnically concentrated areas among first-generation immigrants, especially for those with low levels of English proficiency. There are other aspects of immigrant politics that may also be affected by residence in ethnic enclaves, including the level of party outreach, the involvement of transnational actors, the viability of immigrant candidates, and the policy responsiveness of elected officials and local government bureaucracies. While this study does not address these various issues, future studies of immigrant politics can indeed help broaden the debate among social scientists on the relationship between ethnic enclaves and immigrant well-being.

Also, a significant relationship may exist between processes of political incorporation such as interest group activity and aspects of immigrant adaptation such as occupational specialization or the granting of refugee status. Studies of political institutions can also provide insights into the ongoing debates over immigrant adaptation and assimilation. While the sociological literature points to segmented assimilation and divergent outcomes, political institutions hold the potential to play a more integrating role. For instance, the two-party system in the United States may constrain the extent to which immigrants from different national origins lead separate lives and experience diverse outcomes. Other institutions and social processes—such as religious associations, occupational specializations, and settlement patterns—can lead to greater divergence in group trajectories over time. Of course, the ability of parties to channel immigrants into one of two political camps is constrained by the limited party outreach to immigrant-heavy areas and the greater proportion of Independents among first-generation immigrants. Also, there have been instances where an immigrant group is subject to "electoral capture," where their votes are so taken for granted by one party that they become marginal players in the policy process (Frymer 1999). Still, the two-party system has the potential to bring together immigrants of different national origins, occupations, and religious affiliations and it is important to understand why such integration takes place under certain circumstances but not in others.

Just as the literature on political participation can contribute to the study of immigrant adaptation, studies of immigrant politics can also help reshape the theoretical frameworks used to study political participation. For instance, this study has shown that time-related aspects of immigrant adaptation have a significant place in explanations of voting participation. It does not matter simply whether people identify as Asian American, white, Latino, or black; it also makes a difference whether they are long-term residents or recent arrivals, first-generation immigrants or in the third generation and beyond. Country-of-origin factors also matter, with significant differences in participation associated with whether one comes from a country ruled by a repressive or democratic regime, or whether one's country of origin allows for dual nationality. Thus the role of race and ethnicity in shaping contemporary political behavior can no longer be considered without taking seriously various aspects of immigrant adaptation that are highlighted in this study. What this means at a more practical level is that future surveys of public opinion and political behavior need to include questions related to immigrant adaptation and qualitative studies of racial and ethnic politics need to consider immigration-related factors in a more systematic manner.

Findings from the wider literature on immigrant adaptation also have the potential to explain some of the puzzles uncovered in this analysis, such as why second-generation whites are more likely to vote and more likely to identify with the Democratic Party than those in the third generation and beyond. They may also suggest other factors that bear a significant relationship to political outcomes, such as residence in ethnic enclaves, intermarriage patterns, remittance behavior, and frequency of travel to the homeland. The literature on immigrant adaptation can also provide some insights into studies of political socialization, including the question of how the transfer of party identification, issue preferences, and ideology from adults to children may vary among parents in the first, second, or third immigrant generations. Finally, studies of immigrant adaptation can also provide important insights on the racial identification of first- and second-generation immigrants—developments that will surely have a bearing on the future of racial and ethnic politics in the United States.

Description of Data Sources

1. Current Population Survey

Data on individual characteristics and voting participation were obtained from the Voter Supplement to the Current Population Survey (CPS) in November of 1994, 1996, 1998, and 2000. Data sources for other variables are noted below. The full sample contains all respondents who answered questions to the voting and registration questions in the CPS. Interviews were conducted in English and Spanish. Puerto Ricans are excluded from the sample because it is unclear to which immigrant generation they should be assigned. Also, foreign-born individuals who have lived in the United States for less than six years and claim that they are U.S. citizens are excluded because of their higher propensity to misreport their citizenship status. In general, misreporting of the vote is lower in the CPS than in other surveys such as the National Election Studies (Presser, Traugott, and Traugott 1990). For a more detailed discussion of vote misreporting, see Chapter 2.

Race/Ethnicity and Other Demographic Variables

Race/ethnicity: Non-Hispanic white as the omitted category
Black: 1 if black, non-Hispanic, 0 otherwise
Asian: 1 if Asian, non-Hispanic, 0 otherwise
Latino: 1 if of Hispanic origin (any race), 0 otherwise
First generation: 1 if born outside the United States or outlying territories, 0 otherwise
First generation less than fifteen years in the United States: First generation and lived in the United States less than ten years

First generation fifteen to thirty years in the United States: First generation and lived in the United States ten to nineteen years

First generation more than thirty years in the United States: First generation and lived in the United States more than twenty years

Second generation: 1 if born in the United States or outlying territories and either parent *not* born in the United States or outlying territories, 0 otherwise

Third or later generation: 1 if born in the United States to parents born in the United States, 0 otherwise

Female: 1 if female, 0 otherwise

INDIVIDUAL RESOURCES

Age: Series of dummy variables with "Age 18–29" as the omitted category

Income: Series of dummy variables with "Family income below $25,000" as the omitted category

Education: "Less than high school" as the omitted category

High school graduate: 1 if respondent graduated from high school or obtained GED or equivalent, 0 otherwise

Some college: 1 if respondent received associate's degree or did not complete college, 0 otherwise

College graduate: 1 if respondent received a bachelor's degree or higher, 0 otherwise

SOCIAL INCORPORATION

Long duration at address: 1 if respondent has lived at the same address for five years or more, 0 otherwise

Married: 1 if married, 0 if unmarried, widowed, divorced, or separated

Employed: 1 if currently employed, 0 otherwise

INSTITUTIONAL BARRIERS

Liberal absentee eligibility: 1 if universal eligibility (anyone can vote absentee) or expanded eligibility (automatic eligibility for citizens of a certain age or who live a certain distance from the polls), 0 otherwise (Oliver 1996)

Restrictive registration: Individual lives in state where one has to register at least twenty-one days prior to election day. Data obtained from the League of Women Voters (www.lwv.org)

MOBILIZATION CONTEXTS

Presidential toss-up: 1 for states ranked as "Clinton slightly favored," "Dole Slightly Favored," or "Toss-up"; 0 otherwise (Associated Press 2000; Yoachum 1996)

Senator or governor toss-up: 1 if ranked as "highly vulnerable" or "vulnerable" (or in some years, "toss-up") by the *Congressional Quarterly*. During each election season, the *Congressional Quarterly* comes up with a survey of Senate and gubernatorial races based on opinion polls and surveys of candidate and party organizations (Babson and Groppe 1994; Benenson 2000; Cassata 1998; Cranford 1994; Foerstel 1998; Greenblatt 1996; Greenblatt and Wells 1996; Yoachum 1996).

OTHER VARIABLES

Election year: Series of dummy variables with the 2000 election as the omitted category

State voting history: Average of percentage voting in each state from 1972 to 1992 (Federal Election Commission www.fec.gov / votregis / turn / turn.htm)

From repressive regime: 1 if respondent came from a repressive regime at the time of entry to the United States, 0 otherwise. Regime coded as "repressive" if it was ranked as "partly free" or "not free" by Freedom House. Freedom House rankings of countries began in 1972. For years prior to 1972, countries were coded as repressive if they were communist countries or if they were ranked as repressive in 1972 and continued to be repressive for more than 75 percent of the years since 1972 (Freedom House www.freedomhouse.org).

Parents from repressive regime: 1 if one or both of respondent's parents are from repressive regime, 0 otherwise

In Spanish ballot area: 1 if respondent lives in a county, state, or metropolitan area with Spanish-language ballots (United States General Accounting Office 1997)

Percentage of state that is black, percentage Asian, percentage Latino: State ethnic proportions are based on Census reports that take into account the total state population (U.S. Bureau of the Census, "1990 to 2000 Annual Time Series of State Population Estimates By Race and Hispanic Origin," www.census.gov / population / www / estimates / st_srh.html).

State voting history: Average of percentage voting in each state from 1972 to 1992 (Federal Election Commission www.fec.gov / votregis / turn / turn.htm)

Consistency of Model Predictors

A replication of the analysis for presidential years and midterm elections produces results that are consistent with those found during the entire time period. Thus, for instance, the same top factors (age, education, residential duration, marital status, and income) that are significant in the full sample are also significant when the analysis is confined to presidential elections or midterm elections. Overall, the correlation between the significance rankings for the full sample and the presidential election sample is 0.85. The correlation for midterm elections is even higher, at 0.99. Finally, separating the voting decision into its component parts of registration and turnout reveals a similar picture with respect to the significance of the traditional sets of variables. The rank correlation of the registration stage with voting is 0.89 for the variables considered, and the figure for turnout is similarly high, at 0.90. Thus, as far as the traditional sets of factors are concerned, the findings as presented in Chapters 4 and 5 are consistent across both presidential and midterm elections and also when we split the voting decision into its component elements of registration and turnout.

2. National Election Studies

Data on individual characteristics and voting participation were obtained from the National Election Study from 1964 to 1994. Sample is of white respondents only.

First generation: 1 if born outside the United States or outlying territories, 0 otherwise

Second generation: 1 if born in the United States or outlying territories and either parent *not* born in the United States or outlying territories, 0 otherwise

Third or later generation: 1 if born in the United States to parents born in the United Sates, 0 otherwise

Age: Respondent's age (in the voting estimation, presented as a series of dummy variables with "Age 18–29" as the omitted category)

Income: Series of dummy variables with "0 to 16th percentile" as the omitted category

Education: "Less than high school" as the omitted category

High school graduate: 1 if respondent obtained diploma or equivalent, 0 otherwise

Some college: 1 if respondent received junior / community college degree or did not complete college, 0 otherwise

College graduate: 1 if respondent received a bachelor's degree or higher, 0 otherwise

Female: 1 if female, 0 otherwise

Married: 1 if married, 0 otherwise

Owns home: 1 if owns home, 0 otherwise

Party contact: 1 if contact by major party, 0 otherwise

Independent: 1 if party independent (no leaners), 0 otherwise

Interest in politics: 1 if respondent follows government or public affairs some of the time or most of the time, 0 otherwise

Internal efficacy: 1 if respondent disagreed with statement "Sometimes politics and government seem so complicated that a person like me can't really understand what's going on," 0 otherwise

External efficacy: 1 if respondent disagreed with statement "I don't think public officials care much what people like me think," 0 otherwise

3. Washington Post / Kaiser / Harvard University Survey of Latinos

Data on individual characteristics and voting participation were obtained from the PKH survey of Latinos in 1999. Sample contains both Latino and non-Latino respondents. The analyses presented examine behavior among Latino respondents only, except in a few cases where comparisons are made between (non-Hispanic) white and Latino respondents. A full description of the PKH survey can be found in Chapter 2. As in the CPS sample, Puerto Ricans are excluded from the analysis. In the estimation for voting, only those who answered the question of whether they voted in the most recent election are included.

First generation: 1 if born outside the United States or outlying territories, 0 otherwise

Second generation: 1 if born in the United States or outlying territories and either parent *not* born in the United States or outlying territories, 0 otherwise

Third or later generation 1 if born in the United States to parents born in the United States, 0 otherwise

Age: Respondent's age (in the voting estimation, presented as a series of dummy variables with "Age 18–29" as the omitted category)

Income: Series of dummy variables with "Less than $30,000" as the omitted category.

Education: "Less than high school" as the omitted category

High school graduate: 1 if respondent obtained diploma or equivalent, 0 otherwise

Some college: 1 if respondent received junior / community college degree or did not complete college, 0 otherwise

College graduate: 1 if respondent received a bachelor's degree or higher, 0 otherwise

Female: 1 if female, 0 otherwise

Independent: 1 if party independent (no leaners), 0 otherwise

Internal efficacy: 1 if respondent disagreed with statement "Sometimes politics and government seem so complicated that a person like me can't really understand what's going on," 0 otherwise

External efficacy: 1 if respondent disagreed with statement "I don't think public officials care much what people like me think," 0 otherwise

4. Pilot National Asian American Political Survey

Data on individual characteristics and voting participation were obtained from the PNAAPS survey from November 2000 to January 2001. Sample contains only Asian American respondents. A fuller description of the PNAAPS survey can be found in Chapter 2 and in Lien, Conway, and Wong 2004.

> *First generation*: 1 if born in Asia, 0 otherwise
> *Second generation*: 1 if born outside Asia and parents born in Asia, 0 otherwise
> *Third or later generation*: 1 if born outside Asia and parents born outside Asia, 0 otherwise
> *Age*: Respondent's age
> *Income*: Series of dummy variables with "Less than $30,000" as the omitted category
> *Education*: "Less than high school" as the omitted category
> *High school graduate*: 1 if respondent obtained diploma or equivalent, 0 otherwise
> *Some college*: 1 if respondent received vocational / technical degree or some college education, 0 otherwise
> *College graduate*: 1 if respondent received a bachelor's degree or higher, 0 otherwise
> *Female*: 1 if female, 0 otherwise
> *Partisan*: 1 if identifies or leans toward Democrats or Republicans, 0 otherwise

5. The Public Policy Institute of California Statewide Surveys

The Public Policy Institute of California (PPIC) Statewide Survey is a telephone survey of approximately two thousand adult residents in California, with interviewees derived from a computer-generated random sample of telephone numbers (Baldassare 2002b). The survey questionnaire is conducted in either English or Spanish. The PPIC surveys are one of the few surveys of public opinion and political participation that contain sufficient numbers of Latinos, Asians, whites, and blacks to provide precise estimates of participation. Pooling the three monthly surveys allows for more reliable comparisons across racial groups, with controls for factors such as age, education, home ownership, and immigrant generation.

First generation: 1 if born outside the United States or outlying territories, 0 otherwise

Second generation: 1 if born in the United States or outlying territories and either parent *not* born in the United States or outlying territories, 0 otherwise

Third or later generation: 1 if born in the United States to parents born in the United States, 0 otherwise

Age: Respondent's age (coded in original dataset as follows: 18 to 24, 25 to 34, 35 to 44, 45 to 54, 55 to 64, 65 and above)

Education: Educational attainment (coded in original dataset as follows: some high school or less; high school graduate; some college; college graduate; postgraduate)

Income: Household income (coded in original dataset as multiples of $20,000 up to $100,000, then $100,000 and above).

White: 1 if white, non-Hispanic, 0 otherwise

Black: 1 if black, non-Hispanic, 0 otherwise

Asian: 1 if Asian, non-Hispanic, 0 otherwise

Latino: 1 if respondent of Hispanic origin (any race), 0 otherwise

Female: 1 if female, 0 otherwise

Owns home: 1 if owns home, 0 otherwise

Political Participation (in the last twelve months)

Vote regularly: 1 if "nearly always" or "always," 0 otherwise

Sign petitions: 1 if "signed a petition such as the signatures gathered for local and state initiatives," 0 otherwise

Attend local meeting: 1 if attended a meeting on local or school affairs, 0 otherwise

Write elected official: 1 if "written or e-mailed a local, state, or federal elected official," 0 otherwise

Give money: 1 if gave money to a political party, candidate, or initiative campaign, 0 otherwise

Attend rallies: 1 if attended a political rally or speech, 0 otherwise

Party work: 1 if worked for a political party, candidate, or initiative campaign, 0 otherwise

6. Dow Jones Interactive News Coding

A listing of the number of newspaper stories dealing with immigration one month prior to the general election starting in 1994. The states that are part of this analysis are California, Texas, and New York. There are six newspapers used in each state: California (*Contra Costa Times, Los Angeles Times, Oakland Tribune, San Diego Union-Tribune, San Francisco*

Chronicle, San Jose Mercury News), Texas (*Austin American-Statesman, Corpus Christi Caller-Times, Dallas Morning News, El Paso Times, Houston Chronicle, San Antonio Express-News*), and New York (*New York Daily News, New York Observer, New York Post, New York Times, Newsday, Village Voice*).

Dow Jones Interactive (www.djinteractive.com) was used to conduct searches for relevant terms in the headline and lead paragraphs of newspaper stories. The results are normalized by the extent of election coverage in those states for the same one-month period. This normalization is done in order to control for factors such as circulation and the extent of political coverage for the newspapers in each state. A search term used for a particular state (Texas) for immigration-related stories, for example, was "immigration not California not New York" and for election-related stories was "election or elections not California not New York."

7. Interviews with Leaders of Ethnopolitical Organizations

Interviews with Latino and Asian organization leaders are based on my fieldwork during the summer of 2000 in the following metropolitan areas: Orange County, Los Angeles, and San Francisco in California; San Antonio, Houston, and Austin in Texas; and New York City. Names of organizations were obtained using community directories as well as the snowball method. The community directory used for Latino organizations is the *Anuario Hispano-Hispanic Yearbook* (2000); that for Asian American organizations is the *OCA National Directory of Asian Pacific American Organizations* (1999). Organizations were chosen for interview if they engaged in any of the following activities: voter registration, voter education, and get-out-the-vote efforts. There were twenty Latino organization leaders or staff members interviewed (one per organization), seven in California and thirteen in Texas. There were seventeen Asian American organization leaders interviewed, fourteen in California and three in New York. Two Latino organization leaders in New York and two Asian American organization leaders in Texas were also interviewed. Most of the interviews (68 percent) were done by phone, the rest in person. The interview followed a questionnaire format, using the following scheme.

1. Can you please give me a brief history of your organization—when it started and how? Who helped to create the organization? Was the creation of the organization prompted by any political event or development?

2. How would you describe your community?
   a. Age?
   b. Class / occupation?
   c. Residential pattern / concentration?
   d. Education?
   e. Generational status (first, second, third, etc.)?
   f. Partisan identification?

3. Has your organization engaged in any of the following efforts? If so, please describe efforts for elections in the past two years and plans for the 2000 election.
   a. Naturalization
   b. Registration
   c. Electoral mobilization (get out the vote)
   d. Rallies / protests
   e. Policy influence in local politics
   f. Policy influence in state politics
   g. Policy influence in national politics

4. If more than one activity, what would you consider your first- and second-order activities in terms of efforts expended? Why do you choose —— as your primary activity? Why do you not choose to expend much effort on ——?

5. In your efforts, what have you found the greatest obstacles to have been for
   a. Naturalization?
   b. Registration?
   c. Electoral mobilization (get out the vote)?
   d. Rallies / protests?
   e. Policy influence in local politics?
   f. Policy influence in state politics?
   g. Policy influence in national politics?

6. Have there been any instances in which *candidates* (at the local, state, or national level) have come to you for support? If so, please describe such instances and your responses to such requests. Did these requests happen during the
   a. 1996 election?
   b. Subsequent statewide election?
   c. 2000 election?

7. Have you attempted to initiate contact in the last two years with any *candidate* at the local, state, or national level in an attempt to influence policy?

8. Have there been any instances in which *party organizations* (at the local, state, or national level) have come to you for support? If so, please describe such instances and your responses to such requests. Did these requests happen during the
   a. 1996 election?
   b. Subsequent statewide election?
   c. 2000 election?

9. Have you attempted to initiate contact in the last two years with any *party organization* at the local, state, or national level in an attempt to influence policy?

10. If your organization is nonpartisan, have you hosted any event for a political candidate in the past four years? Do you plan on doing so during the 2000 election?

11. What are the issues that are most important for your community?
    a. [If foreign policy issues mentioned:] Which are more important for your organization—domestic issues or foreign policy issues?

12. Are there any appointments of members of your community at the local, state, or national levels? Do you think that such appointments were intended as a reward for past support or mobilization? Do you think that such appointments are intended to induce support in the future? If appointments have not yet been made, when do you expect to have such appointments?

13. Is getting coethnic appointments a goal of your organization?

14. Do you think members of your community are more likely to vote when there is a coethnic candidate?
    a. How about if the candidate has a coethnic staff member?
    b. How about if the incumbent has a coethnic person in an appointed position?
    c. How about if the incumbent pushes an issue that your community cares about and succeeds? What if the incumbent fails to get the issue passed?
    d. How about if the candidate attends a cultural event?

Number of Respondents by Race, National Origin, and Immigrant
Generation, CPS 1994–2000

	(a) All Respondents			
	White	Black	Latino	Asian
First generation	5,603	764	3,367	3,614
Second generation	24,389	543	4,062	1,662
Third and later generations	229,010	28,250	6,038	1,692

	(b) Whites			
	Germany	Italy	Poland	United Kingdom
First generation	684	642	441	459
Second generation	819	2,274	1,124	369
Third and later generations	n/a	n/a	n/a	n/a

	(c) Blacks		
	Jamaica	All Caribbean	All Africa
First generation	310	566	124
Second generation	101	222	58
Third and later generations	n/a	n/a	n/a

	(d) Latinos			
	Mexican	Cuban	Central/ South American	Other[a]
First generation	1,470	673	941	283
Second generation	3,120	241	404	297
Third and later generations	4,496	37	166	1,339

(Continued)

[a] Of these respondents, first- and second-generation immigrants are primarily from the Dominican Republic.

	(e) Asian National Origin					
	Filipino	Chinese	Japanese	Southeast Asian	South Asian	Korean
First generation	1,105	931	163	574	534	377
Second generation	468	304	579	77	79	101
Third and later generations	n/a	n/a	n/a	n/a	n/a	n/a

SOURCE: Current Population Survey Voter Supplement, 1994–2000.

Number of Respondents by Immigrant Generation and National Origin, Ethnic-Specific Surveys

	All	German	Italian	British	Polish	Irish
	(a) Whites[a]					
First generation	1,122	105	72	45	28	23
Second generation	3,349	295	312	99	149	148
Third and later generations	20,914	2,212	428	1,281	284	1,554

	All	Mexican	Cuban	Central/ South American
	(b) Latinos			
First generation	504	127	153	130
Second generation	537	196	58	67
Third and later generations	402	161	10	10

	All	Chinese	Filipino	Indian	Japanese	Korean	Vietnamese
	(c) Asian Americans						
First generation	913	279	180	121	41	157	135
Second generation	172	20	58	14	72	6	2
Third and later generations	122	3	27	6	82	4	0

SOURCE: National Election Studies, 1964–1994 (Whites); Washington Post / Kaiser / Harvard University Survey of Latinos, 1999 (Latinos); Pilot National Asian American Political Survey, 2000 (Asian Americans)

[a] Based on those who reported their ethnicity. The variable in the NES is as follows: "In addition to being an American what do you consider your main ethnic group or nationality group? (If more than 1 group mentioned:) With which of these groups do you most closely identify?"

Logit Regression of Voting Among First-Generation Immigrants, CPS 1994–2000

	Whites		Blacks		Latinos		Asian Americans	
	β	s.e.	β	s.e.	β	s.e.	β	s.e.
1994 election	-0.434***	0.107	-1.198***	0.294	-0.706***	0.138	-0.465***	0.129
1996 election	0.085	0.106	-0.433	0.301	0.225*	0.123	0.099	0.118
1998 election	-0.585***	0.108	-1.200***	0.258	-0.795***	0.129	-0.874***	0.125
Age								
30–39	-0.207	0.173	0.481	0.337	0.371**	0.148	0.165	0.145
40–49	0.135	0.169	0.775**	0.352	0.806***	0.154	0.351**	0.144
50–59	0.344**	0.176	0.420	0.369	1.164***	0.171	0.622***	0.160
60–69	0.794***	0.184	0.992**	0.448	1.203***	0.187	1.103***	0.190
70–79	0.880***	0.192	0.680	0.521	1.347***	0.213	1.268***	0.226
80–89	0.567***	0.201	0.551	0.641	1.244***	0.270	1.163***	0.379
Education								
High school graduate	0.420***	0.090	0.277	0.268	0.444***	0.107	0.409***	0.159
Some college	0.952***	0.104	0.474*	0.274	0.966***	0.121	0.657***	0.166
College graduate	1.175***	0.106	0.919***	0.316	1.392***	0.143	1.145***	0.155
Income								
$25,000–$50,000	0.276***	0.096	-0.247	0.238	0.095	0.102	0.083	0.130
$50,000–$75,000	0.198*	0.112	0.206	0.289	0.044	0.147	0.222	0.139
> $75,000	0.576***	0.116	0.214	0.403	0.084	0.157	0.562***	0.139
Not reported	-0.088	0.106	-0.386	0.312	-0.340***	0.149	0.165	0.166
Long duration at address	0.626***	0.073	0.606***	0.193	0.505***	0.086	0.212**	0.086
Married	0.305***	0.075	0.450**	0.194	0.362***	0.091	-0.075	0.101
Employed	-0.016	0.090	0.248	0.255	-0.020	0.115	0.210*	0.116
Female	-0.027	0.067	0.104	0.181	0.064	0.084	-0.129	0.082
Liberal absentee eligibility	0.137	0.096	-1.087**	0.466	-0.339**	0.156	0.401***	0.141

	Whites		Blacks		Latinos		Asian Americans	
	β	s.e.	β	s.e.	β	s.e.	β	s.e.
Restrictive registration	-0.137	0.115	-0.522	0.424	-0.158	0.266	-0.147	0.175
Presidential toss-up	0.155	0.127	0.353	0.372	-0.084	0.144	0.370**	0.176
Senator/ governor toss-up	0.165**	0.069	-0.246	0.220	0.341***	0.101	0.063	0.096
First genera-tion < 15 years in U.S	-0.660***	0.128	-0.524	0.325	-0.753***	0.141	-0.393***	0.152
First genera-tion 15–30 years in U.S	-0.476***	0.088	0.075	0.305	-0.227**	0.103	-0.389***	0.136
From repres-sive regime	-0.241***	0.072	-0.013	0.194	-0.146	0.111	0.164*	0.088
State percent-age black	-0.007	0.008	-0.002	0.016	0.003	0.011	0.009	0.010
State percent-age Latino	0.007	0.006	0.027	0.025	0.005	0.009	0.004	0.006
State percent-age Asian American	-0.002	0.010	-0.014	0.040	0.063***	0.015	0.012***	0.004
Lives in Spanish ballot area	-0.109	0.077	0.740***	0.268	0.115	0.101	0.096	0.102
State voting history	0.007	0.009	0.006	0.027	0.016	0.013	0.027**	0.012
Constant	-1.244*	0.658	-0.935	1.774	-2.302**	0.923	-3.148***	0.847
N	5,603		764		3,367		3,614	
Pseudo R-squared	0.114		0.162		0.145		0.100	
Log likeli-hood	-3,322.77		-435.70		-1,995.45		-2,238.83	

NOTE: Samples are of adult citizens.

*** $p < 0.01$; ** $p < 0.05$; * $p < 0.1$

Logit Regression of Voting Among Second-Generation Immigrants,
CPS 1994–2000

	Whites		Blacks		Latinos		Asian Americans	
	β	s.e.	β	s.e.	β	s.e.	β	s.e.
1994 election	-0.480***	0.061	-0.702**	0.347	-0.643***	0.141	-0.291	0.236
1996 election	0.063	0.060	-0.108	0.342	0.010	0.112	0.309	0.198
1998 election	-0.723***	0.061	-0.956***	0.299	-1.010***	0.130	-0.736***	0.223
Age								
30–39	0.431***	0.069	0.330	0.283	0.249**	0.111	0.709***	0.200
40–49	0.779***	0.070	0.975**	0.381	0.501***	0.129	0.876***	0.229
50–59	1.131***	0.072	0.953*	0.490	1.215***	0.147	0.937***	0.294
60–69	1.772***	0.073	0.680	0.452	1.621***	0.164	1.875***	0.268
70–79	1.994***	0.073	0.978**	0.488	2.062***	0.191	1.747***	0.280
80–89	1.579***	0.078	0.619	0.645	0.978***	0.289	1.179***	0.381
Education								
High school graduate	0.666***	0.049	0.306	0.369	0.606***	0.111	0.837***	0.252
Some college	1.264***	0.059	0.414	0.357	1.381***	0.118	1.511***	0.268
College graduate	1.776***	0.064	0.989**	0.411	2.005***	0.159	1.937***	0.286
Income								
$25,000–$50,000	0.265***	0.048	0.104	0.275	0.148	0.097	0.012	0.196
$50,000–$75,000	0.343***	0.061	0.017	0.347	0.409***	0.134	-0.018	0.227
> $75,000	0.400***	0.063	0.676*	0.410	0.590***	0.154	0.345	0.219
Not reported	0.121**	0.059	-0.113	0.340	-0.014	0.162	-0.132	0.275
Long duration at address	0.666***	0.039	0.685***	0.241	0.529***	0.082	0.109	0.143
Married	0.475***	0.038	0.226	0.246	0.295***	0.085	0.328**	0.152
Employed	0.090*	0.048	-0.047	0.257	0.017	0.105	0.243	0.176
Female	0.067*	0.035	0.136	0.207	0.170**	0.078	0.202	0.128
Liberal absentee eligibility	0.121***	0.046	0.009	0.293	0.032*	0.140	0.015	0.242

	Whites		Blacks		Latinos		Asian Americans	
	β	s.e.	β	s.e.	β	s.e.	β	s.e.
Restrictive registration	-0.009	0.053	0.420	0.378	-0.104	0.250	0.312	0.307
Presidential toss-up	0.170***	0.066	-0.158	0.430	-0.017	0.155	0.362	0.344
Senator/ governor toss-up	0.184***	0.036	0.214	0.231	0.201*	0.105	0.409**	0.174
Parents from repressive regime	-0.011	0.039	-0.140	0.229	-0.059	0.152	-0.179	0.136
State percent-age black	0.002	0.003	0.002	0.014	0.018*	0.011	-0.016	0.015
State percent-age Latino	0.004	0.005	0.032	0.061	0.047***	0.012	0.010	0.006
State percent-age Asian American	0.011***	0.003	0.006	0.023	0.012*	0.007	0.009	0.010
Lives in Spanish ballot area	-0.036	0.044	-0.368	0.259	0.079	0.096	-0.071	0.178
State voting history	0.028***	0.005	0.017	0.026	0.037***	.013	0.026	0.021
Constant	-3.809***	0.312	-2.042	1.734	-4.467***	0.901	-4.431***	1.389
N	24,389		543		4,062		1,662	
Pseudo R-squared	0.151		0.107		0.167		0.149	
Log likeli-hood	-12,780.20		-335.67		-2,320.27		-977.59	

NOTE: Samples are of adult citizens.

*** $p < 0.01$; ** $p < 0.05$; * $p < 0.1$

Logit Regression of Voting Among Third- and Later-Generation Immigrants, CPS 1994–2000

	Whites		Blacks		Latinos		Asian Americans	
	β	s.e.	β	s.e.	β	s.e..	β	s.e.
1994 election	-0.610***	0.018	-0.849***	0.046	-0.653***	0.124	-0.693***	0.253
1996 election	-0.062***	0.017	-0.102**	0.046	0.179*	0.095	-0.269	0.213
1998 election	-0.854***	0.018	-0.762***	0.047	-0.732***	0.107	-0.673***	0.257
Age								
30–39	0.408***	0.017	0.439***	0.043	0.586***	0.089	0.003	0.191
40–49	0.737***	0.017	0.762***	0.045	0.795***	0.095	0.461**	0.198
50–59	1.079***	0.020	1.094***	0.054	1.062***	0.123	0.544**	0.224
60–69	1.702***	0.024	1.584***	0.063	1.661***	0.165	1.135***	0.340
70–79	1.851***	0.027	1.693***	0.072	2.208***	0.203	1.135***	0.378
80–89	1.467***	0.034	0.922***	0.094	1.778***	0.324	2.079***	0.623
Education								
High school graduate	0.856***	0.018	0.597***	0.041	0.655***	0.092	0.432	0.298
Some college	1.505***	0.020	1.150***	0.046	1.412***	0.102	0.653**	0.307
College graduate	2.122***	0.022	1.712***	0.063	1.889***	0.141	1.463***	0.320
Income								
$25,000–$50,000	0.271***	0.015	0.255***	0.038	0.348***	0.083	0.535***	0.203
$50,000–$75,000	0.500***	0.018	0.411***	0.057	0.478***	0.111	0.491**	0.229
> $75,000	0.577***	0.020	0.687***	0.082	0.875***	0.136	0.851***	0.238
Not reported	0.299***	0.021	0.235***	0.051	0.316**	0.129	0.707***	0.258
Long duration at address	0.601***	0.012	0.607***	0.032	0.563***	0.070	0.474***	0.144
Married	0.462***	0.012	0.170***	0.034	0.303***	0.071	0.447***	0.141
Employed	0.100***	0.015	0.221***	0.037	0.195**	0.090	0.277	0.192
Female	0.069***	0.011	0.222***	0.031	0.176***	0.067	0.187	0.133
Liberal absentee eligibility	0.111***	0.013	0.052	0.041	0.115	0.132	0.333	0.301

	Whites		Blacks		Latinos		Asian Americans	
	β	s.e.	β	s.e.	β	s.e..	β	s.e.
Restrictive registration	-0.086***	0.016	0.088	0.054	-0.027	0.185	0.577	0.380
Presidential toss-up	0.037***	0.018	0.079	0.050	0.030	0.124	-0.170	0.450
Senator/ governor toss-up	0.141***	0.011	0.139***	0.032	0.537***	0.093	0.334	0.221
State percentage black	0.005***	0.001	0.016***	0.002	0.028***	0.010	0.020	0.018
State percentage Latino	0.011***	0.002	-0.007	0.006	0.027***	0.007	0.021***	0.007
State percentage Asian American	0.008***	0.001	-0.004	0.003	0.018***	0.005	0.019	0.013
Lives in Spanish ballot area	-0.110***	0.017	0.376***	0.043	0.191**	0.089	-0.236	0.263
State voting history	0.026***	0.001	0.035***	0.003	0.056***	0.012	0.088***	0.027
Constant	-3.779***	0.088	-3.831***	0.198	-6.473***	0.797	-8.136***	1.824
N	229,010		28,250		6,038		1,692	
Pseudo R-squared	0.174		0.155		0.172		0.141	
Log likelihood	-127,699.44		-16,435.61		-3,405.76		-999.94	

NOTE: Samples are of adult citizens.

*** $p < 0.01$; ** $p < 0.05$; * $p < 0.1$

NOTE: Additional appendix tables (A.6 to A.14) can be found at the author's Web site at http://www.karthick.com.

Notes

CHAPTER 1

1. Even in the case of amnesty, negotiations with Mexico were under way in January 2002 to provide a limited form of legalization for undocumented workers from Mexico (Slevin and Sheridan 2002).

2. For a more detailed overview of this literature, see Chapter 4.

CHAPTER 2

1. It should be noted that Milton Gordon's notion of immigrant adaptation is different from Oscar Handlin's in one significant respect: Handlin posits that institutions and practices from the Old World are irrelevant to life in the United States but that it still takes some time for immigrants to cope with life in the United States. On the other hand, Gordon argues that immigrant groups often retain traditional structures and customs, which in turn helps determine the pace at which cultural assimilation proceeds.

2. The same is also true of Nathan Glazer and Daniel Patrick Moynihan's *Beyond the Melting Pot* (1963), which provides an analysis of political power among different ethnic groups in New York City. In the book, Glazer and Moynihan pay attention to party allegiance and office holding but do not examine differences in the extent of voting participation per se.

3. Women of all ethnic groups (including native-born "Yankees") had low levels of registration until the mid-1930s. According to Gamm (1989), what changed during the New Deal for Jewish immigrants was that they switched from party registration along class lines (working-class Jews were registered Democrats, whereas upper-class Jews were Republicans) to registering and voting solidly with the Democratic Party.

4. There is also an extensive literature on border crossing among undocu-

mented immigrants, with some studies examining the relationship between border crossings and immigrant outcomes in the United States (Espenshade and Huber 1998; Cornelius et al. 2004).

5. The authors provide "native-born versus foreign-born" tabulations for social and demographic characteristics such as education, income, language ability, and religious affiliation, but not for measures of political participation. However, one can examine nativity data at the individual level from public datasets of the LNPS at the Inter-university Consortium for Political and Social Research (ICPSR) http://www.icpsr.umich.edu.

6. It is quite likely that the nonsignificance of the first-generation variable is due to its collinearity with the acculturation variable. Other studies using the same dataset (Uhlaner, Cain, and Kiewiet 1989; Tam Cho 1999) find that the percent of one's life spent in the United States has a significant effect on voting among Asian Americans. Lien does not provide a correlation between her acculturation variable and immigrant generation. However, one can surmise that the two variables are collinear since the former includes two immigrant-relevant policy issues—support for employer sanctions for hiring illegal immigrants and opposition to bilingual ballots for non-English-speaking voters.

7. Pei-te Lien is the principal investigator of the Pilot Study of the National Asian American Political Survey (PNAAPS). The survey's sample is limited to ethnic-heavy zip codes in five metropolitan areas: Chicago, Honolulu, Los Angeles, New York, and San Francisco.

8. The authors do not explain or speculate on why the strength of these variables differs for Asian Americans and Latinos.

9. She does note, however, that education has a weak effect on direct political participation among Asian Americans (without taking into account their immigrant generation).

10. Since 1990, there has been a significant rise in the number of foreign-born citizens nationwide and in California, especially in metropolitan areas such as Los Angeles and the San Francisco Bay Area. Other developments that have changed the decision-making structure of naturalization and political participation for immigrants include the passage of Proposition 187 in California during the 1994 election, the passage of welfare reform and immigration reform at the national level in 1996, and the rise in the number of countries allowing dual citizenship.

11. One notable exception is the Philip Kasinitz, John Mollenkopf, and Mary Waters (forthcoming) study of the immigrant second generation in New York City, which includes samples of second-generation Russian immigrants. Another exception is Jane Junn's (1999) analysis of the 1990 Citizen Participation Study, which tests one measure of immigrant adaptation for whites—foreign-born status.

12. The racial classification scheme used here is found in many other contemporary studies of race and ethnicity in the United States: whites are non-Hispanic whites; blacks are non-Hispanic blacks; Asians are non-Hispanic Asians; Latinos are of Hispanic origin and can be of any race. Finally, the terms

Asian and *Asian American* are used interchangeably and refer to those respondents who indicate Asian as their primary racial identification.

13. A more detailed overview of the variables in the pooled CPS dataset and the other data sources used in this book can be found in the Appendix.

14. A more detailed overview of the interview questionnaire and methods can be found in the Appendix.

CHAPTER 3

1. Although the U.S. Census stopped including questions on the nativity of parents after 1970, it is now possible to estimate the size of the second-generation population in 2000 using the Current Population Survey, which has consistently asked questions on the nativity of parents since 1994.

2. While the term *Hispanic* was not used as a measure of ethnicity until the 1970 Census, national origin data from the 1900 Census reveal that immigrants from Latin America accounted for only 1 percent of the foreign-born population and that those from Europe and Canada accounted for over 97 percent.

3. There have been a few reasons offered as to why the number of naturalizations rose so sharply during this period (U.S. Immigration and Naturalization Service 1997). One was that the passage of restrictionist legislation at the state and national level prompted immigrants to secure their rights and benefits through naturalization. Another factor was that many of the 2.7 million undocumented immigrants who were granted legal status in 1986 under the Immigration Reform and Control Act (IRCA) became eligible for naturalization in the early to mid-1990s. Other factors include the decision of some Latin American countries to allow dual nationality and the implementation of a "Green Card Replacement Program" that reduced the relative cost of seeking American citizenship.

CHAPTER 4

1. In the standard theoretical literature on voting participation, "external efficacy" refers to the extent to which respondents believe that their participation matters and "internal efficacy" refers to the extent to which respondents feel that they understand government and politics.

2. As discussed in the section on socioeconomic status, the positive relationship between socioeconomic status and voting has been found for Latinos in various studies (de la Garza et al. 1992; DeSipio 1996a; Shaw, de la Garza, and Lee 2000), but such relationships have been found to be less consistent among first-generation immigrant Latinos (Tam Cho 1999; Hritzuk and Park 2000).

3. The share of naturalized citizens among the total population increased by 19 percent between 1985 and 2000. During the same period, the number of long-term residents (living in the United States for fifteen years or more) increased by 68 percent (United States Census Bureau 2001). Other developments that have changed the decision-making structure of naturalization and political

participation for immigrants include the legalization of immigrants under the Immigration Reform and Control Act in 1986, the increased number of countries allowing dual citizenship, the passage of Proposition 187 in California during the 1994 election, and the passage of welfare reform and immigration reform at the national level in 1996.

4. It should be noted, however, that although the dip in participation among the very elderly may be substantial, it is not statistically significant for most groups because of small sample sizes.

5. For first-generation Korean and Japanese immigrants, the relationship between age and voting is erratic.

6. Among second-generation Cuban Americans, Southeast Asians, and Afro-Caribbeans, the number of respondents older than fifty years of age is so low as to produce unreliable estimates of the effect of age on voting.

7. As indicated in Chapter 3, the same results hold true whether one conducts the analysis for first-generation immigrants who have higher levels of English proficiency (self-reported responses) or for those with lower levels of English proficiency (not self-reported responses).

8. Other measures of social incorporation can include involvement in religious institutions or civic associations.

9. In her study of Los Angeles neighborhoods, Min Zhou notes that Korean immigrants who have moved to the suburbs continue to spend the weekends in Koreatown, attending religious services and consuming products and services offered in the neighborhood. She does not find the same phenomenon in nearby Mexican neighborhoods.

10. Several scholars of African American family structures, including Melvin Wilson (1989), have noted that the system of extended social support among blacks extends back to the days of slavery and has eased the burden of child rearing among single black women.

11. The only exception is for second-generation blacks.

12. There still remain significant questions relating to the effects on turnout of factors such as race-based districting and English-only ballots. The Current Population Survey does not include information on respondents' congressional districts. However, it is possible to determine the effects of racial diversity at the level of county and metropolitan area. It is also possible to determine the effects of bilingual ballots on participation because such policies are implemented at the county level. Both of these effects will be considered in Chapter 7.

13. North Dakota does not have any registration; all resident citizens can vote.

14. As indicated earlier, Oliver (1996) shows that party mobilization efforts also matter. Oliver based his findings on his original survey of state party chairs. There is no comparable information that is publicly available for 1996, 1998, and 2000 to test whether Oliver's analysis of CPS data from 1994 still holds true today.

15. It is possible that registration deadlines are significant only in the registration stage of participation (registration among eligible citizens), while ab-

sentee ballot eligibility is significant for the turnout stage (voting among those previously registered). Separate analyses with registration or turnout as the dependent variable also reveal an inconsistent relationship between institutional barriers and the likelihood of participation.

16. In his comparative study of Southern politics, Key (1949) noted that states with higher partisan or factional competition had higher levels of voter turnout. Indeed, Key attributed the low turnout among poor Southern whites not as much to poll taxes or literacy tests, but to the lack of two-party competition in the South.

17. Given that a significant proportion of Asian Americans and Latinos live in these states, utilizing measures that exclude such states may lead to biased estimates of the effects of political culture on participation.

18. Differences in voting across immigrant generations for whites, blacks, Latinos, and Asian Americans will be considered in greater detail in Chapter 5.

CHAPTER 5

1. Some scholars have noted that English language ability has a significant relationship to the likelihood of participation (Tam Cho 1999). Questions on language ability are not present in cross-racial surveys of participation such as the November CPS Voter Supplements. However, since language ability is related primarily to duration of stay in the United States, immigrant generation, and region of origin (Espenshade and Fu 1997), the factors included in this analysis serve as adequate proxies for English language ability.

2. As noted in Chapter 1, much of the early scholarship on immigrant adaptation considered political participation to be part of this larger process of cultural and civic assimilation (Handlin 1951; Gordon 1964).

3. The "percentage of life in the United States" question fails to differentiate between second-generation and third-generation immigrants, since all native-born respondents regardless of their immigrant generation have spent 100 percent of their lives in the United States.

4. Processes relevant to immigrant incorporation may also extend beyond the third generation. However, it is not possible in the CPS to differentiate between the third generation and later immigrant generations. Furthermore, even if we had data available on the nativity of each respondent's grandparents, the problem of mixed nativity origins (grandparents from different immigrant generations) is so prevalent that it would make it difficult to distinguish third-generation respondents from those in later immigrant generations.

5. It is possible that the confusion associated with having a dual identity may decrease the motivation of second-generation respondents to participate. It is likely, however, that if such confusion exists, it is more prevalent among first-generation immigrants than among those in the second generation.

6. Indeed, most Asian immigrants were not able to naturalize until 1952.

7. First-generation Latinos in the PKH survey actually display a higher level of participation than those in later immigrant generations, a finding that is un-

affected by the inclusion or exclusion of attitudinal factors. This higher participation among first-generation respondents may be partly due to the fact that California and Florida account for a larger proportion of PKH respondents than their share in the national Latino population. Thus, the higher level of immigrant participation would reflect the higher level of participation among Latino immigrants in California noted in Chapter 6 and the traditionally high levels of participation among Cuban immigrants in Florida.

8. The MCSUI does not contain information on voting or on whether the parents of respondents were born in the United States.

9. One prominent example is Jesus Galvis, a member of the City Council of Hackensack, New Jersey, who ran unsuccessfully for a simultaneous seat in Colombia's senate in 1998 (Fritz 1998).

10. One notable exception is Michael Jones-Correa's study of immigrants from Latin America in *Citizenship Studies* (2001). Also, a recent unpublished paper by Bruce Cain and Brendan Doherty (2003) addresses the issue of participation among dual nationals using the PKH survey of Latinos, but the data are marked by unusually high proportions of respondents claiming dual citizenship (even among Cuban Americans, who are not eligible for it).

11. The results are from multivariate regressions that control for all of the factors outlined in Chapters 4 and 5 other than country of origin and originating from a country ruled by a repressive regime. This is done because there is a high degree of collinearity between dual citizenship policies and these variables. Controlling for these factors reduces the statistical significance of the findings for white and Asian immigrants to the .15 level.

12. A separate test of Anglophone country origin reveals that the variable is significant only in the case of Asian immigrants.

13. Not only has the dominant model of Anglo conformity been noted by early scholars such Milton Gordon (1964); it is also seen as the normative goal of immigrant incorporation by conservative commentators such as Pat Buchanan and others.

14. Anglophone origin may also be relevant, but a separate analysis reveals that it is not significant in the case of black immigrants.

15. The variable is significant only for Asian immigrants.

16. Another relevant distinction here may be between those who come from communist countries and receive refugee assistance and help with settlement (such as immigrants from Vietnam) versus those who come from communist countries and do not receive such benefits (Chinese immigrants, for instance).

17. It should be noted, however, that the same does not apply to immigrants from Europe or black immigrants. It is possible that the greater homogeneity of racial identification among white immigrants and black immigrants than among Asian immigrants diminishes the influence of Anglophone origin among the former but not among the latter.

18. Also, Leighley's (2001) findings are based on the 1990 Citizen Participation Survey. As indicated in Chapters 3 and 6, several important changes during the 1990s make surveys from 1990 less useful in understanding immigrant electoral participation today.

19. The effect of racially charged measures on voting will be considered in more detail in Chapter 8.

20. Note, however, that ethnic concentration at the county level is also significant for first-generation Latinos when the presence of Spanish language ballots is not controlled for. One reason to separately analyze the effects of county-level concentration and the presence of Spanish language ballots is that the two measures have a relatively high degree of correlation (0.51).

21. Janelle Wong (2001) notes the low level of mobilization of Asian Americans by mainstream party organizations at the local level. It is not clear from her analysis, however, if this lack of mobilization is also present among state-level party and campaign organizations.

22. Similarly, outside of Hawaii and the San Francisco Bay Area, over one-half of Asian American respondents live in counties where they constitute less than 7 percent of the electorate.

23. The provisions have since been renewed in 1982 and 1992 and are set to expire in 2007.

24. In the case of political subdivisions, a numerical minimum of ten thousand citizens of language minorities may be used instead.

25. Although there are clear demographic guidelines regarding the implementation of Spanish language ballots, prosecution and advocacy by civil rights organizations has often been necessary to make sure that election boards comply with such provisions. Furthermore, mobilization may have also played a role in the handful of jurisdictions that offer Spanish language ballots even in the absence of being required to do so by law.

26. Two cases that deserve mention are ballots in Queens that switched the Democrat and Republican labels in Chinese translations (Young 2000) and the complaints by the U.S. Department of Justice (2002) regarding the lack of Spanish language assistance at polling places in Orange and Osceola Counties in Florida during the 2000 election.

27. Controlling for the poverty level in the county maintains the significance of the effects of Spanish language ballots on voting among second-generation immigrants and those in later immigrant generations, but the effects for first-generation immigrants are negative and nonsignificant. Controlling for the proportion of noncitizens in addition to poverty levels in the county removes the significance of living in Spanish ballot areas for all three immigrant generation groups.

28. Latinos who are proficient in English may still prefer to speak in Spanish during survey interviews, as indicated by the PKH survey of Latinos (Lee 2001). However, the use of language of interview as a proxy for English proficiency in the CPS is justifiable for several reasons. First, the PKH survey indicates that the unique effects of language of interview (after controlling for English proficiency) are far stronger for public opinion and ethnic-oriented political participation than for general reports of voter turnout. Also, imputed values of English proficiency based on a previous study of English proficiency in the CPS (Espenshade and Fu 1997) do not produce substantively different results than the ones found using language of interview. Finally, we can expect

language of interview in the CPS to bear an even stronger relationship to English proficiency than in other surveys such as the PKH survey of Latinos, in which there is a 0.80 correlation between language of interview and English proficiency. This is most likely due to the fact that respondents in the CPS need to answer a vast array of questions regarding demographics and labor force participation—hundreds of questions more than the typical political or social survey. Given the greater language skills demanded to complete the CPS survey, it is unlikely that respondents who are only marginally proficient in English will choose to be interviewed in English or that those who are marginally proficient in Spanish will choose to be interviewed in Spanish.

29. The only exception is for those in the first generation with some college education.

30. See Appendix Tables A.3, A.4, and A.5 for coefficients from the multivariate regressions that do not take into account group-specific means in the other variables considered.

CHAPTER 6

1. This does not mean that the surge in naturalizations during the mid-1990s was due entirely to these legislative changes. Other factors include the rising costs of the Green Card Replacement program, an increase in countries allowing dual nationality, and a wave of immigrants eligible for citizenship who were legalized under the 1986 Immigration Reform and Control Act.

2. According to Key, party contestation was kept low in states where lower-class whites could unite with blacks.

3. Micheal Giles and Melanie Buckner (1993) argue that the feeling of racial threat among whites increases with the proportion of blacks in their area because of interethnic competition for jobs and other scarce resources. Stephen Voss (1996a) argues that white feelings of racial threat are based on symbolic factors and that white support for racist candidates does not increase with residential proximity to blacks.

4. Data from the Current Population survey indicate that participation among first-generation white immigrants is not influenced by the proportion of nonwhites in their counties. However, the variable is significant for native-born whites, with the likelihood of voting higher in counties with a greater proportion of nonwhite populations. While this finding is not central to this chapter's analysis, it does indicate that even standard notions of political threat may not apply for first-generation white immigrants as they might for whites in later immigrant generations.

5. Given the exceptional and consistently high level of participation among Cuban immigrants, Texas (and not Florida) is included as the relevant comparison to California. Also, Hawaii has the largest proportion of Asian Americans, but New York was chosen as a basis of comparison to California because Asian Americans are not a racial minority in Hawaii.

6. The Dow Jones Interactive search reveals an average of thirteen daily sto-

ries related to immigration or Proposition 187 in the major California newspapers one month prior to Election Day.

7. An article in the *Los Angeles Times* about a student walkout in Oxnard noted that "although most of the students who attended were Latino, student organizers said they tried hard to make the event multicultural to attract different student groups" (Bustillo and Stoll 1994). Other articles also confirm the largely Latino makeup of protests, including the chanting of slogans in Spanish and the waving of Mexican flags (Pyle and Hernandez 1994; Bustillo and Davis 1994).

8. Using an ordinal scale is advantageous over using separate dummy variables for two reasons. First, it is much easier to test for possible interactive effects between threat and mobilization. Second, given the small number of cases (seven state-racial group combinations), it is not possible to control for race of respondent while including three sets of dummy variables for threat and mobilization each. Doing so drops from the estimation those dummy variables that have a high degree of collinearity with one of the race variables.

9. In the model that controls for race, changing the value of threat for black immigrants in New York does not change the estimate for threat and mobilization because there is no variation on the variable "black." However, in the model that does not control for race, the effect of the threat variable is slightly stronger using the threat level of 2 (logit coefficient of 0.33 versus 0.27), but in both cases the variable is statistically significant.

10. Indeed, in contrast to Wilson's attempt to capitalize on racially divisive propositions in 1994, the state Republican Party persuaded the organizers of the petition to end bilingual education to put the measure on the June primary ballot instead of the general election (Lindlaw 1998).

11. Interview with Regional Outreach Chair to Ethnic Communities, California Republican Party (2000).

12. Republican Latino leaders and some leaders of nonpartisan Latino organizations noted that Southwest Voter was too closely tied to the Democratic Party, as its former director was the co-chair of the Democratic National Convention in 2000. Organizers within Southwest Voter report that they are strictly nonpartisan, although one acknowledged that mobilizing poorer Latinos may end up benefiting the Democratic Party in the short run.

13. Interview with Carlos Vaquerano, executive director of the Salvadoran American Legal and Education Fund (2000) and Ruben Villareal, Southwest Voter Registration Education Project (2000).

14. The problem of factionalism was especially prevalent in San Antonio (Bexar County), with little coordination between the Democratic Party chair and candidate organizations (interview with Gabe Quintanilla, executive director of the Bexar County Democrats, 2000).

15. Interviews with staff member, Texas Democrats (2000), and Orlando Sanchez, a city Council member in Houston, Texas (2000).

16. Interview with staff member, Southwest Voter Research and Education Project, Texas (2000).

17. The situation is similar to that found among Irish machine cities, where entrenched Democrats had little incentive to mobilize new immigrants from countries such as Italy (see Chapter 2).

18. Indeed, Samuel Nicolas might have won Assembly District 42 with the support of the Haitian and Caribbean communities in Flatbush were it not for the entry of another Caribbean into the race (Kappstatter and Hutchinson 1998; White 2000).

19. Interview with staff member, Chinese Americans United for Self Empowerment (2000).

20. Interviews with staff members of Asian Pacific American Legal Consortium (2000), Chinese Americans United for Self Empowerment (2000), APIA Vote (2000), and Chinese American Political Association (2000).

21. A similar point about the lack of financial support for white immigrant organizations can be found in Irene Bloemraad's (2002) analysis of the Portuguese community in Massachusetts.

22. As of the fall of 2001, no comparable directory existed for immigrant organizations in California. However, a review of organizations in directories such as the Bay Area Progressive Directory lists only three or four organizations that cater to the needs of Jewish immigrants or other European immigrants (Cheetham 2002).

23. Here I present the results as relative odds, based on weighted logit regressions. The original logit coefficients (presented in the Appendix) represent the log-odds of the independent variable's effect on the dependent variable. Exponentiating the log-odds gives us the relative odds (sometime referred to in terms of "likelihood").

24. The only exception is for second-generation respondents in 1998, for whom the threat variable is not statistically significant.

25. The threat coefficient for second-generation respondents in 1994 is actually the highest, at 0.870.

26. The threat coefficients are 0.772 and 1.55 in 1994 and 1998, respectively, when the sample is restricted to Latino and Asian immigrants. In the full sample, the coefficient values from the national analysis are 0.429 and 0.635.

27. There may be exceptions, however, when an ethnic candidate runs for elected office and ethnopolitical organizations coordinate mobilization strategies with the ethnic candidate's campaign organization. The presence of an ethnic candidate cannot be included in this analysis because the CPS data do not have the level of geographic detail necessary to test for the effects of ethnic candidates on voting.

28. One possible source of variation is the fact that Latino immigrants in California during the 1996 election may have experienced higher levels of threat than other immigrants in the state and Latino immigrants elsewhere because of Proposition 209, which sought to do away with affirmative action in state institutions. Asian immigrants seemed to have been less threatened by such legislation and were the group most likely to split their vote on the measure (Tam Cho and Cain 2001; Field Institute 1997). The threat variable is not a significant

predictor of participation, but this may be because Latino immigrants in California present the only possible source of variation on the measure of political threat.

29. As one article in the *Washington Post* notes, "Several other lawyers with Middle Eastern and South Asian clients said their businesses have been booming, as immigrants have sought to become citizens or legal permanent residents, the first step on the path to citizenship. 'I can tell by the way they are requesting these applications, they're worried,' said Anthony Fatemi, who runs a law practice on Democracy Boulevard in Bethesda" (Sheridan 2002).

CHAPTER 7

1. This relationship may not always hold if members are more likely to write elected officials in places where state and local governments are least efficient. In our examination of racial differences in participation, this is less likely to be an issue. Whites in California are more likely to reside in cities with higher property values and well-financed government services, and yet they are the ones most likely to write their elected officials. Of course, the size of the city also matters, with residents in smaller cities more likely to write their elected officials than those in larger cities. However, the fact that the variable also captures contact with state and national government should lead to a greater equalization among those who reside in small versus large cities. We cannot control for city size or type of city on this measure of writing elected officials. However, in the PPIC Survey on Land Use (2002), whites are more likely to write their local elected officials on land-use issues even after controlling for confidence in local government.

2. Two factors may explain why the gap in participation by English language ability is not greater: (1) those who communicate primarily in Spanish can have either a relative or friend contact elected officials on their behalf, or (2) they may write in Spanish to elected officials who either speak Spanish themselves or have Spanish-speaking staff.

3. This divergence in party mobilization was also noted in interviews with staff members of Asian Pacific American Legal Consortium (2000) and APIA Vote (2000), both based in Los Angeles.

4. For detailed results on the effects of these control variables, see Appendix Tables A.13 and A.14.

5. Similar results hold when first- and second-generation blacks are excluded from the black comparison to third-generation whites.

CHAPTER 8

1. In my fieldwork, I found several organizations that would focus only on helping immigrants with naturalization but little on the subsequent processes of registration and turnout. Or there would be organizations that would encourage immigrants to register and vote as their civic duty but would refrain

from drawing attention to particular issues that might have a disproportionate impact on their welfare.

2. As one article in November 2000 noted, "'Both parties show up at swearing-in ceremonies to try to register voters,' said William A. Carrick, a California Democratic consultant. 'There is a Democratic table and a Republican table. Ours has a lot of business. Theirs is like the Maytag repairman'" (Robinson 2000).

Bibliography

Abramson, Paul, John Aldrich, and David Rohde. 1998. *Change and Continuity in the 1996 Elections.* Washington, DC: CQ Press.

Abramson, Paul, and William Claggett. 1992. "The Quality of Record Keeping and Racial Differences in Validated Turnout." *Journal of Politics* 54 (3): 871–82.

Alba, Richard. 1985. "The Twilight of Ethnicity Among Americans of European Ancestry: The Case of Italians." *Ethnic and Racial Studies* 8 (1): 134–58.

Alba, Richard, and Victor Nee. 2003. *Remaking the American Mainstream: Assimilation and Contemporary Immigration.* Cambridge, MA: Harvard University Press.

Allen, Mike. 1998. "Confrontation in Harlem: The Police." *New York Times*, September 7.

Alvarez, R. Michael, and Lisa García Bedolla. 2003. "The Foundations of Latino Voter Partisanship: Evidence from the 2000 Election." *Journal of Politics* 65 (1): 31–49.

Andersen, Kristi. 1996. *After Suffrage: Women in Partisan and Electoral Politics Before the New Deal.* Chicago: University of Chicago press.

Anderson, Nick. 2000. "In Shift, GOP Proposes Easing Immigration Rules." *Los Angeles Times*, November 26.

Anuario Hispano: Hispanic Yearbook. 2000. McLean, VA: TIYM Publishing.

Arvizu, John R., and F. Chris Garcia. 1996. "Latino Voting Participation: Explaining and Differentiating Latino Voting Turnout." *Hispanic Journal of Behavioral Sciences* 18 (2): 104–28.

Associated Press. 2000. "Look at the Electoral Map." *Washington Post*, September 23.

Babson, Jennifer, and Maureen Groppe. 1994. "Governors' Races May End in November Surprise." *Congressional Quarterly Weekly Report* 52 (30): 2165–68.

Baldassare, Mark. 1998. *PPIC Statewide Survey: April 1998.* San Francisco: Public Policy Institute of California (dataset).

———. 2002a. *A California State of Mind: The Conflicted Voter in a Changing World.* Berkeley: University of California Press.

———. 2002b. *PPIC Statewide Surveys.* San Francisco: Public Policy Institute of California (dataset).

Barreto, Matt A., and Nathan D. Woods. 2000. *Voting Patterns and the Dramatic Growth of the Latino Electorate in Los Angeles County, 1994–1998.* Claremont, CA: Tomás Rivera Policy Institute.

Bartels, Larry. 2000. "Partisanship and Voting Behavior, 1952–1996." *American Journal of Political Science* 44 (1): 35–50.

Bass, Loretta, and Lynn Casper. 1999. "Are There Differences in Registration and Voting Behavior Between Naturalized and Native-Born Americans?" *Population Division Working Paper No. 28.* Washington, DC: US Bureau of the Census.

Benenson, Bob. 2000. "Proudly Worn Party Label Missing in Key Contests." *Congressional Quarterly Weekly Report* 58 (35): 2182–85.

Benford, Robert, and David Snow. 2000. "Framing Processes and Social Movements: An Overview and Assessment." *Annual Review of Sociology* 26: 611–39.

Berestein, Leslie. 1994. "Asian Groups United to Educate Residents on Impact of Prop. 187." *Los Angeles Times*, September 25.

Bloemraad, Irene. 2002. "Ethnic Leaders and the Immigrant Settlement Industry: The Development of Community Advocates." Paper presented at the Immigration Workshop, Harvard University, March 7.

Bobo, Lawrence, and Franklin Gilliam Jr. 1990. "Race, Socioeconomic Status, and Black Empowerment." *American Political Science Review* 84 (2): 377–94.

Borjas, George. 1987. "Self-Selection and the Earnings of Immigrants." *American Economic Review* 77 (4): 531–53.

———. 1999. *Heaven's Door: Immigration Policy and the American Economy.* Princeton, NJ: Princeton University Press.

Brady, Henry. 2003. "Adverse Impact of Punch-Card Voting on Minorities." *UC Berkeley News.* September 15.

Burns, Nancy, Kay Schlozman, and Sidney Verba. 2001. *The Private Roots of Public Action: Gender, Equality, and Political Participation.* Cambridge, MA: Harvard University Press.

Bustillo, Miguel, and Maia Davis. 1994. "Students Stage Walkout in Protest of Prop. 187." *Los Angeles Times*, October 22.

Bustillo, Miguel, and Ira Stoll. 1994. "Proposition 187 Student Rally in Oxnard Ends at Park." *Los Angeles Times*, November 5.

Cain, Bruce, and Brendan Doherty. 2003. "The Impact of Dual Citizenship on Political Participation." Paper presented at the Nation of Immigrants Conference, University of California, Berkeley, May 2.

Cain, Bruce, Roderick Kiewiet, and Carole Uhlaner. 1991. "The Acquisition of Partisanship by Latinos and Asian Americans." *American Journal of Political Science* 35 (2): 390–422.

Calvo, Maria A., and Steven J. Rosenstone. 1989. *Hispanic Political Participation.* San Antonio, TX: Southwest Voter Research Institute.

Camarota, Steven. 1999. "Immigrants in the United States—1998." *January 1999 Backgrounder*. Washington, DC: Center for Immigration Studies.

Campbell, Angus, Philip E. Converse, Warren E. Miller, and Donald E. Stokes. 1960. *The American Voter*. Chicago: University of Chicago Press.

Carnegie Center for International Peace. 1997. "New Americans and Co-Ethnic Voting." *Research Perspectives on Immigration* 1 (3).

Cassata, Donna. 1998. "California, the Coveted Prize." *Congressional Quarterly Weekly Report* 56 (28): 1865–68.

Cauvin, Henri. 1998. "Rally for Louima." *New York Daily News*, August 10.

Cheetham, Ken. 2002. "The San Francisco Bay Area Progressive Directory." www.bapd.org/.

Chiswick, Barry. 1977. "Sons of Immigrants: Are They at an Earnings Disadvantage?" *American Economic Review* 67 (1): 376–80.

Cohn, D'Vera. 2001. "Illegal Immigrant Total Is Raised." *Washington Post*, October 25.

Collett, Christian. 2000. "The Determinants of Vietnamese American Political Participation: Findings from the January 2000 Orange County Register Poll." Paper prepared for presentation at the annual meeting of the Association of Asian American Studies, Scottsdale, AZ.

Converse, Philip. 1972. "Change in the American Electorate." In *The Human Meaning of Social Change*, ed. Angus Campbell and Philip Converse. New York: Russell Sage Foundation.

Cornelius, Wayne, Takeyuki Tsuda, Philip Martin, and James F. Hollifield, eds. 2004. *Controlling Immigration: A Global Perspective*. 2nd ed. Palo Alto, CA: Stanford University Press.

Cranford, John. 1994. "The Senate: Election Slate Full of Close Calls Puts Democrats on the Edge." *Congressional Quarterly Weekly Report* 52 (41): 2996–99.

Dahl, Robert. 1961. *Who Governs? Democracy and Power in an American City*. New Haven, CT: Yale University Press.

Davidson, Chandler, and Bernard Grofman. 1994. *Quiet Revolution in the South: The Impact of the Voting Rights Act, 1965–1990*. Princeton, NJ: Princeton University Press.

de la Garza, Rodolfo O. 1996. "The Effects of Primordial Claims, Immigration, and the Voting Rights Act on Mexican American Sociopolitical Incorporation." In *The Politics of Minority Coalitions: Race, Ethnicity, and Shared Uncertainties*, ed. Wilbur C. Rich. Westport, CT: Greenwood Press.

de la Garza, Rodolfo O., Louis DeSipio, F. Chris Garcia, John Garcia, and Angelo Falcon. 1992. *Latino Voices: Mexican, Puerto Rican, and Cuban Perspectives on American Politics*. Boulder, CO: Westview Press.

DeSipio, Louis. 1996a. *Counting on the Latino Vote: Latinos as a New Electorate*. Charlottesville: University Press of Virginia.

———. 1996b. "Making Citizens or Good Citizens? Naturalization as a Predictor of Organizational and Electoral Behavior Among Latino Immigrants." *Hispanic Journal of Behavioral Sciences* 18 (2): 194–213.

———. 1999. "The Second Generation: Political Behaviors of Adult Children of

Immigrants in the United States." Paper prepared for presentation at the annual meeting of the American Political Science Association, Atlanta.

Directory of Services to Immigrants. 2000. New York: New York City Mayor's Office of Immigrant Affairs and Language Services.

Downs, Anthony. 1957. *An Economic Theory of Democracy.* New York: Harper and Brothers.

DuBois, W. E. B. 1935. *Black Reconstruction in America.* New York: Harcourt Brace & Company.

Edsall, Thomas, and Cheryl Thompson. 2001. "Alliance Forms on Immigrant Politics." *Washington Post*, August 7.

Eljera, Bert. 1994. "Wilson Hails Efforts of Legal Immigrants." *Los Angeles Times*, October 18.

Erie, Steven. 1988. *Rainbow's End: Irish-Americans and the Dilemmas of Urban Machine Politics, 1840–1985.* Berkeley: University of California Press.

Espenshade, Thomas J., and Haishan Fu. 1997. "An Analysis of English-Language Proficiency Among U.S. Immigrants." *American Sociological Review* 62 (2): 288–305.

Espenshade, Thomas J., and Greg Huber. 1998. "Antecedents and Consequences of Tightening Welfare Eligibility for U.S. Immigrants." *Immigration, Citizenship, and the Welfare State in Germany and the United States.* Stamford, CT: JAI Press.

Espiritu, Yen L. 1992. *Asian American Panethnicity.* Philadelphia: Temple University Press.

Feldman, Paul. 1994. "California Elections: Proposition 187—Opponents of Measure Vow to Sue If It Passes." *Los Angeles Times*, November 11.

Field Institute. 1997. "A Review of Voting and Political Demography in 1996." *California Opinion Index* (1). San Francisco: The Field Institute.

Fishman, Joshua. 1972. *The Sociology of Language.* Rowley, MA: Newbury House.

Fix, Michael, and Jeffrey Passel. 1999. *Trends in Noncitizens' and Citizens' Use of Public Benefits Following Welfare Reform, 1994–97.* Washington, DC: Urban Institute.

Foerstel, Karen. 1998. "Senate Hopefuls' Trial by Fire." *Congressional Quarterly Weekly Report* 56 (28): 1860–64.

Foo, Lora. 1994. "Asian Workers and Prop. 187." *Los Angeles Times*, November 5.

Frey, William H. 1996. "Immigration, Domestic Migration and Demographic Balkanization in America: New Evidence for the 1990s." *Population and Development Review* 22 (4): 741–63.

Fritz, Mark. 1998. "Pledging Multiple Allegiances." *Los Angeles Times*, April 6.

Frymer, Paul. 1999. *Uneasy Alliances: Race and Party Competition in America.* Princeton, NJ: Princeton University Press.

Fulwood, Sam. 1998. "Decision '98: The Final Count." *Los Angeles Times*, November 5, p. 2.

Gamm, Gerald. 1989. *The Making of New Deal Democrats: Voting Behavior and Realignment in Boston, 1920–1940.* Chicago: University of Chicago Press.

Gans, Herbert. 1992. "Second-Generation Decline: Scenarios for the Economic and Ethnic Futures of the Post-1965 American Immigrants." *Ethnic and Racial Studies* 15 (2): 173–92.

García, Edwin. 2002. "Courting Minorities After Low Turnout." *San Jose (CA) Mercury News*, November 29.

García, James. 1994. "Immigration Is Key Issue in California." *Austin (TX) American-Statesman*, October 9.

Gibson, Campbell J., and Emily Lennon. 1999. "Historical Census Statistics on the Foreign-Born Population of the United States: 1850–1990." *Population Division Working Paper No. 29*. Washington, DC: U.S. Census Bureau.

Giles, Micheal, and Melanie Buckner. 1993. "David Duke and Black Threat: An Old Hypothesis Revisited." *Journal of Politics* 55 (3): 702–13.

———. 1996. "Beyond Racial Threat: Failure of an Old Hypothesis in the New South: Comment." *Journal of Politics* 58 (4): 1171–80.

Gimpel, James. 1999. "Migration, Immigration, and the Politics of Places." Washington, DC: Center for Immigration Studies.

Gimpel, James, and Karen Kaufmann. 2001. *Impossible Dream or Distant Reality? Republican Efforts to Attract Latino Voters*. Washington, DC: Center for Immigration Studies.

Glastris, Paul, Kenneth T. Walsh, Julian E. Barnes, and Josh Chetwynd. 1997. "Immigration Boomerang." *U.S. News and World Report*, March 17.

Glazer, Nathan, and Daniel P. Moynihan. 1963. *Beyond the Melting Pot: The Negroes, Puerto Ricans, Jews, Italians, and Irish of New York City*. Cambridge, MA: M.I.T. Press and Harvard University Press.

Goldsborough, James. 2000. "Politicians Fall Silent on Immigration." *San Diego Union-Tribune*, November 6.

Gonzalez, Juan. 1998. "A Giant Awakens and Votes." *New York Daily News*, November 11.

Gordon, Milton. 1964. *Assimilation in American Life*. New York: Oxford University Press.

Green, Donald, and Jonathan Cowden. 1992. "Who Protests: Self-Interest and White Opposition to Busing." *Journal of Politics* 54 (2): 471–96.

Greenblatt, Alan. 1996. "Open Governorships Provide a Measure of Suspense." *Congressional Quarterly Weekly Report* 54 (40): 2961–63.

Greenblatt, Alan, and Robert Wells. 1996. "Senate Elections: Still Anybody's Call." *Congressional Quarterly Weekly Report* 54 (40): 2954–59.

Greenhouse, Steven. 2000. "Coalition Urges Easing of Immigration Laws." *New York Times*, May 16.

Guendelman, S., J. B. Gould, M. Hudes, and B. Eskenazi. 1990. "Generational Differences in Perinatal Health Among the Mexican American Population: Findings from HHANES, 1982–84." *American Journal of Public Health* 80 (suppl.): 61–65.

Hajnal, Zoltan, and Mark Baldassare. 2001. *Finding Common Ground: Racial and Ethnic Attitudes in California*. San Francisco: Public Policy Institute of California.

Hajnal, Zoltan, and Hugh Louch. 2001. *Are There Winners and Losers? Race, Eth-*

nicity, and California's Initiative Process. San Francisco: Public Policy Institute of California.

Hajnal, Zoltan, and Taeku Lee. 2003. "Beyond the Middle: Latinos and Multiple Dimensions of Political Independents." Paper prepared for presentation at the annual meeting of the Midwest Political Science Association, Chicago, April.

Handlin, Oscar. 1951. *The Uprooted*. Boston: Little, Brown.

Hansen, Marcus L. 1938. *The Problem of the Third Generation Immigrant*. Rock Island, IL: Augustana Historical Society.

————. 1987. *The Problem of the Third Generation Immigrant: A Republication of the 1937 Address with Introductions by Peter Kivisto and Oscar Handlin*. Rock Island, IL: Swenson Swedish Immigration Research Center and Augustana College Library.

Hero, Rodney. 1992. *Latinos and the U.S. Political System*. Philadelphia: Temple University Press.

————. 2003. "Social Capital and Racial Inequality in America." *Perspectives on Politics* 1 (1): 113–22.

Hero, Rodney, and Anne Campbell. 1996. "Understanding Latino Political Participation." *Hispanic Journal of Behavioral Sciences* 18 (2): 129–41.

Hill, Kevin, and Dario Moreno. 1996. "Second-Generation Cubans." *Hispanic Journal of Behavioral Sciences* 18 (2): 175–93.

Hill, Laura, and Hans Johnson. 2002. *Understanding the Future of Californians' Fertility: The Role of Immigrants*. San Francisco: Public Policy Institute of California.

Hritzuk, Natasha, and David Park. 2000. "The Question of Latino Participation: From an SES to a Social Structural Explanation." *Social Science Quarterly* 81 (1): 151–65.

Iritani, Evelyn. 1996. "Foreign Donation Furor Dampens Fund-Raising." *Los Angeles Times*, October 21.

Jacobson, Matthew Frye. 1999. *Whiteness of a Different Color: European Immigrants and the Alchemy of Race*. Cambridge, MA: Harvard University Press.

Jennings, Kent, and Richard Niemi. 1981. *Generations and Politics: A Panel Study of Young Adults and Their Parents*. Princeton, NJ: Princeton University Press.

Johnson, Hans, Belinda Reyes, Laura Mameesh, and Elisa Barbour. 1999. *Taking the Oath: An Analysis of Naturalization in California and the United States*. San Francisco: Public Policy Institute of California.

Johnson, Martin, Robert Stein, and Robert Wrinkle. 2003. "Language Choice, Residential Stability, and Voting Among Latino Americans." *Social Science Quarterly* 84 (2): 412–24.

Jones-Correa, Michael. 1998. *Between Two Nations: The Political Life of Latin American Immigrants in New York City*. Ithaca, NY: Cornell University Press.

————. 1999. "Different Paths: Gender, Immigration, and Political Participation." *International Migration Review* 32 (2): 326–49.

————. 2001. "Institutional and Contextual Factors in Immigrant Citizenship and Voting." *Citizenship Studies* 5 (1): 41–56.

————. 2002. "Under Two Flags: Dual Nationality in Latin America and Its Consequences for the United States." *International Migration Review* 35 (4): 997–1029.

Junn, Jane. 1999. "Participation in Liberal Democracy: The Political Assimilation of Immigrants and Ethnic Minorities in the United States." *American Behavioral Scientist* 42 (9): 1417–38.

Kahn, Joan R. 1994. "Immigrant and Native Fertility During the 1980s: Adaptation and Expectations for the Future." *International Migration Review* 28 (3): 501–19.

Kang, Connie. 2000. "Asian Americans Lean to Democrats, Poll Says." *Los Angeles Times*, November 10.

Kappstatter, Bob, and Bill Hutchinson. 1998. "Battles for Legislature Raging Around the City." *New York Daily News*, November 16.

Kasinitz, Philip. 1992. *Caribbean New York: Black Immigrants and the Politics of Race*. Ithaca, NY: Cornell University Press.

Kasinitz, Philip, John Mollenkopf, and Mary Waters. (Forthcoming). *The Immigrant Second Generation in Metropolitan New York*. New York: Russell Sage Foundation.

Kellstedt, Lyman. 1974. "Ethnicity and Political Behavior: Inter-Group and Inter-Generational Differences." *Ethnicity* 1: 393–415.

Key, V. O., Jr. 1949. *Southern Politics in State and Nation*. New York: Vintage Books.

Kim, Claire Jean. 1999. "The Racial Triangulation of Asian Americans." *Politics and Society* 27 (1): 105–38.

————. 2000. *Bitter Fruit: The Politics of Black-Korean Conflict in New York City*. New Haven, CT: Yale University Press.

King, Peter. 1994. "They Kept Coming." *Los Angeles Times*, November 9.

Lamare, James. 1982. "The Political Integration of Mexican-American Children: A Generational Analysis." *International Migration Review* 16 (1): 169–88.

Lee, Taeku. 2001. "Language-of-Interview Effects and Latino Mass Opinion." John F. Kennedy School of Government Faculty Research Working Paper Series 01-041.

Leighley, Jan. 2001. *Strength in Numbers? The Political Mobilization of Racial and Ethnic Minorities*. Princeton, NJ: Princeton University Press.

Lewis, Paul, and S. Karthick Ramakrishnan. (Forthcoming). *Governing Cities in Transition: How Local Policymakers React to Immigration and Change*. San Francisco: Public Policy Institute of California.

Liang, Zai. 1994. "Social Contact, Social Capital, and the Naturalization Process: Evidence from Six Immigrant Groups." *Social Science Research* 23 (4): 407–37.

Lien, Pei-te. 1994. "Ethnicity and Political Participation: A Comparison Between Asian and Mexican Americans." *Political Behavior* 16 (1): 237–64.

————. 1997. *The Political Participation of Asian Americans: Voting Behavior in Southern California*. New York: Garland Publishing.

————. 1998. "Does the Gender Gap in Attitudes and Behavior Vary Across Racial Groups?" *Political Research Quarterly* 51 (4): 869–95.

———. 2001. *The Making of Asian America Through Political Participation.* Philadelphia: Temple University Press.

———. 2004. *Pilot National Asian American Political Survey (PNAAPS), 2000–2001.* Ann Arbor, MI: Inter-university Consortium for Political and Social Research (dataset).

Lien, Pei-te, Christian Collet, Janelle Wong, and S. Karthick Ramakrishnan. 2001. "Asian Pacific American Public Opinion and Political Participation." *PS: Political Science and Politics* 34: 3.

Lien, Pei-te, M. Margaret Conway, and Janelle Wong. 2003. "The Contours and Sources of Ethnic Identity Choices Among Asian Americans." *Social Science Quarterly* 84 (2): 461–81.

———. 2004. *The Politics of Asian Americans: Diversity and Community.* New York: Routledge.

Lindlaw, Doug. 1998. "State GOP Faces Uphill Battle to Win Over Latino Voters." *Los Angeles Times*, November 1.

Lollock, Lisa. 2001. *The Foreign Born Population in the United States: March 2000.* Washington, DC: U.S. Census Bureau.

López, David E. 1999. "Social and Linguistic Aspects of Assimilation Today." In *The Handbook of International Migration—The American Experience*, ed. Charles Hirschman, Philip Kasinitz, and Josh DeWind. New York: Russell Sage Foundation.

Lubman, Sarah, Hallye Jordan, and Karen De Sa. 2001. "Vicente Fox, Davis Pledge Cooperation." *San Jose (CA) Mercury News*, March 22.

Massey, Douglass, and Nancy Denton. 1987. "Trends in Residential Segregation of Blacks, Hispanics, and Asians: 1970–1980." *American Sociological Review* 52 (6): 802–25.

McAdam, Doug. 1982. *Political Process and the Development of Black Insurgency, 1930–1970.* Chicago: University of Chicago Press.

McCarthy, Robert J. 1994. "Cuomo Defeat Tied to Poor Urban Showing; in Big Cities, Blacks, Other Traditional Supporters, Didn't Go to Polls." *Buffalo (NY) News*, November 20.

McClain, Paula, and Joseph Stewart. 1999. *"Can We All Get Along?": Racial and Ethnic Minorities in American Politics.* Boulder, CO: Westview Press.

McDonnell, Patrick. 1997. "Prop. 187 Found Unconstitutional by Federal Judge." *Los Angeles Times*, November 15.

McDonnell, Patrick, and Chip Johnson. 1994. "70,000 March Through L.A. Against Prop. 187." *Los Angeles Times*, October 17.

McDonnell, Patrick J., and Robert J. Lopez. 1994. "L.A. March Against Prop. 187 Draws 70,000." *Los Angeles Times*, November 17.

McDonnell, Patrick, and George Ramos. 1996. "Latinos Make Strong Showing at the Polls." *Los Angeles Times*, November 8.

Miller, Warren. 1992. "The Puzzle Transformed: Explaining Declining Turnout." *Political Behavior* 14 (1): 1–43.

Miller, Warren, and J. Merrill Shanks. 1996. *The New American Voter.* Cambridge, MA: Harvard University Press.

Mollenkopf, John, Timothy Ross, and David Olson. 1999. *Immigrant Political Participation in New York and Los Angeles*. New York: Center for Urban Research, City University of New York.

Moreno, Dario. 1997. "The Cuban Model: Political Empowerment in Miami." In *Pursuing Power: Latinos and the Political System*, ed. F. Chris Garcia. Notre Dame, IN: University of Notre Dame Press.

Nakanishi, Don T. 1986. *The UCLA Asian Pacific American Voter Registration Study*. Los Angeles: Asian Pacific American Legal Center.

Neal, Terry, and Richard Morin. 1998. "For Voters, It's Back Toward the Middle." *Washington Post*, November 5.

Nguyen, Tina. 1994. "Chinatown: Coalition of Groups Denounce Prop. 187." *Los Angeles Times*, October 30.

Nie, Norman, Jane Junn, and Ken Stehlik-Barry. 1996. *Education and Democratic Citizenship in America*. Chicago: University of Chicago Press.

OCA National Directory of Asian Pacific American Organizations. 1999. New York: Philip Morris Management Corp.

Olson, Mancur. 1965. *The Logic of Collective Action*. Cambridge, MA: Harvard University Press.

Oliver, J. Eric. 1996. "The Effects of Eligibility Restrictions and Party Activity on Absentee Voting and Overall Turnout." *American Journal of Political Science* 40 (2): 498–513.

Pantoja, Adrian D., Ricardo Ramirez, Gary M. Segura. 2001. "Citizens by Choice, Voters by Necessity: Patterns in Political Mobilization by Naturalized Latinos." *Political Research Quarterly* 54 (4): 729–50.

Passel, Jeffrey, and Rebecca Clark. 1998. *Immigrants in New York: Their Legal Status, Incomes and Taxes*. Washington, DC: Urban Institute.

Passel, Jeffrey, and Jennifer Van Hook. 2000. "Adult Children of Immigrants: Integration of the Second Generation." Paper presented at the annual meeting of the Population Association of America, Los Angeles, March 23–25.

Pear, Robert. 2002. "Bush Plan Seeks to Restore Food Stamps for Noncitizens." *New York Times*, January 10.

Pickus, Noah. 1998. *Becoming American/America Becoming: Final Report of the Duke University Workshop on Immigration and Citizenship*. Durham, NC: Duke University.

Portes, Alejandro, and Dag MacLeod. 1999. "Educating the Second Generation: Determinants of Academic Achievement Among Children of Immigrants in the United States." *Journal of Ethnic and Migration Studies* 25 (3): 373–96.

Portes, Alejandro, and Rafael Mozo. 1985. "The Political Adaptation Process of Cubans and Other Ethnic Minorities in the United States: A Preliminary Analysis." *International Migration Review* 19 (1): 35–63.

Portes, Alejandro, and Rubén G. Rumbaut. 1996. *Immigrant America: A Portrait*. 2nd ed. Berkeley: University of California Press.

———. 2001. *Legacies: Story of the Immigrant Second Generation*. Berkeley: University of California Press.

Portes, Alejandro, and Min Zhou. 1993. "The New Second Generation: Segmented Assimilation and Its Variants." *Annals of the American Academy of Political and Social Science* 530: 74–96.

Presser, Stanley, Michael W. Traugott, and Santa Traugott. 1990. "Vote 'Over' Reporting in Surveys: The Records or the Respondents." *Technical Report No. 39*, National Election Study. www.umich.edu/~nes/.

Pulido, Laura. 2000. "Rethinking Environmental Racism: White Privilege and Urban Development in Southern California." *Annals of the Association of American Geographers* 90 (1): 12–40.

Putnam, Robert. 2000. *Bowling Alone: The Collapse and Revival of American Community*. New York: Simon & Schuster.

Pyle, Amy, and Greg Hernandez. 1994. "10,000 Students Protest Prop. 187." *Los Angeles Times*, November 3.

Pyle, Amy, and Simon Romero. 1994. "Measure Fuels a New Latino Campus Activism." *Los Angeles Times*, October 25.

Quintanilla, Gabe. 2000. Personal interview with author, June 1.

Radelat, Ana. 2000. "Power SURGE: More Latino Candidates Running for Office This Year." *Hispanic*, September 1.

Ramakrishnan, S. Karthick. 2002. "Voters from Different Shores: Electoral Participation in Immigrant America." PhD diss., Princeton University.

Ramakrishnan, S. Karthick, and Mark Baldassare. 2004. *The Ties That Bind: Changing Demographics and Civic Engagement in California*. San Francisco: Public Policy Institute of California.

Ramakrishnan, S. Karthick, and Thomas J. Espenshade. 2001. "Immigrant Incorporation and Political Participation in the United States." *International Migration Review* 35 (3): 870–909.

Rehnson, Stanley. 2001. *Dual Citizenship and American National Identity*. Washington, DC: Center for Immigration Studies.

Roane, Kit. 1998. "Black Sergeants Sent to Troubled Precinct Sue." *New York Times*, November 19.

Robinson, Walter. 2000. "Surge in Immigrant Voters Favors Gore." *Boston Globe*, November 4.

Rogers, Reuel. 2000. "Between Race and Ethnicity: Afro-Caribbean Immigrants, Afro-Americans, and the Politics of Incorporation." PhD diss., Princeton University.

Rosenstone, Steven J., and Mark Hansen. 1993. *Mobilization, Participation, and Democracy in America*. New York: Macmillan.

Rumbaut, Rubén. 1997. "Assimilation and Its Discontents: Between Rhetoric and Reality." *International Migration Review* 31 (4): 923–60.

Sanchez, Orlando. 2000. Personal interview with author, June 2.

Sapiro, Virginia, Steven J. Rosenstone, and the National Election Studies. 2001. *1948–2000 Cumulative Data File*. Ann Arbor: University of Michigan, Center for Political Studies (dataset).

Scales, Amy. 1998. "Blacks, Especially in South, Answered the Democrats' Call." *Boston Globe*, November 5.

Schachar, Ron, and Barry Nalebuff. 1999. "Follow the Leader: Theory and Evidence on Political Participation." *American Economic Review* 89 (3): 525–47.

Schattschneider, E. E. 1960. *The Semi-Sovereign People: A Realist's View of Democracy*. New York: Holt, Rinehart and Winston.

Schwartzman, Howard. 2003. "Johnson Thinks Locally, Campaigns Globally." *Washington Post*, February 10.

Scioneaux, Horton. 2001. "Hispanic Voters: The Sleeping Giant Has Awakened." *Desert Democrat*. www.democrats-hd.org/writers/scioneaux/hispanicvoters.pdf.

Segal, Adam. 2003. *The Hispanic Priority: The Spanish-Language Television Battle for the Hispanic Vote in the 2000 U.S. Presidential Election*. Washington, DC: Hispanic Voter Project, Johns Hopkins University.

Shaw, Daron, Rodolfo de la Garza, and Jongho Lee. 2000. "Examining Latino Turnout in 1996: A Three-State, Validated Survey Approach." *American Journal of Political Science* 44 (2): 338–46.

Sheridan, Mary. 2002. "Citizenship Applications Up Sharply." *Washington Post*, January 20.

Slevin, Peter, and Mary Beth Sheridan. 2002. "Administration, Mexico 'Advancing' on Immigration Issues." *Washington Post*, January 11.

Smith, James, and Barry Edmonston, eds. 1997. *The New Americans: Economic, Demographic, and Fiscal Effects of Immigration*. Washington, DC: National Academy Press.

Smith, Rogers. 1997. *Civic Ideals: Conflicting Visions of Citizenship in U.S. History*. New Haven, CT: Yale University Press.

Southwest Voter Registration and Education Project. 1996. *Latino Vote Reporter* 1 (2). Montebello, CA: Southwest Voter Research Institute.

Southwest Voter Research Institute. 1995. *Southwest Voter Research Notes*, 9 (1). Montebello, CA: Southwest Voter Research Institute.

Stevens, Gillian. 1992. "The Social and Demographic Context of Language Use in the United States." *American Sociological Review* 57 (2): 171–85.

Tam Cho, Wendy. 1999. "Naturalization, Socialization, Participation: Immigrants and (Non-)Voting." *Journal of Politics* 61 (4): 1140–55.

Tam Cho, Wendy, and Bruce E. Cain. 2001. "Asian Americans and Immigration: An Exploration of Attitudes and Initiative Vote Patterns." In *Asian American Politics: An Exploration*, ed. Gordon Chang. Palo Alto, CA: Stanford University Press.

Tate, Katherine. 1991. "Black Political Participation in the 1984 and 1988 Presidential Elections." *American Political Science Review* 85 (4): 1159–76.

Tobar, Hector. 1998. "In Contests Big and Small, Latinos Take Historic Leap." *Los Angeles Times*, November 5.

Tomás Rivera Policy Institute. 1996. *Post-Election Survey*. Los Angeles: Tomás Rivera Policy Institute (dataset).

Tsuda, Takeyuki, Zulema Valdez, and Wayne A. Cornelius. 2003. "Human Versus Social Capital: Immigrant Wages and Labor Market Incorporation in Japan and the United States." In *Host Societies and the Reception of Immigrants*, ed. Jeffrey Reitz. La Jolla, CA: USMEX Press, University of California, San Diego.

Uhlaner, Carole. 1989. "Rational Turnout: The Neglected Role of Groups." *American Journal of Political Science* 33 (2): 390–422.

Uhlaner, Carole, Bruce Cain, and Roderick Kiewiet. 1989. "Political Participation of Ethnic Minorities in the 1980s." *Political Behavior* 11 (3): 195–231.

Uhlaner, Carole, Mark Gray, and F. Chris García. 2000. "Ideology, Issues, and Partisanship Among Latinos." Paper presented at the annual meeting of the Western Political Science Association, San Jose, CA, March.

United States Census Bureau. 2001. *Profile of the Foreign-Born Population in the United States: 2000.* Washington, DC: United States Census Bureau.

United States Citizenship and Immigration Services. 2002. *2002 Yearbook of Immigration Statistics.* Washington, DC: United States Citizenship and Immigration Services.

United States Department of Justice. 2002. "Justice Department Announces Resolutions in Two Florida Voting Matters." Washington, DC: United States Department of Justice. www.usdoj.gov / opa / pr / 2002 / June.

United States Department of State. 2001. "Bush Remarks at Ellis Island (New York) Naturalization Ceremony." Washington, DC: United States Department of State. usinfo.state.gov / usa / race / diversity / 10july01.htm.

United States General Accounting Office. 1997. "Bilingual Voting Assistance— Assistance Provided and Costs." *GAO-GGD-97-81.* Washington, DC: United States General Accounting Office.

United States Immigration and Naturalization Service. 1997. *1997 Statistical Yearbook of the Immigration and Naturalization Service.* Washington, DC: United States Department of Justice.

———. 1999. *September FY 1999 Year End Report.* Washington, DC: United States Department of Justice.

———. 2000. *2000 Statistical Yearbook of the Immigration and Naturalization Service.* Washington, DC: United States Department of Justice.

———. 2001. "General Naturalization Requirements." Washington, DC: United States Department of Justice. http://www.ins.usdoj.gov / text / services / natz / general.htm.

Valle, Victor, Rudolfo Torres, and Saskia Sassen. 2000. *Latino Metropolis.* Minneapolis: University of Minnesota Press.

Vaquerano, Carlos. 2000. Personal interview with author, July 17.

Verba, Sidney, and Norman H. Nie. 1972. *Participation in America.* Chicago: University of Chicago Press.

Verba, Sidney, Kay Lehman Schlozman, and Henry E. Brady. 1995. *Voice and Equality.* Cambridge, MA: Harvard University Press.

Villareal, Rubén. 2000. Personal interview with author, March 29.

Voss, Stephen. 1996a. "Beyond Racial Threat: Failure of an Old Hypothesis in the New South." *Journal of Politics* 58 (4): 1156–1170.

———. 1996b. "Familiarity Doesn't Breed Contempt: A Rejoinder to 'Comment.'" *Journal of Politics* 58 (4): 1181–83.

Waldinger, Roger, ed. 2001. *Strangers at the Gates: New Immigrants in Urban America.* Berkeley: University of California Press.

Waters, Mary. 2001. *Black Identities: West Indian Immigrant Dreams and American Realities.* Cambridge, MA: Harvard University Press.

Wattenberg, Martin. 1998. *The Decline of American Political Parties, 1952–1996.* Cambridge, MA: Harvard University Press.

White, Andrew. 2000. "Ethnic Politics and the Changing Face of New York." *GothamGazette.com.* www.gothamgazette.com / iotw / ethnic /. August 7.

White, Michael J., and Afaf Omer. 1997. "Segregation by Ethnicity and Immigrant Status in New Jersey." In *Keys to Successful Immigration,* ed. Thomas J. Espenshade. Washington, DC: Urban Institute Press.

Wilkerson, Isabel. 1994. "The 1994 Elections: Voters Minorities; Many Blacks See Betrayal in This Year's Campaign." *New York Times,* November 10.

Wilson, Melvin N. 1989. "Child Development in the Context of the Black Extended Family." *American Psychologist* 44 (2): 380–85.

Wolfinger, Raymond E., and Steven J. Rosenstone. 1980. *Who Votes?* New Haven, CT: Yale University Press.

Wong, Janelle. 2000. "The Effects of Age and Political Exposure on the Development of Party Identification Among Asian American and Latino Immigrants in the U.S." *Political Behavior* 22 (4): 341–71.

———. 2001. "Political Participation Among Asian Americans: Mobilization or Selective Recruitment?" Paper prepared for presentation at the annual meeting of the American Political Science Association, San Francisco, August 29–September 2.

———. 2002. "The Role of Community Organizations in the Political Incorporation of Asian American and Latino Immigrants." Paper prepared for presentation at the Conference on Race and Civil Society, Racine, WI, January 11–12.

Yamamoto. Eric. 1999. *Interracial Justice: Conflict and Reconciliation in Post-Civil Rights America.* New York: New York University Press.

Yang, P. Q. 1994. "Examining Immigrant Naturalization." *International Migration Review* 28 (3): 449–77.

Ybarra, Steve. 2000. Telephone interview with author, July 21.

Yoachum, Susan. 1996. "Clinton Seems to Have Enough Electoral Votes." *San Francisco Chronicle,* November 1.

Young, Fiona. 2000. "Chinatown Ballot Shows 'Republican' as 'Democrat.'" *Village Voice,* November 15.

Zhou, Min. 1997. "Segmented Assimilation: Issues, Controversies, and Recent Research on the New Second Generation." *International Migration Review* 31 (4): 975–1008.

———. 2001. "Immigrant Neighborhoods in Los Angeles: Structural Constraints, Ethnic Resources, and Varied Contexts for the Adaptation of Immigrant Children." Paper presented at the Wiener Inequality and Social Policy Seminar, John F. Kennedy School of Government, Harvard University, October 29.

Index